I AM MADE FOR M.A.G.I.C.

I AM MADE FOR M.A.G.I.C.

*Finding inner peace in
30 seconds*

PAUL S DUNNE

Paul Dunne

CONTENTS

1	The Invitation	1
2	An Explanation	11
3	You Need To Understand	19
4	Before You Step In	39
5	The Principles of M.A.G.I.C.	43
6	Using a Holistic Approach	59
7	Meditation	81
8	Appreciation	105
9	Grounding	129
10	Insight	145
11	Connection	167
12	Applying M.A.G.I.C. the Practice	199
13	The Thirty-Second Practice	213
14	Challenges You May Encounter	217
15	Daily Maintenance	225
16	Which practice, when?	231
17	Extra M.A.G.I.C. tricks	239

Guidance behind the book	247
Notes about the author	253
References	255

CHAPTER 1

The Invitation

From those who came before you,
A truth, a wink, an invitation into what to think.
For there is no truth other than what you think;
Think of love or think of fear;
This answer to truth is taught by every master and seer.
- Paul Dunne

Have you read the books, watched the videos, and bought the T-shirt? Many of us have. The first thirty years of life had me looking for **the T-shirt**. I was questioning my half-Lebanese heritage; being baptized and confirmed a Catholic; deciding if I wanted to be a priest or a farmer; unravelling the good luck, bad luck story of being a farmer; being inspired by the philosophy of Buddhist teachings; being fascinated by the truths of the Tao; wondering what Zen had to do with motorcycles; and challenging everything I thought I knew to be the infallible truth. Talk about pulling down fences and moving foundations!

The next thirty years of my life were more of a relief when I focused on my relationship, children, and starting my journey of working with people. The farmer had become an extension officer working in communities with young people, and the philosopher was becoming a psychologist. There were lots of rumblings in my head and heart, lots of uncertainties, and big questions. I wanted to know what someone needed to do to become a master. Why did a master believe what they believed? How did they live with such contentment in this world of contrast? What did these masters do to heal people? Which practices did they use for personal expansion and happiness? Who knew these answers, where were they, and how would I go about accessing them?

When I was a seven- or eight-year-old kid, it was difficult to explain what a psychologist did. Somehow, they could look inside people's heads and "fix" them. I was fascinated by the idea of understanding other people's minds and being able to help them. Most of all, it was about helping others to feel better after something had made them unhappy. My earliest memory on the subject took place as I was sitting in a pickup truck with my dad on one side and my uncle on the other. I said something about wanting to be a psychologist when I grew up. The response from two of the most influential people in my life wasn't exactly what I wanted to hear. I guess they meant well, hoping to motivate me to study and take up the school challenge. It had the opposite effect; there wasn't a year in those twelve years when I didn't want to be somewhere else. I enjoyed the learning; in fact, I loved the learning, especially in science. My problem was teachers and tests.

What I heard was that if you want to be a psychologist, you would have to study hard, get good grades, and go to college. Well, for a little fat kid with big eyebrows, poor self-esteem, and anxiety about teachers, that left me with only one choice. Hearing this comment, I threw my dream out the window. There was no way I was going to put myself through the trauma of dealing with any more teachers or tests than I had to. This left me with two choices: to become a farmer, or a priest. When the time arrived and I had to decide, I looked at the priest gig and decided that it was a little too restrictive for me. So, I became a farmer, following in the footsteps of my dad and his dad. From that moment on, I developed an appreciation for—and lived and breathed—the land.

Farming provided me with plenty of opportunities for self-improvement without having to read all the books. I didn't have to study what I wasn't interested in, and I didn't have to deal with teachers who just weren't interested in me. Sitting on a tractor all day, going around and around in circles, had a magical way of allowing me to grow and expand my mind.

Over the years, I read the books I was interested in, and I asked thousands of questions. I was hungry to learn. I asked things like, "Why doesn't that stalk of wheat grow up and become a gum tree?" and "How does it know what to do when it's planted in the soil?" It was during these nowhere years of adolescence that the confirmed Catholic started questioning the traditions of the church and patriarchalism. The search had begun for nontraditional information about someone called Jeshua and a way of life called Buddhism.

The way of farming and the appeal of farming changed as I moved into my mid-twenties and married life became more appealing—so much so that I questioned the relevance of farming in my life. There was something bigger and better calling in the distance. It hurt to stay, and it hurt to go. Much to the sadness of my dad, and to my own astonishment, I left the farm and returned to studying. Two years of studying farm management was a way of feeding this void inside of me. Two years of studying showed me that I could ace the class and play the game of "study to secure a piece of paper."

This was the turning point. The cosmic realization to come out of this was that I had the intellectual capacity to become a psychologist if I so chose. Little did I know what this really meant in the grander scheme of things. I began eight years of part-time study in psychology—and then, in my seventh year, I walked away. Maybe I was having a bad day; maybe I was tired. Regardless, I arrived home to declare that I was quitting college. I looked around me and noticed the discrepancies between what I was learning in college and what I was seeing in the community while working with young people. There was an enormous gap. Six weeks later, the somewhat-wiser-than-me mother of our children lovingly reminded me that while it was my choice, a great deal of energy had already gone into chasing this dream.

It was then that I made a contract with myself. I committed to finishing school, getting the piece of paper, and becoming the bestest psychologist I could become. Twenty-nine years later, my success rate with clients was ninety to ninety-five percent. I was a non-traditional psychologist working with young people. I decided it was time to be free from the system, and I subsequently surrendered my dream of being a psychologist.

After twenty-nine years, a repressed insight rose up to bite me. It was the proverbial phoenix rising from the ashes as I realized, through all my stubbornness, that I simply wanted to make a difference, especially for young people. I didn't really need to become a psychologist to make a difference. That was only my ego's way of feeling good about me being intelligent, of feeling smart, and a way of negotiating with the system. It had been a journey, negotiating roundabouts, and it certainly had been worth it.

At that point in my life, I had read the books, seen the videos, and even had the T-shirt. But it wasn't enough! My success with my clients didn't flow into my inner world. The song played over and over in my head: what did I need to change, what did I need to do differently, and what was I missing that would fill the internal nothingness? This was the same search as before, but with a different perspective.

I spent most of my life journey looking beyond the bounds of mainstream psychology and personal growth literature. While I was searching and continually fascinated by what I found, my everyday behavior and my profession stayed mainstream. Finally, when I stopped looking outside of myself for the answers, quieted my mind, stopped thinking I knew the answers, and finally stopped trying to fit into the mainstream, the guidance flowed. It may have been flowing for a long time before this, but I had been too busy searching to notice. In some ways, the searching was a way of masking my conformity with mainstream psychology.

Like most people, I knew about meditation in different forms, and I knew about self-reflection and journaling. I also used Energy Psychology techniques. I knew about the benefits of exercise, a healthy diet, good sleep, and avoiding stress. These seemed somewhat obvious, but nothing appeared to be enough. I rationalized that I was going to have to learn some advanced practices if I was to make a difference for myself or anyone else. What follows is one answer to my quest. (I figured there were others, but I probably missed them.)

What eventually emerged out of the ashes was an acronym. The acronym came as insight, intuition, instruction, synchronicity, and guidance from those I refer to as "my team." I never intended to come up with an acronym. My only intention was to have something better than what I had—something I could happily give to anyone searching for personal expansion and a sense of inner peace. My preferences were simple: I wanted to know what I had to do—something simple, easy to understand, and quick and powerful enough for me to see tangible results.

It was important for me to find a practice that was simple and relatable in the "real" world. This is not intended to diminish any of the practices used around the globe for personal growth and inner peace. Each of us is unique, and we are not bound to the practices of our neighbors. We owe it to ourselves to seek until we find the practice/s that best aligns with our makeup, belief system, and lifestyle. Use what you feel drawn to, and leave the rest.

What if you had a personal practice at your fingertips made from five of the most powerful practices known and taught across time? Would it help if someone fashioned this practice specifically for you and your life? Would it be of any benefit if this practice nourished and enhanced your physical, mental, emotional, and spiritual worlds? What would you say if you knew this integrated practice was at your fingertips in a user-friendly form to practice throughout your day, and you could complete this practice within thirty seconds? This book will explain and teach you how to practice five individual practices interlaced as one practice called M.A.G.I.C. Each individual practice provides a vast array of benefits on its own, but when combined as one, there is energetic magic.

Equipped with a great deal of evidence accumulated over thirty years of practicing my art, combined with a lifetime of asking questions, I have attempted to provide the reader with hands-on evidence or links to evidence that support the use of this personal practice. These are the same practices consistently taught by sages, mystics, teachers, gurus, shamans, medicine men and women, and healers throughout the ages. This is my attempt to provide a mixture of ancient teachings, empirical evidence, anecdotal evidence, and mature faith as guidance toward a more fulfilling and joyous life. The following pages will provide you with one road map for your journey.

For those readers who would like scientific evidence for each of these five practices, there is evidence-based research supporting their efficacy. You will find reference links to observational and demonstrated evidence supporting the use and benefits of each practice. This document is a compilation of research on what presents as the five most powerful personal practices for growth and inner peace that I could find—a type of meta-analysis of the research if you like.

This practice will enhance any practice you may already use and will not exclude nor detract from other practices. Flexibility within the practice allows—if not encourages—you, the student, to meld it into your everyday life experience. The heart of this practice rests in its ability to allow you to bring about a change in your life from the inside out. It recognizes and acknowledges your power as an individual to change your world while you evolve with this planet, on this planet.

The instruction in this book is not about training you to do anything. It is not about teaching you how to meditate, ground, or engage in any other practice. This book is an introduction to and explanation of a practice that combines five proven and powerful practices into one simple practice. This book is about awareness—conscious awareness in using what you already have and what you already do naturally every day to increase your levels of joy and excitement in life.

The acronym M.A.G.I.C. comes from the combination of five practices: meditation, appreciation, grounding, insight, and connection. Each individual practice will provide support and stimulation for the holistic self. The complete practice nurtures the spiritual, mental, emotional, physical, and energetic parts of the self.

Meditation serves to calm and attune the "mental self." Meditation comes in many forms and is probably the most studied of all the practices presented. The mental self refers to the mind, both conscious and unconscious. Most people think of this as their head, but it is far more inclusive than just the head. Increased inner peace and conscious awareness of the now moment is the result.

Appreciation serves to nurture our "emotional self." We can say thank you for life's blessings with the practice of appreciation. More than this, it allows us to recognize that all of life is a blessing, even when it is not perceived as something we want. The emotional self embraces all parts of us involved in our emotional or feeling life. The result is acceptance and nonattachment to any outcome, which brings freedom and joy.

Grounding is for the "physical self." We use our five senses to interpret our physical world, and this is part of the physical self. There is the physical body and the physical world, which can be touched. More specifically, this is the practice of connecting our body's energy system with the energy system of planet Earth. It is through this connection with the earth that we exchange electrons, which brings about forms of healing.

Insight is for the "energetic self." The energetic self includes the set of pathways in the body along which vital energy is said to flow, called meridians. It also includes the chakra system, the surrounding energy field, and your emotional state of being. Insight is the practice of intuitively accepting guidance from aspects of the unseen self. This includes what we refer to as Spirit. It is an inner knowing that turns props in life into guidance and inspiration for life's expansion, delivered through the energetic system.

Connection is for our "spiritual self." We can understand this spiritual self as the unseen life force that saturates and surrounds the experience we are having as a human consciousness. Rather than the people, places, events, and objects that appear in our lives, this is the energetic relationship we have with these things. It is a connection with self, with life on this planet, and with the spirit of All-That-Is.

By taking the simplistic and innate power of mindfulness meditation, integrating this with the practice of appreciation for what life offers (no matter how it appears), combining this with grounding our energy into the earth, adding a little insight and intuition, and then finally connecting with self, all of life, and the unseen, we end up with the five practices of M.A.G.I.C.

M.A.G.I.C. is a holistic, therapeutic approach to an inner sense of peace and personal empowerment. The practice offers a means for building on that which has already happened and is now in the past. It provides inner strength, and a knowingness to help us accept the present for what it is: the present moment. Finally, consistent practice will keep the mind from getting caught up in the "what ifs" of the future. This book has been written to provide some explanation and insight, with links to supporting evidence, as well as practical applications for those who choose to make this their personal practice.

Some individuals will never allow themselves to believe in things they cannot see, and there are those who need to see a double-blind, placebo-controlled, randomized clinical study before they allow themselves to believe. These individuals hold to the notion that "seeing is believing." M.A.G.I.C. promotes a philosophy that says, "Believing is seeing." Dr. Wayne Dyer argued that it is indeed a case of believing is seeing, and he wrote the book *You'll See It When You Believe It: The Way to Your Personal Transformation*[1]. Dr. Dyer wrote about how the universe responds to what we believe rather than what we see. The rule is, you will see it when you believe it and not, you will believe it when you see it.

There are indeed many aspects of this physical world that are unseen, and yet the general population still accepts them. Most people accept that the wind exists, even though they cannot see it. Magnetism, electricity, and gravity, along with the greater part of the light spectrum, are also aspects accepted but unseen. That being said, this isn't about believing anything you don't want to believe. And while it may do so, this isn't about challenging your belief system. The idea is for you to accept what you believe, at least in the beginning, and experiment with the rest until you are prepared to choose.

One underpinning principle of M.A.G.I.C. is that there are no coincidences in this universe, and everything is the observed effect of a cause.

Explaining the concept behind this cause and effect can fall on deaf ears, especially exploring the concept that "I cause my effect." This is sometimes a little difficult for our limited minds to grasp. This book can be something like that. View it as fuel for your expansion and happiness, and remind yourself that it is always your choice whether to open the door or not. This requires some dedication to undertake your own research and exploration of the topics covered here. Then again, you may feel you don't need more. This is a personal invitation for you to play, investigate, and reflect, then play, investigate, and reflect some more.

Each individual practice of M.A.G.I.C. is powerful and proven as a standalone practice for personal change and expansion. As a standalone practice, each will provide an increased sense of inner calm and personal awareness. When any single practice is engaged, it has the power to change your life and raise the vibrational frequency of your holistic being. We can measure the effects of this as physical, mental, emotional, and spiritual well-being. Here you will discover what will happen when you combine five powerful practices into one by choosing to practice M.A.G.I.C.

What is your story? What are you observing in your world that has brought you to this place? Your story is important and relevant to everything in this book. Maybe you don't know it, or maybe you don't believe it, but there are no coincidences in this universe. There are situations and events we cannot explain, but just because we do not have an explanation doesn't mean there isn't one. One of the most powerful concepts binding the pages of this book is that things are always working out for us. Even though we may not see any sign of this, and there are times when we don't believe it, in retrospect, I've found that things are always working out for me. Use this book to help you understand your story, and use your story to understand your life. When we trust the journey, the process, we can let go of the drama.

Throughout this book, we will hear from some fellow adventurers and how they have used the practice of M.A.G.I.C. These are down-to-earth personal stories, and like the reference links to empirical evidence related to each of the practices, these stories are points of reference. In including these stories, I acknowledge and appreciate all those individuals who have provided me with feedback, and especially those who have shared their stories. (Please note that the names have been changed.)

Enjoy this practice as you allow it to complement and compliment your life experience. Play with the practice in a way that allows you the freedom of molding it to suit your uniqueness and lifestyle. As you allow this practice to be integrated into your everyday life, look for inspiration rather than motivation. Inspiration comes from the heart, while motivation comes from the head. Remind yourself that even though you are using physical and mental tools, this is a heart-centered practice as much as it is a spiritual practice.

In appreciation of All-There-Is,
Paul Dunne

CHAPTER 2

An Explanation

> I KNOW THE SMELL OF RAIN AS IT COMES ACROSS THE FIELD;
> I KNOW THE SMELL OF MINT AND LEMONGRASS, AND THE SOIL JUST TILLED;
> I KNOW THE FEELING OF A SMILE SENT MY WAY, OR A HIGH FIVE, JUST TO SAY,
> THE MOST IMPORTANT THINGS IN LIFE ARE UNSEEN AND FREE.
> IN THIS FREEDOM, I DEAL WITH MY PAST BY CREATING MY FUTURE, IN THE NOW.
> -PAUL DUNNE

M.A.G.I.C. is the combination of five of the most powerful practices taught for well-being and health. The practice of M.A.G.I.C. merges mindfulness meditation with the practices of appreciation, grounding, insight, and connection. It takes less than one minute to perform. This is a practice like no other that enhances the physical, mental, emotional, and spiritual quadrants of the self. As change comes about, it will be noticed first by the seeker as changes happening within—changes in his or her physical, mental, emotional, and energetic states of being. As is the universal rule, these benefits will then ripple out into the external world as verifiable observations.

The beauty of this simple practice is that it brings about a change in your internal state of being. This "state of being" refers to how a person feels at any moment. This is the frequency at which the atoms that make up the physical body are vibrating. At any moment, your cells reflect the frequency at which your atoms are vibrating. If you knew what this frequency was, you could do something to adjust it, so that you could feel "happy" (or "sad," if you prefer that). The simple truth is that each of us does have a means of gauging what our vibrational frequency is in any moment: our emotions or feelings. A low vibration is revealed through a heavy emotion, such as anger, depression, helplessness, or hopelessness. A high vibration is revealed through a light emotion, such as hope, excitement, joy, appreciation, or love.

The other way we can gauge our state of being is through the feedback provided by the world around us. The people, places, objects, and events in our lives are always reflecting to us the thoughts, beliefs, and current emotional state we hold in relation to any subject. The emotional state is reflected to us as a vibrational frequency of energy. We call this vibrational energy by different names, and we recognize it through our six senses. Sound and light are the easiest examples to understand because most people know that these phenomena travel through the air as vibrations (light waves and sound waves). They then enter our eyes or ears and are transformed into electrical messages for the brain. What you may not know is that emotions work similarly; they travel through the air from one person to another as electromagnetic waves carrying information and data. Our emotional state, or how we feel, is the effect of how we react to this feedback.

The practice of M.A.G.I.C. recognizes that how we are feeling at any moment is not determined by the people, places, objects, or events in our external world. This practice recognizes that it is not what someone says or does to us that causes positive or negative sensations in the body. The people, places, and things in our lives are not the cause of our joy, nor are they the cause of any pain. M.A.G.I.C. considers these things to be props—nothing more. They have no meaning until our brains and inner minds give them meaning. This is why different people can interpret the same event in different ways.

It is how we interpret or perceive the things in our world that ultimately brings about the sensations we experience. Yes, people can press our buttons, and sometimes this will not be pleasant. Ultimately, this story starts with the core beliefs we hold about ourselves as individuals living in this world, in relation to any subject. M.A.G.I.C. allows us to take charge of how we respond to any circumstance by providing a space for observation of the story, rather than interaction with the story. The result is reassurance and empowerment, irrespective of the circumstances.

The intention of M.A.G.I.C.

The intention behind M.A.G.I.C. is to initiate a change within the individual towards inner joy and peace through practicing what they innately have available. By combining five separate practices into one practice, we simplify and simultaneously amplify the change process. This internal change will bring about an observable external change. The increase in vibrational frequency within the individual then follows the rules of quantum physics; it activates a change in the outer world.

The intention of this practice will become the intention held by the one who practices it. M.A.G.I.C. as a practice can be used to address a particular issue in an individual's life, such as anxiety or depression, or something more general, such as attracting a relationship or abundance. Eventually, the seeker who is reading this book will collaborate with the wiser, more loving part of himself or herself. While there are necessary challenges for us to face that will support our evolution as humans on this planet, when we choose to accept M.A.G.I.C. as a personal practice, we will be supported and guided by that aspect of us that represents the Creator: our authentic self.

The function of M.A.G.I.C.

The function of M.A.G.I.C. is to support the retraining and reframing of the one who is practicing M.A.G.I.C. in terms of her or his thinking, while simultaneously inspiring them to reach their grandest version of their greatest self. By dissolving emotional responses such as anxiety, anger, and depression, M.A.G.I.C. nurtures alternative positive responses, such as hope, appreciation, and joy. The practice coaches the seeker into a place of alignment with their authentic self. This results in the restructuring of the very thing that causes all disharmony in life: our perceptions. Through this practice, we focus forward on our expansion, rather than focusing on the past and reenergizing it. We do not remember our past; we remember with it. That is, we relive it.

Practicing M.A.G.I.C. leads us to question the very foundations underlying our thinking, providing the opportunity to rewrite these scripts. There is a critical difference between attempting to change what and how we think and redesigning the very foundations of our thinking. Change the foundations or underlying core beliefs, and we influence everything that sits on those foundations, including what and how we think. It is the function of M.A.G.I.C. to retrain the thinking of you, the user, and re-establish this thinking from the perspective of your creator-established belief system.

The uniqueness of M.A.G.I.C.

M.A.G.I.C. is a self-generated, self-directed practice applied in less than a minute, resulting in the reactivation of personal power in a soft and gentle way. It is a simple, personalized, efficient tool that uses what the seeker already does naturally in his or her life to bring about change from the inside out. By adopting an inside-out approach, the practice revitalizes an individual's personal power. While we can never really lose our freedom to choose or our personal power, we do have the freedom to focus on living life from a place of powerlessness and bondage, or from a place blessed with power and freedom. Sometimes it takes an extreme circumstance for us to recognize that we have this power, but the power is always there. It is often in such extreme circumstances that we are shaken out of a mundane trance, or stubbornness, thereby encouraging us to call on our inner being for guidance. This helps to remind us that we have access to personal power as we continue to make choices.

As a multifaceted holistic approach recognizing and incorporating the physical quadrant of life, the practice of M.A.G.I.C. integrates the power of a meditative mind, the exhilaration of an appreciative heart, and the connection with a higher power through a transcendent relationship with Spirit, while grounding our energy and offering insightful guidance. This combination can't help but impact us on all levels of our existence. The simplicity and brevity of the practice, the small amount of effort required, the adaptability and flexibility to fit into an individual's everyday life, and the power generated by the practice qualifies it as totally unique.

What to expect from M.A.G.I.C.

Expect a reduction and eventual elimination of the underlying causal factors of pain. This practice provides an alternative, a means for inciting change by building and developing resilience against triggers and risk factors. Expect a reduction in intense emotions, such as anxiety, depression, despair, loneliness, and rage. Practicing M.A.G.I.C. delivers immediate and positive results, providing relief from pain. It does so while actively supporting a sense of self and personal control in life.

By practicing M.A.G.I.C., anyone can expect to accumulate all the benefits attributed to each of the individual practices, only in exponentially greater degrees. While this progress is gentle in nature, it should not be any surprise if the ego mind offers resistance. Expect some resistance from the ego mind in practicing M.A.G.I.C., because what we are doing is taking back from the ego mind the job description, role, and responsibility for choosing our own emotional and spiritual life.

The innate power of M.A.G.I.C.

This innate power is who we are, and when we combine it with free will, a thinking mind, and a feeling heart, we can activate the power of the practice simply by being rather than doing. You and me, we are the one, and only one. Each of us controls our own thinking, and as a result, we control our emotional state. The people, places, events, and objects in our lives give us cause to think something or feel something, but they don't actually cause us to think or feel anything. (It might be wise to read that again.)

We, as distinct beings, operate as the only variable in this story. What we unconsciously believe about ourselves living in this world, what we believe about where we came from, what we believe about our essence —each of these is under our control. It is a nice feeling when we come to the realization and acceptance that we do indeed have the power to manage our experience. There is only one variable in this story, and in reality, each of us has total influence over this one variable. We are the one and only variable.

It should be noted that accepting triggers for what they are is not about accepting or condoning disrespectful or abusive behaviors. The importance of accepting triggers for what they are—triggers—is about letting go of any attachment or expectation we allocate to those triggers. Recognizing triggers as opportunities to experience joy or growth is one way of using our freedom of choice to dissolve the influence of those triggers. When we accept triggers for what they are, it provides a means for staying detached from the drama. Of course, some individuals like the drama. This is a choice: to play out the drama, or to choose personal empowerment, and often we need to retrain our thinking to overcome this pattern. M.A.G.I.C. allows us to step back from the triggers that create the drama, so that we can make more choices of integrity for ourselves and the collective consciousness.

Practicing M.A.G.I.C. allows us to acknowledge triggers for what they are, recognize and appreciate the emotional responses within, gain clarity on the resulting thoughts, and connect with a part of ourselves that is truly authentic. If nothing else, practicing M.A.G.I.C. allows us to let go of the drama in a way that lifts our vibrational frequency. It is as simple as, when we are not focused on what we don't want, and we are finding it difficult to focus on what I do want, the best place to be is in a place of acceptance and neutrality. We allow Life to open to our greatest good in this place of acceptance and neutrality. It is literally as if we are in a continuous state of meditation.

18 - PAUL S DUNNE

CHAPTER 3

You Need To Understand

You Need To Understand?

You do not need this book

While it may serve to take it on your journey, you do not need this book. The answers you are looking for may come from the questions that arise as you read this book. My thinking is that by practicing any or all the five practices that make up M.A.G.I.C., questions will arise. It is by answering these questions that arise that you will come to know that the answers were always within and accessible to you.

If you are looking for a how-to-find-happiness book, this isn't it. This book will tell you one thing: you are happiness; you are love. The title *I Am Made for M.A.G.I.C.* could just as well have been *I Am Made for Love/Happiness*. The underlying message here is that if you simply stop doing that thing you do—the thing where you are trying to "make" things happen—and instead revert back to the five practices, life will unfold seemingly miraculously. The truth is, for some people, for some of the time, sitting on this book while meditating would serve as the most powerful means for finding inner peace.

You think, therefore, you are

You are a thinking, feeling being, with a consciousness that is aware of this. Forcing yourself to stop thinking or feeling is not only unnatural, it is self-defeating. You think, therefore, you are experiencing. You must think because it is your nature to think; it is the way you function. Your brain is the center for conscious activity, where you crystalize all your thoughts into experiences. Everything you experience grows out of a thought. Everything you observe in this world has grown out of a thought. Your thinking brain has an enormous role to play in deciding what kind of experience you have in the world. And yet, the brain isn't the captain of the ship. It may come as a shock to many people, but the majority of decisions are not made by our brains.

So, the question needs to be asked, "What is the purpose of the brain?" We can see our brain as the conscious mind. It is the engine room and chemist's warehouse, but it is not the deciding voice. Decisions relating to issues of safety from physical harm, homeostasis, and happiness take place somewhere other than in the brain. These decisions are made by the inner mind, what is often referred to as the subconscious mind. While the inner mind is accessing every experience since before you were born, and deciding the safest, most normal route forward, the conscious mind is deciding how to carry out these instructions. The word *normal* is important here because it distinguishes from *natural*. Normal is what you have learned and now refer to as "normal." Natural is what you were conceived with in this world before you were trained in the ways of thinking of the world.

It is the purpose of the brain to work out how to best carry out the instructions of the inner mind and manage the distribution of chemicals, blood flow, and general mechanics of the body. You can see the brain as an amazing computer you carry around within your person. While you can survive with very little brain, you cannot function without the brain. It is magical how the lower body continues to function even when the stem between the brain and the lower body is severed. There may not be movement, but there is still existence/life without the brain.

So, where is the captain, if not in the conscious mind? The brain (conscious mind) collaborates with the inner mind (subconscious mind), working as a central processing unit and distributor of commands, while you go about your everyday affairs. It is sometimes easy to discount the supremacy of the inner mind in this partnership. The inner mind is the part of each of us that records every single experience we've had since before we were born, up until this very moment ... and this moment ... and this moment. These recordings are in full color, surround sound, 5D, and HD, with an attached energetic charge (emotion). The inner mind has recorded and stored every experience you have ever had since before birth. It accesses these recordings whenever there is a stimulus, or what you might refer to as a "trigger." Once triggered, these memories are activated as if they are happening in the here and now. For the inner mind, everything is in the here-and-now present moment.

If a memory has a positive or good-feeling charge attached to it, you will experience the effects of something enjoyable. Likewise, if the memory has a negative or bad-feeling charge attached to it, you will experience the effects of that so-called pain memory. You experience these effects because your inner mind depends on experiences to make associations. Otherwise, you wouldn't have the reactions that you do. The inner mind is powerful; it has the power to convince the conscious mind that our legs won't work, and subsequently, they won't. The inner mind also has the power to convince your conscious mind that you are in danger, even if you aren't. The conscious mind will then react as if danger is imminent, because even though it sees no danger, the inner mind has convinced it otherwise.

When someone has a nightmare, they will commonly find themselves physically triggered, bringing about palpitations and sweats. This is because even though they are asleep, the inner mind believes the "dream" to be real and reacts accordingly. What is anxiety, worry, or stress, if not physical changes resulting from the inner mind believing something "bad" is about to happen or has happened, and providing this information to our conscious minds? The core beliefs or programs held in the inner mind not only influence but control your everyday perceptions. It is these perceptions—the way you interpret things—that govern the millions of choices you make each day.

There is a redemptive aspect in all of this: each of us has the freedom and the capacity to think different thoughts, select different actions, and focus on different issues, if we so choose. We can change our thinking—what we think about, and how we think about it. The problems arise when we live unconsciously, basically hopping from rock to rock, hoping the next rock will be handy and firm to keep us from falling into the deep. Living unconsciously means we go about our day without choosing what or how to think. Most of us do not realize we have this freedom to choose how we play out our day—or better said, how we create our day. Consciously choosing is consciously creating. This requires a commitment to retraining the brain, and we do this through the practice of M.A.G.I.C.

Just as you must think, you must feel. It is the nature of the beast. All sentient beings have something like emotions or feelings. When you shut down your feeling facility, you close off an essential part of who you are, as well as who you could become. You close off the holistic function of your heart, through which all higher-level guidance comes. We each have an amazingly powerful part of us guiding us and letting us know if what we are thinking at any moment is based in love or fear. This part communicates through the heart.

The heart's language is emotion, and when any of us rejects emotion/feeling from our experience, we reject the heart's guidance that comes from our wiser self. In his book *Conversations with God*, Neale Donald Walsch shares this insight from God: "Feeling is the language of the soul. If you want to know what's true for you about something, look to how you're feeling about it. Feelings are sometimes difficult to discover—and often even more difficult to acknowledge. Yet hidden in your deepest feelings is your highest truth. The trick is to get to those feelings."

Sadly, our thoughts and feelings are often blamed and shamed as the problem. Today's mainstream health system promulgates the need to control our thoughts and feelings, if not shut them down altogether.

This has not helped the cause. We use substances (prescribed or self-medicated) to quiet the mind and numb the emotions. Nothing in this approach serves our greater good.

Thoughts are powerful. They never die. Just as energy never dies, thoughts either continue until they join with like thoughts, or they convert into another form. Thoughts of a particular vibrational frequency attract other thoughts that vibrate at the same frequency. When this happens, the thoughts gain momentum and grow stronger. You can test this for yourself. Take any of your thoughts—just one—and give it some of your attention. As you continue to give this thought attention throughout your day, be aware of how it changes, and furthermore, be aware of what might change in your life. Do you recognize anything that has shown up in your day that reflects the thought with which you started the day?

The other interesting thing about thoughts is that every thought creates a unique experience. Today's thoughts create tomorrow's experience. Even when the experience comes from the past, the current thought about it is now creating an additional part of your life, a fresh experience that includes the same energy as the original thought. The difference now is that you have had many other experiences along the way. Now this existing thought is using the original foundational belief, plus all the experiences you have had in the meantime, to create a new unique experience. Similar feeling, new experience. Same bathwater, different bath. In so many ways, we are doing nothing more than re-living the same old stuff.

Recognizing that we have power over our thinking and which thoughts we give energy to is transformational. Recognizing that we have power over our emotions is another step up. All emotions are valuable, including anxiety, anger, depression, despair, and so on. An emotion of appreciation is no more valuable than an emotion of anxiety. Each comes to us as a message, letting us know what we think and believe. Both serve our greater good and growth as evolving humans. The insight lies in learning to appreciate our emotions as increments on a gauge providing us with information. The information tells us what we believe about ourselves living in this world.

An anxious thought, by its very nature, excites sensations in the physical body. It is the sensation that we feel as something uncomfortable. Similarly, a thought of appreciation will excite an emotional response in the physical body that feels "happy" or "loving." Both sets of sensations are there to tell us something. And here is the key: all of these emotional responses are messages from the heart to let us know we are thinking and believing something—on the one hand, something self-defeating, and on the other hand, something self-assured. Thoughts are not painful or joyous in themselves; it is the effect on our gauge that can be termed "painful" or "joyous." Change our thinking, and we will alter the reading on our gauge. If we do this enough times, we eventually change how we think, because we change our beliefs. After all, beliefs are just thoughts repeated over and over. Change what we believe about who we are in this world, and we become the change we want to see in this world.

A basic premise of M.A.G.I.C. says, "Because we think, therefore we can choose what to think about." Consider this in light of the fact that a painful thought cannot exist in the same space as a thought fueled by appreciation. It is truly a choice of where we place our focus. The practice of M.A.G.I.C. doesn't mean we are thinking "positive" thoughts all day—usually not. Rather, with this practice, we stay longer and more often in the here-and-now moment, which is neutral. Without judgment or attachment, we do not need to avoid anything. Add to this the practice of connection, grounding, and insight, and we can enjoy accepting responsibility for our creations.

Life is an inside-out process

As children, we are taught that what we can "see" is what is "real." We come to understand how important it is to change what is happening in the world outside of ourselves if we want to be happier on the inside. Make the people, places, and events on the outside happy, and this will make us happy on the inside. Upset these people, and we will suffer. While this is the mode of operation for most people, it is back-to-front thinking. Most of us interpret thoughts, feelings, and triggers as an outside-in process: there is something happening on the outside that is causing an effect on the inside. This is far from the truth.

Consider it from this perspective: what we believe about ourselves (or anyone else) in this world is what we project onto the screen we call "the world." We are always projecting onto this screen. The light never stops shining through us, even when we filter it with our thinking. Imagine it like a projector shining a clean white light onto a screen. In front of the projector, we then place a film rolling past the light. Now the image on the screen becomes that of the filtered light rather than the pure light. Change the film, and we change the image on the screen. What we project onto this screen is what we perceive to be the truth in some form. It may not be conscious, but it is a truth we hold within. And what we thus perceive or observe in our world becomes our experience. Our screen—the world—becomes our reality. The more we see it, the more we come to believe it must be true. But as master teachers have decreed throughout time, all permanent change must start from the inside, as the cause for change on the outside. This is a reminder that when there is chaos within, there is chaos without; peace within, peace without; love within, love without.

Triggers are just that - triggers

We all have powerful triggers in our lives. Triggers exist and will always exist. There will be people, places, and events that leave us feeling "good," and there will be abusive, disrespectful, and challenging people, places, and events in this world that leave us feeling "bad." That is the way of the world. But it is this contrast that gives birth to creativity, invention, and the story of evolution from the beginning of time. As I've mentioned, when we don't like a particular trigger in our outer world, we are taught how important it is to change something about those external conditions so we can feel okay. But the hidden reality is that we cannot truly change something on the outside if we don't change it on the inside. It may be possible to change something outside of ourselves for a short time, but ultimately it will return to the same or similar status, and always with a similar vibrational frequency.

Have you ever wondered why we attract people into our lives who mirror our parents, or how some people seem to attract photocopies of their last partner? Have you ever wondered why an individual who was bullied in school seems to attract this same treatment as she or he goes into adulthood? If we only change the circumstances or situation on the outside without changing what is happening on the inside, we will repeat the undesired experience over and over.

Instead, by making choices to change how we perceive the world—and in particular, how we see ourselves in the world—we can hold onto our power rather than giving it away in reaction to the external trigger. The only power triggers have in our lives is the power we give them as we stew over them in bed at night or wrestle with them as we go about our day. So, by remaining firmly committed to our life principles and living consciously, we not only reverse the impact of external triggers, we align with the superhero within. From this place, we naturally access creativity, spontaneity, strength, and guidance. This teaching goes back in time and across borders. It is one of the underpinning principles of M.A.G.I.C.: life is an inside-out job.

Natural flow

M.A.G.I.C. is a personal tool that places us in a state of natural flow. Perhaps the best way to illustrate natural flow is to have you remember a time when your creativity and synchronicity were peaking. It is in such times that things appear to be working out the best for you. You may even notice that in these times, your dis-stress levels are much lower, if not nonexistent. We experience the state of natural flow as creativity, being "in the zone," feeling inner peace and contentment, and the feeling of being one with nature. Each of us knows this state of natural flow in our own way in different circumstances. When we are in the state of natural flow, everything in life seems to flow with ease. This is not to say that life is all "happy-happy, joy-joy"; it was never meant to be that. After all, it is the contrast in life that gives us variety. But natural flow is a time when, even if circumstances are challenging, we operate from a calm and optimistic state of mind. And by practicing M.A.G.I.C., we challenge the ways of thinking and behaving that take us out of our natural flow state.

M.A.G.I.C. practiced in conflict situations alters what is happening for the people and events involved, within moments, and it always moves things towards a return to flow state. It has been reported that engaging with M.A.G.I.C. has helped people meet the black dog of depression at the door and make friends with it, allowing them to get on with their lives. M.A.G.I.C. has been successfully practiced in eliminating a growing feeling of anxiety or the threat of a panic attack, leaving a feeling of inner calm. These outcomes underline the crux of being in a natural flow state.

As with the athlete, musician, parent, teacher, gardener, performer, artist, mechanic, or surgeon, when we are in the moment, allowing the innate part of us to come to the surface, there is a flow present. It matters not who we are, where we are, or the circumstances that appear in our lives; the practice of M.A.G.I.C. provides a way to be in a state of flow more often and with more consistency, allowing us to be consciously aware of the effects. Because we are the cause, we can always choose our preferred effects. The only proviso is that we have to choose.

Everywhere and for everyone, there is a natural flow of Source energy that functions in our lives at all times. This can be seen as Love, God, Source, All There Is, the quantum field, or simply as the light shining through the prism, presenting as the all-pervasive, ever-flowing field we call life. There is no source of darkness; there is only a source of light. But that light can be filtered or dimmed by our thinking, and what we end up with is an absence of light. It is this absence that we call darkness.

Each of us has baggage that limits the natural flow. The baggage doesn't stop the Source light from flowing, of course, but it certainly restricts it. It acts as a filter or a film through which the light must pass. The more baggage we have, the less light that can come through. To help us with this, we all have a gauge to let us know how much of our origin light or life we are allowing to flow through. The gauge measures this flow in increments of emotion. The greater the amount of light we are allowing to flow through, the more the gauge will tell us that all is full of love. The less light we allow through, the more the gauge will tell us there is a lack of light, which equals pain. One end of the gauge registers fear emotions, and the other end registers love emotions. The love emotions end basically says, "I am allowing all or most of the light to flow through my filter." Note: it is not the trauma or the experiences we have in life that act as the filter of the light; it is the beliefs, the interpretations we hold of these experiences that act as the filters.

Most people do not understand the simplicity of this concept, or they do not know how to adjust the flow of light, so they adjust the next most accessible thing: the gauge itself. The reasoning for this is that if we disconnect the gauge or alter what it is telling us, then we don't have to deal with the feedback. The feedback can be uncomfortable, and if we do not understand how to adjust the light flow, the next best thing is to turn off the alarm bells. So, we can hide the gauge, we can dumb it down, or we can try ignoring it. But ultimately, we cannot stop it from working. It is part of our makeup, and it functions continuously to let us know the state of play. In the middle of the game of life, it is helpful to know the score. It is our gauge (emotional status) that gives us the score in any moment. We use many things to mute the gauge, like drinking, drugs, medication, food, work, sex, adrenaline stimulation, and religion. But no matter what we try, soon enough, the pressure of discomfort builds up to a point where we can no longer ignore it. This can become so painful that we want to leave this life experience. To the immature, unaware, or altered mind, opting out of life can appear to be the only option.

Allowing this light to shine through is our purpose, because it creates a new world, and another, and another. This is our evolution as individual aspects of the creative force and as a collective. By focusing on shining the light, rather than focusing on our discomfort and blaming the gauge, we engage the laws of the natural universe to energize this intention. Where focus goes, energy flows. To put this another way, what you look at and give your attention to grows in size and strength. This is a universal law that operates in all sections of society, from school playgrounds to multimillion-dollar board rooms. The force of energy that maintains this universe does not judge your choice of where you place your focus; it simply magnifies your intention. It makes tangible that which you give focus to, and so if you can focus on the light—or at least stop focusing on the lack of light—your life will reflect this.

The obvious question here is, how do you move your focus away from the pain, the discomfort, the lack of light and inspiration, toward seeing the light showing up in the world you see, hear, and feel? Practicing M.A.G.I.C. will lead you into shining your light. Rather than expending your energy on trying to move the clouds in the sky, start by moving the clouds in your mind. See the clouds moving and changing in your mind, then notice what happens in the sky.

Using the power of now

M.A.G.I.C. is a gentle way to return to and stay in the now moment. Focusing on the now moment makes letting go of fear related to thinking about the past and future effortless. Being in the now moment is practicing acceptance. There is no attachment or expectation. We accept the gift of the present and the present as a gift, letting go of past pain and future worries. When we commit to this practice, life becomes a "now" experience. It is in this "now" that we have access to our divine power, awakening all the energies of the universe.

An important outcome here is that we get out of our own way, allowing our inner being to highlight any opportunity for manifesting our dreams. "Your entire life only happens at this moment. The present moment is life itself. Yet, people live as if the opposite were true and treat the present moment as a stepping-stone to the next moment—a means to an end." When we harness the power of now, we are in a much better place to recognize what is taking place in terms of our emotional state. This allows us to make conscious choices about the type of thoughts we entertain, intentionally adjusting our emotional state.

You already do this

Practice anywhere, anytime, everywhere, all the time. In fact, the more situations and circumstances in which M.A.G.I.C. is practiced, the more the effects will be noticed. The practice of M.A.G.I.C. needs to fit into your day in a way that allows you to get on with your day without too much extra effort. Look at the various segments of your day and consider how practicing M.A.G.I.C. can fit in. For example, if exercise is a regular activity for you, ask yourself, "How can I practice M.A.G.I.C. while exercising?" If you practice yoga, then you will find that there are ways that you already practice M.A.G.I.C. If it is a team sport or an individual workout routine, then you may need to think about it. You may already be engaging with some aspects of M.A.G.I.C. without being aware of it.

Additional questions to consider might include: Do I practice mindfulness while I exercise? Do I practice mindfulness while I am eating? Am I practicing appreciation throughout or after my exercise session? Do I practice appreciation during my day, without noticing it? Do I ground myself during exercise through intention or by going outdoors? Do I connect with my fifty trillion cells, other people, or Spirit while exercising? Am I aware of my connection with myself, others, or Spirit during my day? You may be surprised to find that you already do this. For instance, maybe you connect with your cells by registering pain or discomfort when exercising. This is your cells talking to you. In any case, every time you have a thought, it is communication with your cells. Think "thin," think "fat," think "can't," and this is a direct communication to your trillions of cells.

Let us consider the practice of meditation. "Meditation? I don't like it!" "I can't do that!" "I can't sit still long enough to meditate." These are common complaints about the practice of meditation, which all have one thing in common: they suggest the need to "do" something. But the practice of meditation is not about doing anything; it is about *being*. Without even knowing it, we can practice mindfulness and being meditative. Recognizing this and making it a little more conscious means we are choosing to be proactive about our practice. If you have ever watched the clouds float by, gazed into a fire, connected with a body of water, or spaced out while listening to music, then you can meditate. If you can notice your breathing or your heart beating, then you can meditate. This is mindfulness meditation, and everyone does it in some way some of the time.

Sitting cross-legged, chanting, breathing, and grappling with a "monkey mind" that is constantly thinking about everything (including thinking itself) is not all that appealing to most people. The strict rules that come with many practices serve only to discourage potential practitioners. But M.A.G.I.C. does not have a set of rules to limit you. Rather, this practice is to be molded into everyone's unique frame of reference. There are principles and guidelines, but these are there to support the seeker and help fine-tune the practice into his or her own unique customized design. It is the individual who decides to practice for only a minute or to extend the practice period. It is entirely up to each individual. Cross your legs, or keep driving; it is up to the individual. Several one-minute practice periods throughout the day are the suggested format. However, it is your choice whether you want to combine short with extended practice periods. Rather than practicing a meditation during your day, making the day a meditation is the aim.

If someone enjoys spending time in nature, they are intuitively practicing grounding. If someone listens to their intuition (their gut feeling), or spends time with an advisor or counselor looking for answers, this is practicing insight. M.A.G.I.C. is part of who we are and part of our everyday experience. There are no special skills required. This is a natural practice made conscious. Finding the best and most suitable way to engage in this practice is part of the fun, part of the experience. It is important to fit M.A.G.I.C. into our everyday activities, not pile it on top of them.

It becomes personal

M.A.G.I.C. is a choice. It requires embracing yourself in your own unique way, with your own unique needs and preferences. We each have our own needs, lifestyles, quirks, likes, and dislikes. Because it is a way of living, the practice adjusts to each individual's unique characteristics and lifestyle. Even when there are demands on time or resources, M.A.G.I.C. is flexible enough in its content and design to fit into anybody's day. We can use the practice while changing a diaper, in a business meeting, in the middle of a heated discussion, driving a six-hundred-horsepower machine, or sitting on a horse. It can be used in a working, social, or study environment. Different individuals use the practice to enhance their personal life journeys, change their relationship status, support conscious parenting, or redesign their lives. When considered as an application in an organization, M.A.G.I.C. is activated by the individual to have far-reaching ramifications within that organization.

Mother of invention

There have been times in my life when I have found myself on the edge of the precipice, at my wit's end, overwhelmed by nothing and everything at the same time. Times when I recognize that the world has expectations of me to perform. Times when I realize that I have expectations of myself to save the world and do it with a smile, to make sure everyone is happy, and to achieve success in a materialistic framework. In these times, I am far too busy to make any sense of it. It is only after the fact that I recognize that there is another way of seeing my world. But there is something more important I have realized in such insightful moments. I realize, as a result of the "crisis moment," that while I may not have come through it unscathed, I have gained insight, appreciation, and connection, and in many ways, I have become mindful of my growth. Indeed, crisis is an opportunity, and necessity is the mother of invention.

We cannot always do anything about the way our families, schools, workplaces, or society demand that we perform in the way they want us to perform. In fact, we cannot always do anything about the way *we* demand that we perform in the way we think we need to perform. The good news is that we can do something about the feelings and emotions that present as stress, tension, and anxiety when we feel this pressure. Feelings of guilt, failure, not being good enough, hopelessness, anger, frustration, and despair are a few of the many uncomfortable feelings experienced and brought about by everyday triggers. That being said, it needs to be recognized that everyday triggers can also bring about feelings of joy, excitement, happiness, inspiration, calm, and hope. A subtle but powerful insight exists here.

We are not taught about the power of our thoughts and the purpose of our emotions during our development. We are taught how to control our emotions and told how to think, but neither of these is empowering. Consequently, it is not the bullying per se that causes a person to self-harm or consider suicide; it is the inability to distance oneself from the effects of the thoughts and feelings triggered by the bullying. The inability to understand and effectively manage the mind and the resulting emotions has us cut off from our natural flow of joy. This means we experience an ongoing internal discord, which results in us focusing on a lack of joy. The result is that we experience an increased lack of joy. A major contributing factor that drives any individual to harm himself or herself, or to harm another person, is not (for many reasons) assuming the response-ability for his or her emotional state. Many individuals do not know about this ability to respond to underlying emotions. If she or he doesn't know of this ability to respond to charged emotions, or does not know how to respond to charged emotions, the experience can be overwhelming. This, of course, means the thoughts he or she thinks and the style of thinking he or she uses will leave them little choice in how they deal with their pain.

Negative triggers will always exist in life, just as there will always be positive triggers. This isn't about the individual, but about the way the world works. There has always been bullying, domestic violence, expectations, and pressures to perform, shame and blame, and judgment and criticism, just as social exclusion, racism, bigotry, and isolation have always existed. There are as many types of triggers in this world as there are conscious minds to react to them. Triggers cause some individuals to react with scripted thinking, or patterns of thinking, learned over a lifetime. Scripted thinking always comes from the ego self. This is the unique, personalized databank of beliefs such as "I am broken," "I am not enough," "I am not good enough compared to what they expect," "I am unsafe and insecure," "I am alone and lonely, isolated," "I am different and don't fit the script," "I should be this, I should be that," and a variety of other core beliefs learned during our younger years.

As we have seen, triggers provoke thinking, and the resulting thoughts excite our emotions. The brain recognizes these emotions as sensations in the body. We can understand the sensations of different emotions in our bodies as messages from our hearts. If these messages feel nice, then we will usually move on, and if these feelings or messages are painful, it can be all too easy to believe something is broken inside of us.

Emotions are a natural occurrence. It is the way we are made. These sensations we call feelings are natural wonders taking place in a world of electricity, magnetism, chemicals, and minerals: our bodies. It is important to remind ourselves that these sensations result from electromagnetic and chemical changes in and between our trillions of cells. Both pleasant feelings and painful feelings are amazing events happening in our bodies. When we shut this emotional response off, or dumb it down with drugs, then we break off from ourselves.

Most of us learn that feelings that show up as emotional discomfort are "bad." We learn to avoid, repress, resist, and deny all feelings that represent emotional pain. Sometimes these emotions are too painful to deal with alone, and so they are repressed, until the pain is so big that it cannot be ignored. It doesn't get much worse than this. When an individual believes they have no way out of their pain, the experience that emerges is a sense of powerlessness. Even depression is a better feeling than powerlessness, and anger is better than depression. At least if someone is angry rather than depressed, they are energized to change something about their circumstances. But if they are depressed rather than powerless, they can still do something.

It is at this point that necessity can become the mother of invention. The idea is to move from powerlessness through despair, through depression, through rage and anger to hope, all the way up the emotional scale to appreciation and love. I have often felt that my most important role as a practitioner is to give my clients some hope.

Most of us learn young—and we learn very well—how to engage in thinking that is stuck in the past or in the imagined future. Past thinking can elicit feelings of guilt, depression, sadness, anger, and general victim thinking, while thinking based in the future often causes feelings of fear, anxiety, anger, and powerlessness to be activated. This type of thinking builds on itself. The result is an increased emotional response to escalating thoughts of pain. In the end, the only way to stop the pain is to stop thinking and feeling. Here there is little or no hope, and the mother of necessity is powerless to change the circumstances.

No one can make another person happy or sad. We do this ourselves, with our thinking. And if anyone thinks that sounds too much like a cliché rather than a reality, it may be time to look at how much response-ability we are taking for our choices. We think we feel terrible because of what someone says or does to us. In fact, we are unhappy because we are judging them for their judging. The truth is that when someone says something or does something that leaves us feeling unhappy, we are not unhappy because of what they have said or done. The reason we feel this way is that we depend on them to like us so that we can feel happy. As a result, we just gave away our power. We cannot control what is going on in another person's life, and we can't control how they feel, and yet we often depend on them being happy with us so we can be happy.

We each carry core beliefs about ourselves living in this world. Many of these core beliefs tell us we are not worthy, not good enough, or less than enough. When a negative core belief is triggered, we feel the associated pain, plus the pain associated with any charged memories of a similar vibration. A trigger for anxiety will activate all charged memories vibrating at the same vibration as the emotion of anxiety. Similarly, a trigger for anger will not only elicit anger as a reaction, it will activate all charged memories vibrating with a similar frequency of anger. When this happens, it can present as overwhelming or out of control. Old pain is created from memories reenergized, presenting as energy moving in the body: emotion.

When we recognize, acknowledge, and transmute painful charged memories, we activate our authentic self, which always supports self-love. With this release, this cutting of ties to past pain, the bully loses power over his or her target, the partner loses power over the other, and parents lose power over their child. This is because deactivating the trigger eliminates any messages, we may have been sending out about being a victim. This is particularly important when we are considering bullies and victims. No victim means no target for the victim bully. In actuality, because the perpetrator is a victim in their own right, they are vibrating at the same frequency as the victim. Provided one of these players changes their vibration to send out a different message, the game will cease.

Practicing M.A.G.I.C. moves the focus from victim thinking to neutrality, if not to feeling good about the self. The mother of invention comes out of everyday challenges, along with the problems and painful contrasts experienced in this life, as we consciously choose to focus on the solutions. That being said, we need to know about and allow the warrior part of each of us to stand up so that we can believe in ourselves.

No, it's not always that simple! While personal resilience protects an individual from the effects of triggers in his or her life, there are more and more young people who are extremely sensitive not only to "other people's" opinions, but they are sensitive to other people's energy. Another persons' energetic field can often influence us just by us being around them. Michael Faraday's Law of Induction describes how an electric current produces a magnetic field, and conversely, how a changing magnetic field generates an electric current in a conductor. The body is a conductor of electromagnetic flow. The human heart sends out an electromagnetic wave we can scientifically measure, about three meters in all directions. That means each of us is sending out these waves, so we are communicating all the time. These waves carry information that is received by all of life. It is basic physics that we influence and are influenced by those around us energetically.

We are desperate in our heads

As I moved into adulthood, I came to realize how important it was for me to use my head to make rational decisions and solve problems. It wasn't until my later years that I came to the realization that my brain was not the solution-creating machine it was made out to be. I came to realize that solutions are more about creativity than they are about weighing the pros and cons. After reading *Psycho-Cybernetics* by Maxwell Maltz, *Think and Grow Rich* by Napoleon Hill, and *The Power of Your Subconscious Mind* by Joseph Murphy, I came to the realization that the brain isn't the simple answer to my success.

But it was too late. By the time I had settled into my profession, there was a war taking place within. On one side, there was an arrogant conviction that I had to be logical, rational, and systematic about my thinking and my way of living. Problems were to be solved using clear, rational, logical thinking processes. While one part of me was studying the philosophies of the East, the other part of me was studying the power of thinking and how using the brain is the only way to find happiness and success. I came to understand that there was a different intended message than the one most people concluded from the writings of the great proponents of goal-setting, motivation, and success. The underlying message is the spirit of the teachings, not the mechanics of the teachings. Goal-setting is about the power of intention and how it influences the universal force field. The underlying message of motivation is about the power of inspiration and attracting people to aspire rather than moving them with fear. Success is more about living one's passion, or as Joseph Campbell says, "Follow your bliss."

The problems we face as individuals and as a collective come from within. Thus, the solutions also come from within. While this may be the truth, this will remain nothing but intellectual mind-chatter until we know this to be the truth. Intellectualizing this will not help unless we move into feeling, and then move into knowing. We need to know we are powerful beyond measure, not simply say it. M.A.G.I.C. the practice comes out of a need to highlight an individual's personal power to take charge of their life. Practicing M.A.G.I.C. provides a foundation for this change, by helping you understand that "I am not the victim of the world I see."

The ego is focused on the physical plane. It argues that our physical presence and experience are the only important areas of focus. It focuses on the physical, while using the physical as leverage to convince us to live and behave from a fear-based mindset. There is no room for any spiritual, irrational, or illogical discussion. The ego is desperate to keep us in fear mode. Otherwise, we could ignore the ego's masterminded-ness and trust in our own empowerment. If we did this, the ego would suffer and shrink. It is clear that the ego, which operates through the head, is desperate enough to try anything.

While this practice allows a seeker to observe corresponding changes coming about on a physical level, the mechanics of M.A.G.I.C. require our acceptance and use of a nonphysical, no-control approach. In other words, we are operating on a spiritual or energetic foundation. Each of the five practices nurtures and activates our spiritual operating system, our internal processes. This is an inside-out process, and as such, we need to start by changing our energetic frequency. This means we stop listening to the desperation of the ego speaking through the head and listen to our wiser self speaking through our heart.

CHAPTER 4

Before You Step In

Before You Step In

Like many people, I have spent much energy and many hours looking for answers, guidance, and solutions—all while knowing that the journey around the globe will always bring us back to find what we are searching for deep within. And while the answers are within, the means for digging up those answers can vary enormously from person to person. What is right for me is not necessarily right for you. Here are some things you might want to take into consideration before you start riding this horse.

Using M.A.G.I.C. as a personal practice is not for everyone. Each of us finds our own path for personal peace and growth on this planet. This is one practice, one way to make the experience of chopping wood and carrying water more enjoyable, entertaining, and expansive for you. While there is much in this practice that can support you, it isn't the only option, so recognize that you may need to keep searching.

This practice is not governed by religion, culture, race, gender, or socioeconomic status. It is indeed a spiritual practice—but then again, so is living. We cannot get away from the fact that we are energetic beings, clumps of energy interacting in what appears to be a physical reality. Whatever we are, do, or have is spiritual in nature, and as such, any practice that nourishes this has to benefit us holistically. M.A.G.I.C. as a practice will nourish you and your life experience.

Not a quick fix

If you want a quick fix, this may not be for you. Then again, it may very well serve your purpose. M.A.G.I.C. is a personal practice for achieving an inner calm, not a quick fix—nor is it offered as the solution to all your problems. It is offered on the premise that problems are normal, and we need these problems in our lives for our individual and collective expansion. How you view your problems and how you subsequently deal with those problems will hopefully be supported by using this practice.

More than physical

In authentic martial arts play, the solution never originates in the physical dimension. It always originates in the spirit, finds impetus in the heart, and formulates in the head, and only when this protocol is followed will it carry into the physical realm, where action occurs with the hands and feet. Without the spirit, heart, and mind, the body loses its stability and efficiency.

This protocol, when there is an alignment of the heart, head, and hands, is a proficient and effective protocol for opening up to solutions. If you always need to "fix" problems with a physical or mental response, rather than considering the spirit of the problem, this may not be for you. If you are looking for external solutions to internal matters, this may not be for you. M.A.G.I.C. is an experience to help you navigate the physical experience. You need to decide whether you are living in an energetic/spiritual world, or if you are completely constrained by the physical.

Meditation, meditation

If you are not willing to consider engaging in a little meditation each day, this may not be for you. Some form of meditation—*your* form of meditation—is of the essence for this practice. It is essential for life. The form of meditation has to be your choice, and to meditate or not to meditate has to be your choice. M.A.G.I.C. promotes the practice of meditation and suggests the use of mindfulness meditation as a way of turning your day into a meditation, as opposed to having a meditation during your day.

Importance of questioning

If you accept the information presented here as all you need, without doing your own research, this may not be for you. Reading the books, watching the videos, and buying the T-shirt is only part of the journey. If you believe everything you read here without questioning or challenging it or undertaking a little of your own research, this may not be for you. Read the book, consider the information, and then undertake your own research through practice, experimentation, gathering data, and sharing through connection. Most importantly, repeat the last sentence to the point that you are living it. While words can inspire and guide, words don't teach. Your personal experience is the best teacher.

Commit to change

This practice was developed for everyone, but not everyone will want to practice what has been developed. It is not intended to serve all your needs. It is flexible enough to meet everyone where they are, offering practical options for accessing inner peace. Anyone who commits to understanding and engaging in the practice regularly guarantees change. Most of all, this is a practice to be lived. While understanding isn't necessary, it can support the commitment. As with all new things, there is a need to educate the mind. Focus, belief, and action need to be your allies. If you think that just reading and remembering the information in this book is enough without actually applying the practice, this may not be for you. We think with the head; we feel with the heart; we come to know with our spirit self, our inner being; and then we can live it physically once we know.

CHAPTER 5

The Principles of M.A.G.I.C.

The Principles of M.A.G.I.C.

After walking beside many individuals in a bid to provide support, guidance, and hope, I have learned one thing: while I may not have been the "best" practitioner around, I made it my priority to live with integrity. Integrity matters when it comes to supporting the spirit of individuals in physical reality. Establishing a sense of integrity demands that one have a set of principles on which one can stand. When the arguments start, and the rules and laws are thrown around, the only standby we have is the set of principles by which we choose to live. Integrity doesn't come from having a strong will or being stubborn. Integrity comes from following the set of principles that governs how we live. Must you have the same principles as me? No! The advantage we each have is that there have been—and there currently are—master teachers who understand the workings of the universe and want to share with those who are interested.

At the foundation of this practice is a set of principles that come from what might be referred to as "universal principles." These universal principles help us focus on the inherent power within the practice. As with universal law, we find these principles in all aspects of life. If there is one thing you take away from this writing, let it be establishing and living by your own set of principles. No, you don't have to accept the principles listed here as your own. In fact, it is a basic principle that anyone adopting a new set of principles has the responsibility and freedom to establish his or her own set of principles. These principles may very well come from other people's principles, but they are yours to do with what you will. The suggestion is for you to consider the following principles, play with them, and commit to having a set of principles you own.

Here, a principle is a foundation or law used to explain how something operates—its origin, source, dogma, or code. It is an acknowledgment that a principle exists, and it operates in a particular manner in all situations. The underlying principles supporting M.A.G.I.C. offer you, the aspirant, some explanation of how the practice operates and how change comes about. These principles are fundamental to our individual and global evolution on this planet. What follows is a set of principles you can adopt as your own to guide your daily practice, as well as to support you when making your life decisions. Consider your principles as a base you can return to for your own sense of peace and reassurance. In this way, practicing M.A.G.I.C. acts as a reset button.

There is no compromise with these principles. There is no exclusion of any individual, no coercion of any individual, and no judgment of any individual by the spirit within each principle. They are what they are and do what they do—period. Adopt an attitude of love and respect for you regarding the set of principles, no matter what principles you decide to accept.

The following are the key principles underpinning the model. Use these principles as a reference point or reset button if challenges arise as you use this practice. These are not the only principles underpinning the practice. They are presented as a guide for the practice and to help you appreciate the spirit of the practice while imparting a base on which integrity can be built.

1. **We are One, living in separation.**

2. What you put out is what you get back.
3. Life is an inside-out job.
4. Follow your highest excitement.
5. The power is in the now.
6. All is One; One is vibration.
7. The cause-and-effect principle follows an absolute law.
8. What you resist will persist.
9. Listen to your heart; your head is desperate.

We are One, living in separation

Principle: We are as we were created by Love, with love, for love, to be One with Love, while our ego mind has us believing we are separated.

While we are one consciousness, we are separate experiences. We can never separate from our Source, and so we are forever divine in nature. We are as Love made us, made by love, with love, for love. We choose to experience separation through our ego mind. We live in this world as split energy: the ego self and the authentic self.

It sometimes helps to think that we are being created continuously, rather than thinking we were created once upon a time. To say we were created once upon a time suggests that we were made as separate and distinct, like something coming off an assembly line. To believe we are separate and distinct from that which created us belongs to a belief system held by the ego mind. It is the ego mind's desperate need to see itself as separate from that which created us because if we were One with our Creator, the ego mind would lose all power and control. It is therefore the role of the ego mind to convince us that we are separate from that which created us so that we will continually return to the ego mind for guidance, support, and critical advice.

The nature of that which created us is omniscient, omnipresent, and omnificent. We are what we are as an expression of that which created us because a thought never leaves its source. If our Creator didn't think us up—because it certainly wasn't the ego—one has to wonder, where is our source if not our Creator? While we kept our godly powers, we have forgotten this and instead believe in separation. This separation presents because we have taken on consciousness, which presents as us being in physical form. Consciousness is the domain of the ego, and with consciousness comes perception, which makes the mind a perceiver rather than a creator.[10]

As a perceiver, we innocently use our creative powers to project onto the world whatever our ego mind believes to be the truth. What the mind can conceive and believe, it will perceive, irrespective of whether it is fictional or truth. The information our ego mind relies upon to make decisions is a data bank of fictional stories gathered over a lifetime or many lifetimes. These stories are our life experiences. Because of our consciousness and our awareness of experiencing one reality, it is challenging to consider truth.

Because we perceive what we have projected onto this experience as the truth—our reality—we resist the concept that this is an illusion. All our fears arise from the belief that we have become separate from that which created us. We see ourselves as destructive bodies vulnerable to attack, while simultaneously creating images in our mind that we are under attack. The attack will go wherever we allow the mind to go, and it encompasses everything from microscopic life forces like viruses and bacteria to nuclear disasters and the collision of worlds.

What you put out is what you get back

Principle: All things are attracted to all other things vibrating at the same or similar frequency.

This law, like all universal laws, operates without judgment and without favor. It operates consistently and continuously throughout the entire universe. It operates based on attraction, never coercion. Like all laws, we cannot see it. It is not something to hold, but we can see, hear, and touch evidence that this law exists, along with its measurable effects. "What you put out is what you get back" is a principle operating throughout the universe. We can reword it to read, "That which is like unto itself is drawn." In practical terms, angry people will attract into their lives angry people, places, and events, while individuals who practice appreciation will attract people, places, and events into their lives that resonate with appreciation.

This law explains the physics of how we attract the things, events, and people that we draw into our lives. Everything is vibration. Even our five senses operate based on vibrational frequencies. The basic physics operating within this law shows us how everything we see—and what we don't see—forms out of a universal field of energy, and those aspects that vibrate at the same frequency will be attracted to one another. Our thoughts, feelings, words, and actions produce energies that attract like energies, or energies that vibrate at a similar frequency. Negative energies attract negative energies, and positive energies attract positive energies.

Often, we consider two individuals to be opposites in nature. We even say that opposites attract. The underlying principle operating here is that we are attracted to one another not because we are opposites, but rather because we are vibrating at a similar frequency. What we have in common is our dominant vibrational frequency. Just because we exhibit our dominant frequencies to the world through different choices of actions and words doesn't mean we are vibrating at different frequencies. Two individuals can each hold a core belief that he or she is not good enough, which manifests as insecurity. One person might portray this as mild and meek, with little power to stand up for themselves. The other might portray this as power and control over another, always needing to be powerful in a bid to feel good about themselves.

We exhibit differently because we respond and react to the world in the ways we have learned. When two individuals come together in a situation or relationship, and if they each have a dominant vibration of being a victim of circumstances, people, events, or life, their individual and joint choices will promote a victim-style mentality. What I believe about me living in this world adjusts my vibrational frequency, which in turn attracts people, places, events, and circumstances that match that frequency. This was highlighted for me as a practitioner supporting individuals who were victims of or perpetrators of domestic violence. I found the same blueprint underlies acts of bullying. Alter the vibrational frequency, and you change the behavior.

It's basic physics. What we put out into the world via our thoughts and emotions is what we get back via the manifestation of events, experiences, and matter. This is an energetic universe, and every thought, every emotion is moving outward, influencing the field of energy that saturates and surrounds all things. We have no choice; we are always putting out our thoughts and emotions, and we are always getting something back. But being mindful of this process is another matter.

Intention is the key here. When the power of thought energized by the quantum energy of emotion is focused through intention and attention, the effect is unavoidable. The act of intention causes a change in the quantum field of electrons, which brings about an effect. Science has shown us that the act of studying something will cause it to change on a quantum level. Intention is the act of consciously or unconsciously putting something out. Intention through attention is the key to all things we seek. The act of consciously setting an intention acts like a laser beam focused on a point of attraction. This is attention or focus. With the power of pure intention, an individual can move a mountain, and a group of individuals can change the world. Pure intention is the focusing of thought, emotion, and spirit (energy) to influence the chosen point of attention. What physical force cannot change is often altered through focused intention.

Setting an intention to remain vigilant, and monitoring our emotional indicators throughout the day, allows us to make conscious choices to cultivate our happiness... or not! When we neglect to set an intention for ourselves, we accept the intention of our ego mind or other people's egos. The trick isn't to be conscious of our every intention; that would drive us crazy. It would be like trying to "think positive" all the time and watching our thoughts all the time. Because our emotional state provides us with an indication of where we are focusing our attention, through our emotions, we are guided to make moment-by-moment choices of intention.

"The essence of that which is like unto itself is drawn. And what that means is, if I feel unappreciated because of circumstances that have recently occurred in my experience, the Law of Attraction cannot now surround me with people who appreciate me. That would defy the Law of Attraction. If I feel fat and unhappy about the way my body looks and feels, I cannot discover the process or state of mind that is necessary to achieve a good-feeling, good-looking body. That would defy the Law of Attraction. If I feel discouraged about my financial situation, it cannot improve. Improvement in the face of discouragement would defy the Law of Attraction. If I am angry because people have been taking advantage of me, lying to me, dishonoring me, and even defacing my property, no action that I can take can stop those unpleasant things from happening, for that would defy the Law of Attraction. The Law of Attraction simply and accurately reflects back to you in a myriad of ways an accurate response to your vibrational output. In short, whatever is happening to you is a perfect Vibrational Match to the current vibration of your Being—and the emotions that are present within you indicate that vibrational state of Being."[11]

Life is an inside-out job

Principle: We need to change first on the inside what we want to change on the outside.

Our world reflects our core beliefs and the thoughts that arise from those beliefs. To put this another way, we perceive in the world what we project onto the world. The only way we can bring about a change in our external world is to bring about a change in our internal world. Change our thoughts—our old, outdated beliefs—and this will change our moment-to-moment imagery. This will affect a change in our external world. Life is an inside-out job. If we force a change on the outside without the needed change on the inside, the condition will continue, often presenting in another form.

While it may not be groundbreaking news in scientific journals, it is old news in the ancient teachings and modern coaching philosophies that all the power we have comes from within. The world on the outside of us is a reflection of the world within. Charles F. Haanel writes in *The Master Key System*, "Harmony in the world within, will be reflected in the world without by harmonious conditions. The world without reflects the circumstances and conditions of the consciousness within."[12] James Allen writes in *As a Man Thinketh*, "Men do not attract that which they want, but that which they are."[13] Revisit this last quote often and in particular, the part that says, "but that which they are." Contemplate this concept, because this is one of the fundamental principles upon which M.A.G.I.C. is founded.

With an unimaginable amount of time, energy, and money spent each day on diets, the question continues to be asked, "Why is it that so many people try so many diets for so little benefit?" Ever wondered why in our heads we know something to be one thing, but our entire being reacts as if it were something else? And why do we repeat the same behaviors over and over, no matter how much we try not to—like attracting the same types of partners, events, and experiences that we have always attracted in life? Much of the explanation for this observable fact comes from an understanding of the workings of the inner mind. In his book *Self Mastery Through Conscious Autosuggestion*, Emile Coué explains how the unconscious self presides over the functions of our body, but it also controls all of our actions. "It is this we call imagination, and it is this which, contrary to accepted opinion, always makes us act even, and above all, against our will when there is antagonism between these two forces."[14]

The blended practice of M.A.G.I.C. is an inside-out process. It changes our internal environment, thus bringing about changes in our external environment. That which is above is the same as that which is below, and that which we create within becomes the reality we experience without. When we want to influence the perceived world, we must first alter something within our unseen world.

Follow your highest excitement

Principle: When you follow your highest excitement—your greatest joy—at any moment, to the best of your ability with the resources you have available, you open yourself up to the spontaneity of life.

Following your highest excitement will allow the greatest expression of your grandest self to come through—especially in a crisis. This takes place because when we are following our highest excitement relative to the circumstances, we are choosing to be in the highest vibration of energy we can be in that moment. Our cells may not be zinging, but this is not the intention. The idea is to vibrate at a higher rate than we currently are as we observe the circumstances. The focus is on our state of being—our emotional state. It might be difficult to accept at first, but as we lift our emotional state, we draw to us a set of circumstances and events that reflect the vibrational frequency of that emotional state. We actually create our circumstances. Our circumstances do not create us—unless, of course, we allow them to do so.

The power is in the now

Principle: The past has gone; the future is not yet here; the only power you have is in the here-and-now moment.

When we have thoughts of the past, we are essentially playing a movie about something that has come and gone. This old, outdated movie will stimulate emotional responses. This is because our inner mind does not differentiate between what is happening in the now moment and what has happened in the past or what will happen in the future. Our inner mind sees the past, present, and future as happening in the now. This part of us responds to current thoughts of the past as if they represent the present experience. The same goes for current thoughts of the future: the inner mind perceives them as taking place in the now moment. No matter what the subject—relationships, finances, weight—anything in our life will be influenced by moving our thinking into the present moment. Take note of how often you allow old patterns of thinking to determine your choices. Then choose again.

Simple things such as diets are usually goals set in the future, but the way we think about a diet is happening in the now. It is something that is happening in the now for the inner mind. When reliving past events and saying, "if only," though these things are set in the past on a timeline, they happen for the inner mind in the now. Regrets are simply old stories we want to change, and by reliving them, we experience them as if they were happening in the now. Note: we don't remember the past as much as we relive the past. Every time we play a movie about our life events, we relive that event as if it were happening in the here and now. Remind yourself that the inner mind does not distinguish between the past, present, or future. It is all now! Again, the only power anyone has is in the now.

Past thoughts often bring about emotional responses of guilt, depression, anger, and grief, while thoughts of the future provoke emotional responses such as fear, anxiety, powerlessness, and overwhelm. When we ground our thoughts in the present moment, we are exercising our power to create and our sense of freedom. Now we choose another thought, another response, another emotion, and we change the present, which is all we can change. Practicing M.A.G.I.C. directs our attention, our focus, into the now moment. Any of the individual five practices will assist with this, but all the practices combined will deepen this experience.

All is One; One is vibration

Principle: One universal vibrational Source energy makes up all of life, permeating and binding everything seen and unseen.

"THE ALL is MIND": within the Hermetic Principles, they refer to this as the Principle of Mentalism.[15] *The Kybalion* says, "Nothing rests; everything moves; everything vibrates."[16] This principle affirms that everything we can see is in motion, everything is vibrating at its specific frequency, and nothing is at rest because everything is in a state of change. This is also the current belief of science, reflecting ancient teachings. It was Nikola Tesla who said, "If you want to find the secrets of the universe, think in terms of energy, frequency, and vibration."[17] Understanding this—that our very essence is the same stuff that worlds are made of—allows us to appreciate our connection with all of life. We are energy vibrating at a particular frequency, similar to but different from the frequency at which metal, water, light, and so on vibrate, but it is still vibration.

The Law of Oneness states that all around us, and within us is potential—pure potential. There is One Energy, and it is the energy that forms all the universes. "The universal mind is static or potential energy."[18] When we understand this law, it offers a sense of freedom and imposes a duty on us at the same time. Freedom comes from knowing that we can choose for ourselves. Duty comes from knowing that every choice we make causes our life to unfold in a certain way and influences life on this planet. This is known as the "butterfly effect": a thought in one part of the universe affects change in all other parts of the universe.

The formula is simple: thoughts are our skills, our tools of the trade; universal law is our weapon for addressing the challenges of the physical world; and the One Energy is our M.A.G.I.C. for bringing about change. This is the wonderment of life.

The cause-and-effect principle follows an absolute law

Principle: Every cause has its effect, and every effect has its cause.

"Every Cause has its Effect; every Effect has its Cause; everything happens according to Law; Chance is but a name for Law not recognized; there are many planes of causation, but nothing escapes the Law."[19]

In our day-to-day lives, we take cause and effect for granted. It's not something we think about much; it is more like we just do it. If the effect is acceptable, then we say thank you and move on. If the effect is something uncomfortable or painful, then we focus on what our problem-solving deduces to be the cause. We hope that by focusing on the cause, we can change or stop the effect. We learn young and we learn well to intellectualize the cause of events in our lives and set about controlling them. It is the effect that we react to when we judge, analyze, criticize, condemn, or punish. Everything in our perceived world results from our thinking it is so. This includes the people, places, events, and objects that present in whatever form they present in, sometimes acceptable and sometimes unacceptable to our liking. We rationalize that if we can change the effect; we are doing something about what is causing us to feel what we feel. Deal with the perceived cause, and we deal with the effect.

This makes sense in a rational, logical, mechanistic world until we come to realize that our experience depends on our personal perception of the world, and at the same time, it results from our power to influence how life unfolds. The world is a reflection, a mirror of our beliefs. To look at it another way, we project our world outward and confirm it with our perceptions. To be more succinct, we cause our life to unfold through our thinking and feeling, and we experience the effects of this in what we perceive through the six senses. Understanding this is critical because it allows us to manipulate the cause rather than, as most of us do, focus on trying to change the effects.

The masters have taught throughout time that we experience effects in this world (what happens to us), and at the same time, we cause these effects. The world we see reflects what we believe and think, and it becomes the projection we place on our world. The beliefs we hold, and the thoughts that arise from these beliefs, influence the field of energy that binds the entire universe. It is our beliefs and thinking that influence this force to bring about change. We are the cause, and we are the effect. Change the cause, and we change the effects. Practicing M.A.G.I.C. allows us to live as a holistic and holy cause of life unfolding.

What you resist will persist

Principle: What you resist will persist and grow stronger, and what you look at will dissolve.

Our ego mind always recognizes the need for pleasure and the desire to avoid pain. We seek what we think will be a pleasure and avoid what we think will be a pain. But it is important to understand that it isn't the "pleasure" or "pain" that is so powerful here. It is the energy we put into embracing one or resisting the other that is important. It is where we direct our energies that activate the manifesting process.

The learned response for many of us is to resist anything that represents physical or emotional discomfort. If it is going to "hurt," or at least if we perceive it is going to hurt, then we will not put up with it. This is resistance. The level of resistance will vary with each individual, her or his makeup, and the circumstance being resisted. We resist anything we consider a threat to our comfort level, based on a level of priority. We will resist some pain more than other pain. This includes internal processing, such as anxiety, anger, and sadness responses in the body. But the more we resist, the more it will persist and grow stronger. The psychologist Carl Jung believed that what we resist not only persists but will grow.

Thus, it is helpful to learn the art of allowing. This is about allowing yourself to feel the feelings and go through the experience, knowing that where there is no resistance, the universal forces, in collaboration with our inner being, will orchestrate the resources necessary for our highest good and joy. This isn't about allowing what is happening in our world to continue happening, but adjusting what is happening on the inside to effect change on the outside. Note to self: stay out of your own way!

Listen to your heart; your head is desperate

Principle: There is the authentic self, and there is the ego self. Then there is me, the decision-maker who supports one or the other.

Our mind is creative, and the people, places, events, and all experiences in our life result from our habitual or predominant thinking. Understanding this is difficult for the head, even when it reflects and considers the manifested results. It is the job of the heart to *know* this truth. To know we have the power, you have the power, to bring about people, places, events, and all experiences is not an intellectual exercise. It is a *knowingness* nurtured first by the heart. Only then does the head catch on. "The Mind cannot KNOW anything. This is reserved for the

Soul. The Mind assumes and judges and all its judgments are based upon its past experiences. And because it places so much importance on the past, it seeks to make the future like it. It, therefore, drags its limited knowledge of everything like a weight into every experience, never once considering that the very premise of its thought system is insane."[20]

Our ego self will avoid all pain as its prime directive, even if we are not going to end up with the most beneficial outcome. The ego wants to avoid pain and seek pleasure, with no concern for personal growth and expansion. Our ego controls our heads with thousands of untrue stories and programs that have been installed since before we were born. The heart will guide us where we need to go. Our egos will take us away from all things uncomfortable. Staying connected with our heart provides clarity, direction, purpose, and inspiration, without the insecurities of the ego. Our egos are a manifestation of our minds. The mind believes it is alone in this physical world and has to save itself from harm and death. This belief in separation isolates us and makes us dependent on the ego for survival.

"The ego is the mind's belief that it is completely on its own. The ego's ceaseless attempts to gain the spirit's acknowledgment and thus establish its own existence are useless. Spirit, in its knowledge, is unaware of the ego. It does not attack it; it merely cannot conceive of it at all."[21] We learn young and we learn fast to use our heads to avoid pain and find pleasure. We learn to go straight to our heads when confronted with a challenge or problem. Most people most of the time live in their heads and ignore their hearts. Our heads are desperate to live the stories. Our hearts are neither desperate nor do they become caught up in the stories and drama.

The authentic part of us, or our higher self, communicates through our hearts. This part is aware of what we need to reach our full potential in this world. This wiser part of us will guide us through the challenges via the most loving route, but without avoiding pain. The authentic self will not control you, while the ego self will do everything to keep you under its control. The part of you that is accountable for making choices is really the most powerful player. This is the real you, able to decide if you want to give into the ego self or follow the guidance of the authentic self. You have genuine power and freedom here; it is called free will. We are freedom-seeking beings, and when this freedom is challenged by external authorities, we feel disenfranchised. This is an internal pain. By learning to follow our hearts through the M.A.G.I.C. practice, we open up to the omnificent powers of the universal Oneness.

CHAPTER 6

Using a Holistic Approach

Using a Holistic Framework

LIFE IS A SINGULAR EXPERIENCE;
IT REQUIRES A HOLISTIC APPROACH,
SO THAT THE SPIRITUAL CAN BE SEEN IN THE PHYSICAL.
- PAUL DUNNE

M.A.G.I.C. is an integration of techniques/tools/practices that interlock to create a new practice. This is a combination of five of the most powerful practices taught across time and borders for personal growth, personal expansion, well-being, and health in all areas of life. Each of the five practices provides focused attention to different aspects of an individual's life experience. The practice uses a multifaceted, holistic approach that incorporates and recognizes the physical quadrant of an individual's life. It accomplishes this by providing insight and inner knowing as it integrates the power of a meditative mind, the exhilaration of an appreciative heart, the physicality of grounding with the planet, and the connection with a higher power through a transcendent relationship with Spirit.

The practice provides an alternative to being controlled by emotionally charged memories associated with negative triggers. This eventually removes any need to engage in any ongoing dependency on medication, and the desire to engage in destructive behaviors such as violence, self-harm, or suicide. Of course, using M.A.G.I.C. to achieve this does not dismiss the need for professional support. One of the central practices within M.A.G.I.C. is the practice of insight. This often involves interacting with your practitioner of choice.

Until we treat individuals as energetic beings appearing in physical form, we are missing the point. Our health crisis isn't about drugs or smoking, it isn't about pandemics or cancers, and it isn't about obesity or heart disease. Our health crisis starts with a lack of awareness—ignorance, if you like, of our energetic or spiritual nature. If children and young people were taught about their spiritual nature, if they knew their body of cells had the innate knowledge and power to cure disease, maybe their life choices would be more representative of their spirituality rather than representing an "I'm just another body" type of mindset.

Currently, an individual with physical, mental, emotional, or spiritual pain is most likely to be offered pharmaceuticals or Cognitive Behavioral Therapy (CBT). It is acknowledged that there are benefits to both responses, and we often need to stop the bleeding before we address the cause. For many reasons, our response modes, particularly in Western societal systems, are set up to stop the bleeding and erase the symptoms while attributing the cause to an external source. Our method of coping has been to shift into blame and shame thinking. We blame and shame the drug addict, the kid who does not fit into the schooling system, the parent who is losing his or her cool with the kids, and a pandemic for people's psychological and emotional crises. It is our default mode of thinking to look for reasons outside of our ego's fictional victim drama story. It is our default mode partly because we are never taught that we have all the answers within. We are taught to look outside of ourselves for the answers and solutions because we believe this is where the cause of our pain sits.

We cannot treat an issue that is spiritual or energetic in nature by prescribing physical remedies if we want to treat the cause. Current approaches attempt to treat nonphysical problems from a physical mindset. When treatments are prescribed that offer a holistic approach by addressing the physical, mental, emotional, and spiritual quadrants with the intention to eliminate the causal factors, only then will we accept and see the individual as a complete being. Practicing M.A.G.I.C. allows us to operate on and respond to four different aspects of our human experience. It is more like we are acknowledging the four expressions of the one self. The purpose of recognizing four individual aspects is to recognize that life happens from four different perspectives.

There is the physical world, which includes all we can see and touch, such as our body and our possessions. It could be said that our physical world is as expansive as the universe we see when we look out into the galaxy, and as refined as the atoms that comprise our bodies and possessions. The physical body comprises upwards of fifty trillion cells. Each of these cells is like a miniature person. Each cell has innate wisdom, and it is this innate self whom we communicate with when we consult our body language with a pendulum or muscle testing. A cell has all the same structures a person has, such as a digestive system, a reproductive system, a communication system, a brain, and so on. Cells are intelligent and know exactly what they need to be doing. Each cell communicates with every other cell, first via electromagnetic communication, and only after that by way of chemical and physiological changes. A cell has all the information it needs to develop into any part of a body. Dr. Bruce Lipton has demonstrated that a cell can become whatever we direct it to become. Placed in the right environment, it can become a liver cell, or a lung cell, and placed in another environment, it can become a skin cell.[22]

To allow cells to function with their innate wisdom, we need to be in a place of neutrality, if not in a place of acceptance or appreciation. We prevent our cells from following their innate guidance when we are stressed, anxious, angry, depressed, or thinking thoughts that are "less than." The critical note here is that if we want to allow our cells to do what we know they can do—live their purpose—then we need to get out of our own way. Whatever approach we use, it is critical to employ a holistic response. M.A.G.I.C. is a whole-being response, adjusting the external factors in an individual's life by adjusting the internal energetics of that individual. This supports the cessation of emotional responses such as anxiety, anger, depression, and other intense negative emotions. It does this while reframing thoughts, eliminating or adjusting core beliefs, and connecting the individual with her/his own inspiration and empowerment.

It is true that the world is waking up to its own potential, and as individuals, we are more aware of and interested in our own well-being and the miracle taking place within the body. Coming to understand who and what we are in this world brings with it a corresponding process on another level. There is a wiser part of humanity taking up the challenge of considering natural and complementary approaches for health and wellness. In a National Health Interview Survey, ninety-four percent of respondents who practiced yoga and eighty-nine percent of those who used natural product supplements said that they did so for reasons related to wellness; much smaller numbers used these approaches as a treatment for a particular condition.[23] Consider this in light of the principles underpinning the M.A.G.I.C. practice, and we recognize how when we seek holistic wellness—i.e., complete wellness that includes the physical, mental, emotional, and spiritual quadrants—we continue to create more examples of this in our life. Alternatively, when we focus on the problem, we reinforce the problem. Basic quantum physics tells us that wherever thought goes, energy flows. These days, we can measure the impact or the intensity of our thoughts with modern instruments.

We can also recognize changed thinking in the arena of mental health. For example, up-to-date research continues to show the strong connection between the gut and our physical, mental, emotional, and energetic well-being. The gut is another type of brain. Dr. Kelly Brogan teaches how an individual has the power to change his or her mental health by changing the condition of the gut. Research elsewhere shows how inflammation created in the gut of healthy people results in the development of depressive symptoms. On the flip side, anti-inflammatory treatments effectively resolve depression. It is frequently stated that it takes an average of seventeen years for research evidence to reach clinical practice.[24] This poses the question, "What don't we know that we could know?"

These studies, showing how body inflammation creates brain symptoms, support the field of psychoneuroimmunology. Psychoneuroimmunology reveals the connection between all systems and organs and the impact each has on the other. This is literally rewriting the book on psychiatric disorders such as depression. This inclusive framework expands the one-gene, one-ill, one-pill perspective that has stymied effective treatments. The key point here is that the physical body is not a machine built with separate parts. The physical, mental, emotional, and spiritual parts of the body are all interrelated, contributing to our humanness, each aspect cooperating and collaborating while complimenting and complementing each other aspect.

In M.A.G.I.C., each of the five individual practices is a change agent. As change agents, they not only affect positive change in the physical, mental, emotional, and energetic systems, but each practice intensifies each of the other practices. This change builds upon itself and becomes a game-changer. It would be easy if one could simply follow Joseph Campbell's guidance and follow her or his "bliss," but that seems too complicated or too simple. M.A.G.I.C. is a way of supporting someone in following his or her bliss.

Bill Moyers, when interviewing Joseph Campbell, asked, "Do you ever have the sense of ... being helped by hidden hands?", to which Campbell replied, "All the time. It is miraculous. I even have a superstition that has grown on me as a result of invisible hands coming all the time—namely, that if you follow your bliss, you put yourself on a kind of track that has been there all the while, waiting for you, and the life that you ought to be living is the one you are living. When you can see that, you meet people who are in your field of bliss, and they open doors to you. I say, follow your bliss, and don't be afraid, and doors will open where you didn't know they were going to be."[25]

M.A.G.I.C. is a simple, personalized, efficient tool that uses five practices, on top of what an individual already does naturally in his or her life, to bring about a change from the inside out. It is a self-generated, self-directed practice that allows anyone the total freedom and guidance to practice in a manner that compliments their lifestyle. What we can expect from this practice is a reduction and eventual elimination of any sense of powerlessness. By practicing M.A.G.I.C. we develop a genuine internal resilience against triggers and risk factors that are present in our unique worlds.

Consistency provides immediate and positive results, manifesting as relief, concomitant with a supporting sense of self-valuing and personal control. This practice allows us to acknowledge the triggers in our lives for what they are, recognize and appreciate the emotional responses we have, gain clarity about the resulting thoughts, and connect with a part of ourselves that oversees our life journey. This latter part is our spiritual nature—our authentic self.

The practice reinforces the understanding that we are not our circumstances; we are not our emotions; we are not our thoughts; in fact, we are not any of the sensations in our bodies. These things come and go while we continue to exist. We certainly are not the triggers in our lives; they also come and go. We are separate from each of these experiences. We observe these things, and often we become caught up in the stories we attach to these thoughts, feelings, sensations, and triggers, but we are not them. Even if there is a pattern, a habit, or a looped program running resulting in us playing out the drama, this practice will help to re-pattern and reprogram our inner minds.

What we know is that attempting to control or eliminate triggers from our lives is difficult, if not impossible. There will always be triggers in life. It is the nature of living to experience a contrast of triggers to assist us in our evolution. Accepting triggers for what they are isn't about accepting or condoning disrespectful or abusive behaviors. This is not about judging a trigger to be "good" or "bad." This is about mindfulness, nonattachment, and nonjudgment, and always looking for the gift as we assert our right and freedom to live as human beings. Triggers are triggers, reactions are reactions, and having a choice is freedom.

The M.A.G.I.C. practice allows us to recognize and acknowledge the triggers in our lives (and no one else's life). We can then choose how we want to respond to these triggers. This thinking is all about highlighting the importance of accepting triggers for what they are: triggers. It is about letting go of any attachment, expectation, or power we might allocate to these triggers. Recognizing triggers as opportunities to experience joy or growth is another way of using our personal power, and allowing life to unfold. The most important and most potent contribution triggers make to anyone's life is that they act as reflections in a mirror.

The analogy of reflections in a mirror is a reminder to us that what we perceive is a projection of what we believe about ourselves living in this world. The world is the mirror. What we notice in the mirror is our magical way of coming to understand the many parts of ourselves as individuals. Seeing the reflection allows us the opportunity to accept responsibility for our past choices and our next choice. This isn't about ignoring the triggers in our lives or locking into positive thinking. This is about each of us taking responsibility for our own life, owning our feelings, being conscious about our choices, and not handing over the baton to someone else. The mirror simply shows us what we need to look at. It is looking in the mirror that allows me to see that I am responsible for myself. No one is coming to save me, and subsequently, in the decision to "save myself," I find empowerment and hope. Combine this with the practice of M.A.G.I.C., and we have a power plant for inspiration.

We are thinking beings. This is what we do. Our mind is everything because it establishes the germ from which all creations grow. What we think, we become. We create with our thoughts and use our brains to process these thoughts, solve problems, and make decisions. This is the obvious aspect of the thinking self, but there is another aspect to our minds. The conscious mind and the unconscious mind are often seen as two distinct parts of the mind. The conscious mind is the part associated with conscious thinking, problem-solving, and decision-making. This is usually associated with the head. On the other hand, the so-called unconscious or inner mind handles hidden thinking, thoughts, imaginings, body language, visualizations, and dream work.

Nothing is ever really unconscious. More often than not, we are so focused on our conscious mind's interpretation of what is happening around us that we miss the message from the inner mind. While these two parts appear to be separate and behave independently, they are one component: the mind. Some people argue that we are never really in charge of our minds because we are influenced so much by the world around us. The behavior and thoughts of other people in our lives, the impact of advertising, influences from television and social media, and a variety of other sources all contribute to programming our minds, whether we like it or not, whether we believe it or not. Note: we have always and will always have free will.

The brain is an amazing computer installed within the head. Our brain has the power to boost our quality of life or to lessen it. Our brain is the manager of our internal pharmacy and controls the distribution of chemicals to the organs of the body. The brain has an amazing ability for changing itself.[26] It actually rewires itself. It will grow new neural pathways if established pathways are damaged. It does this for learning new skills, for example, learning to play a musical instrument or learning an unfamiliar language. In the brains of stroke victims, it is possible to recognize scar tissue in the brain caused by the stroke long after they have had a stroke, and alongside this are new neural pathways. Whether the brain actually does this of its own accord or another part of us takes over (e.g., the heart or the inner mind) has yet to be established.

There is, however, a downside to this amazing computer we call the mind. The combination of the conscious mind and the unconscious mind acting as a unit isn't all that reliable for distinguishing between fiction and nonfiction stories. The computer aspect of our brains sources its information from our core beliefs housed in the inner mind, and our inner mind cannot tell the difference between what is real and what is imaginary. It treats everything as a current reality. It is ironic that we rely on our brains for making decisions, even when it has no authority or capacity for making many of these decisions. Our brains were not designed to make decisions about emotional or spiritual matters. They were designed for making decisions, but it is a computer—a computer operating with misinformation.

As a computer, the brain depends on stored information and data, a set of established patterns programmed from our reactions to our experiences throughout life. This is an important note regarding children eight years of age or younger when there is no filtering of information or capacity to challenge the validity and reliability of the information. As the brain calculates the best option for avoiding pain and seeking pleasure, it will use programs established when we were a child. "What is wrong with that?" it might be asked. After all, isn't it true that no pain means no gain? If we could avoid pain, we wouldn't be who and what we are today. This is a world of contrast. There will always be opposites; it is natural law and a way of maintaining balance in this universe. It is the contrast that encourages if not inspires us to expand, grow, and become what we are today, do what we do, be what we are, and go where we go. The simple process of walking came out of not walking and the inspiration to do so; talking came out of not talking and the inspiration to communicate; loving came out of not loving and the inspiration to know love; and inner peace came out of chaotic mental chatter and the inner knowing that there had to be something better.

The inner mind, or unconscious, is the part of us that develops as we grow from a baby into adulthood. The inner mind sometimes called the subconscious mind, comprises trillions of stories accumulated over a lifetime. Every experience is a unique story stored like a video in the inner mind. Some of these stories carry a great deal of emotional charge with them. This is the case whether the story recorded is true or false, fiction or nonfiction. The emotional charge, when attached to a memory, is the basis for and the influence of our state of emotional well-being.

Stories that are false or misinterpreted come as misinformation from influential people in our lives as direct instructions and observations via our interactions. This includes but is not limited to, our parents, teachers, television, social media, and friendships. Each of these contributes to the story behind the story we tell. Here is the point: the stories we gather and store during our lives construct our programs or core beliefs. These core beliefs are like programs we have about the self as we go about living in this world. While a belief is only a thought, we have thought it many times. A belief unconsciously directs the choices we make in our lives. Ever wondered why some people repeat the same behaviors, mistakes, or successes time after time? Throughout life, these stories will influence the decisions made about our life matters. The reliability factor of the brain to recall information and use it in different circumstances depends upon these stories. It is no wonder that we each have our own unique take on events in this world; we are unique to our own stories and subsequent beliefs. Note to self: "I don't have to let this control me."

If you are like most people in this world, you will have become so dependent on using your head that it can be difficult to shut it down. When we are stressed, anxious, or worried about life matters, the brain works overtime. The problem arises because we as a species have allowed our heads to protect us from the "what ifs" coming from the fictional stories in the ego mind. The stories of the ego mind are stories of events that we interpreted as children, which we took on board from well-meaning parents. These stories become our life stories, which inevitably means the heart's story is often rejected, abandoned, and ignored for the sake of fiction.

This means we often end up stuck in our heads. The inner part of our minds presents an old story. The thinking mind takes this, looks around for evidence to support the belief, and then adds what it observes in the world, and thus creates another story. This is the ultimate self-fulfilling prophecy. The amount of truth in this story can range from zero to—at a guess—maybe ten percent. This results in overwhelming, confusing thoughts of doubt and fear causing emotional reactions. Eventually, we must engage in unhelpful behaviors to rid ourselves of emotional discomfort.

M.A.G.I.C. acknowledges the existence of what Gary Craig[27] calls the "unseen therapist," the unique individual, while recognizing the collective. The spirit, the energy that lives within each of us is always looking for creative flow, and this practice is a means of letting that flow take place. Like letting the proverbial genie out of the bottle, we can let this spirit flow into each of our creations, no rubbing required, no M.A.G.I.C. carpet rides. It is not the same as waving a wand and *poof*! We need to visualize, imagine, and conceive what we want in life. Then we need to go about life showing up every day looking for the signs. M.A.G.I.C. the practice supports this process by taking the ego's attention away from the doubts, fears, and "what ifs," allowing our authentic self to direct traffic.

We give ourselves a chance when we use meditation for the mental self, as it calms the mind; appreciation for the emotional self by stimulating a sense of joy and acceptance, nonattachment; and grounding, which energizes the physical body through the earth's residual vibrational frequency. Next, we use insight for the energetic part of us or that part that includes our functional energy system. Insight provides the energetic aspect of the individual with intuitive communication and insight for letting go of old, outdated programs, allowing for growth and expansion. Finally, there is a connection to all of life, starting with our own community of cells. Connection acknowledges a relationship with all life on this planet and with Spirit, the higher power with whom we have a personal mystical relationship.

It was originally thought that our brain oversees our emotional world. This was based on the premise that the brain stores all memories and controls all functions, perceptions, and sensations we experience as humans. This school of thought was established long before science had the highly tuned measuring instruments we have today. While measuring changes in the body allows us to see effects on different organs like the brain, it doesn't tell us what causes those effects. There continues to be the age-old question, "What comes first? Is it the chicken or the egg?" For example, it has been scientifically demonstrated that our stomachs and our hearts influence and direct our brains. The brain, being the chemist, then organizes to distribute chemicals and adjust the physiology.

Within the M.A.G.I.C. practice, our emotions or feelings are managed by and associated with the heart. This amazing organ was the first organ to form after conception, it has memory cells like the brain, and it sends more information up to the brain than the brain sends down to the heart. As previously mentioned, studies and research undertaken by the Association for Comprehensive Energy Psychology (ACEP) and the HeartMath Institute have shown a realistic connection between the physiology of the body and the energetic system. Research by the HeartMath Institute has shown that "The heart-brain's neural circuitry enables it to act independently of the cranial brain to learn, remember, decide and even feel and sense."[28] This is not to say that the heart is a brain, but the heart has a brain and operates as part of the body, directing more than the brain. The heart is "a highly complex, self-organized, information processing center, with its own functional brain that communicates with and influences the cranial brain through the nervous system, hormonal system, and other pathways."[29]

The heart is the communication portal between our conscious mind and the inner mind; between our conscious mind and the trillions of cells in our body; between us and every living thing, including the planet; and between us and the unseen: Spirit. One of the most loving and amazing aspects of the heart is that it will always move toward appreciation, growth, acceptance, compassion, and self-acceptance. The heart will take us where we need to go for our greatest good and growth. There is no delusion or misconception in the heart. Our heads operate a little differently by taking us away from pain—any type of pain—and towards what they consider to be a pleasure. Our hearts take us through the pain while supporting our growth and expansion.

We have associated emotions with the brain or the inner mind, or both. We now know that emotions take place throughout the body. Dr. Candace Pert, through her discovery of the bodily opiate receptor and research on neuropeptides, confirmed that emotions are literally encoded throughout our organs and tissues.[30] Perhaps these "emotions" are actually the memories and experiences stored throughout the body. Emotions (emotion = energy in motion) are the messages or responses brought about by the heart because of exciting these memories. If the inner mind records, stores, and retrieves these memories, it is one of the heart's roles to inform our conscious mind that we are "unconsciously" thinking and believing something relevant to the current memories. It is then the brain's role to activate the mechanisms to distribute relevant chemicals and neuropeptides throughout the body.

The inner mind or subconscious mind isn't really hidden. It is obvious and upfront when you know what to look for. What part of you manages your breathing when you are asleep? What part of you manages your healing while you get on with life? What part of you records and stores every experience you have ever had or will have? What part of you blushes when you are embarrassed or has you giggle with nervous laughter? And what part of you gives you dreams at night? Now you are coming to know a small part of your inner mind.

One role of the inner mind is to record and retrieve information, but it does not have the ability or need to distinguish between what has happened in the past, what has happened in the future, and what is happening in the present. It believes everything is happening in the present time, in the now. It has a knee-jerk reaction to what it believes to be happening in the now. What does this mean? It means that if we perceive something with our conscious minds, our inner minds will take this as truth and react to it in the now. "Perceiving something" can refer to sensing something in our external world, or it might be something we have interpreted in our inner world, in the imagination.

If your inner mind believes that you are safe, then it will pass on this information to the conscious mind, along with the evidence. If your inner mind were to believe you are in an unsafe situation, even if you are not, then it passes this information on to the conscious mind, along with its evidence. This is clearly seen when a person is in an altered state of consciousness, such as hypnosis. In these situations, a subject's physical body and brain operate as if the suggestion given to them is real. Why do people become scared and have a physical reaction to something they see on a digital screen when the logical mind says, "It's only TV magic! It's a movie! It's not real"? But logical, rational thinking goes out the window when the inner mind is in control.

Most people see the heart as an amazing pump, but it is far more than a pump. Research over the past thirty years has provided empirical evidence for the amazing role the heart plays in sustaining our quality of life. Indeed, the neurons within the heart enable the heart to learn, remember, and decide independently of the brain's cerebral cortex. We know the activity of the heart can be measured in the brain waves of another person. They have shown that two individuals touching or within three meters of each other have an energetic conversation. Even more extraordinary is the finding that the heart would appear to "psychically" pick up what is happening at least six seconds prior to it happening. In a study undertaken by the HeartMath Institute, findings suggest that "the heart is involved in the processing and decoding of intuitive information."[31]

The heart is the center of emotional alchemy. The alchemist always and in all ways strives to turn any situation into gold, the metaphorical reward in life. The alchemist knows of miracles and M.A.G.I.C. and uses this knowledge to guide you through the galaxy known as life. While the brain is seen as the manager and distributor of chemicals throughout the community of fifty trillion cells, there is an ongoing crossroads between the mind and the heart that influences decisions regarding health and well-being. You are the decision-maker in your life.

The initiation of an emotional response comes from the inner mind when we consciously or unconsciously have a thought, pick up on a trigger, or otherwise have our data bank activated. The indicators of an emotional response are found in our physical cells and in our bodies as chemical and physiological changes, and the responsibility for addressing this lies with our conscious minds. Recognition of an emotional response rests with the heart, which must inform us of what is happening. It is up to the decision-making part of us to then make a choice about what we want to do.

When we are believing something about ourselves, living in this world that contradicts what our authentic self knows to be the truth, our heart will send a message. These messages are like text messages letting us know that we need to consider what we believe about ourselves in this situation and change it if we so choose. These messages are our emotional responses—messages from the heart urging us to reconsider what we are believing about ourselves in this world at that moment.

The belief or thought we operate from, at any moment, will cause feelings of either love or fear. When we become caught up in our heads, "solving the problem" and reliving the drama, we create new dramas that have never actually happened. In these times, we are so busy in our heads that we ignore the messages from our hearts. Anxiety isn't a problem or necessarily something to "get rid of." Anxiety is an emotion, an amazing inner process of mystical quality for guiding us or helping us to deal with unhelpful beliefs about ourselves in this world.

If we have a belief that states we are "not enough," this will influence everything we think, feel, and do. Where does the anxiety come from? It comes from our inner being or "aware self." This aware self uses the heart to send a message to let us know we are thinking or believing something that is conflicting with what our authentic self believes and knows. Our authentic self sends a message through our hearts to let us know there is a discrepancy in our thinking. When our heart communicates this message, it must inform our brain so that our brain can organize the various organs of our bodies to disperse all the correct chemicals, etc. into our cells.

Again, the purpose of this is to urge us to attend to the current state of being, which results from our current thinking. So, it is a good thing, because it is a way of letting us know that our thinking is contradictory to what and who we truly are. By choosing thoughts that support our true essence, we let go of those thoughts and beliefs that contradict our origins. Read that again! Otherwise, attempting to let go of those unwanted thoughts only generates resistance from our egos.

In this writing, there are references to the energetic self and the spiritual self. To some extent, they are different aspects of us. However, it is a little like two waves in the ocean. Each wave is a separate entity, but they are both part of the same source. The "energetic self" is more often used to refer to the energetics of the physical, mental, and emotional quadrants. The word *spiritual* and the term *spiritual self* can be confusing for those who get caught up in words. Here, we refer to the energetic self and the spiritual self as one, with the energetic self-being a part of the spiritual self. Spirituality, as a term here, is not about religion, though it may include religion for some individuals. Spirituality is recognizing the existence and importance of a universal benevolent force or energy, while not getting caught up in the egoistic perspective of any religion.

While the *spiritual self* is used more as an all-inclusive macro-descriptor that also includes the sense of spirituality and the universe, the *energetic self* is comprised of the meridian system, the energy around the body (aura), the chakras, the electric signals of the heart, and electrical communication between cells, all of which are readable and measurable. The spiritual aspect includes these electrical systems along with our personal inner sense of relationship to an all-loving and supportive higher power and our relationship with all that is in the world. Our choice of names for this higher power might include, but is not limited to, Source, Nature, Spirit, Universe, God, Sophia, the Field, and so on.

The bottom line is, this all-pervasive energy is present, and each of us has a relationship with it. The type of relationship depends entirely on our preferences. A relationship or connection with this omnipresent energy is unavoidable; however, the quality of this connection is determined by our everyday choices. We have the freedom and the capacity to enhance the connection or limit the connection. But the connection is always there; otherwise, we would not exist. This could be viewed as an ever-present flow of life force, and we have the freedom and capacity to constrict this flow, or not.

Part of the problem for many people is that they cannot "see" this energy. So, it is easy to dismiss it as something "not real" or "woo-woo." As with gravity, magnetism, or the wind, we do not see this all-pervasive energy, but we can recognize and acknowledge the noticeable effects in our lives. Lynne McTaggart is an award-winning journalist, a principled researcher, and the author of eight books, including the worldwide bestseller *The Field*.³² The book aggrandizes how everything and everyone is connected by the Zero-Point Field (ZPF), a sea of energy that reconciles the mind with matter, classic science with quantum physics, and science with religion. For the ever-present skeptic within, Lynne McTaggart provides a wealth of documented research to quench one's thirst.

The Field has inspired hundreds of thousands of people from various walks of life, including religious leaders, physicists, healers, and most important of all, those who seek scientific evidence for the innate sense that we are not separate, but are part of a greater whole. It's now required reading in some university courses, as well as in courses for many healing disciplines around the world. Most people recognize the magnificence of nature, a force or spirit within life, and an external and internal universe, and they marvel at this magnificence without realizing the connection we have with this field of energy.

How all this works can be mind-blowing, and for some of us, it is interesting, but not that different from so many other aspects of life. Logically, if we go about looking for signs of gravity or the wind, we will find markers. Similarly, if we go about looking for signs, indicators, or the effects of the presence of an omnipresent energetic force in this world, chances are we will find these in numbers. We only see what we allow ourselves to see. Remain skeptical if this is who you are, while remaining curious. Skepticism and curiosity are great buddies in adventure and invention. Be conscious of playing arrogant and ignorant, because those guys are real party poopers.

Dr. Lisa Miller and her team at Columbia University Teachers College, along with a handful of pioneers around the world, have gathered scientific data that supports spirituality as an innate biological part in each of us. Research using fMRI studies shows the effects on a subject's brain when they engage in meditative and spiritual practices, and how this part of the brain responds to spirituality thinking. Dr. Miller describes spiritual development as "the growth and progression of our inborn spirituality as one of many perceptual and intellectual faculties. Spiritual development is the changing expression of this natural asset over time as new words, explanatory models, and ideas ... allow us to feel (or not feel) part of something larger, and experience an interactive two-way relationship with a guiding, and ultimately loving, universe."[33]

Evidence shows convincingly that spirituality is the most robust protective factor against the big three dangers of adolescence: depression, substance abuse, and risk-taking. Dr. Miller's lab confirmed that adolescents who have "a personal sense of spirituality are 80 percent less likely to suffer from ongoing and recurrent depressions and 60 percent less likely to become heavy substance users or abusers."[34] She adds, "There is no single factor that will protect your adolescent like a personal sense of spirituality."

Note to self: matters of spirituality and emotion cannot be addressed via physical or cognitive responses alone. Physical responses might be supportive of the healing process, and they can provide an immediate respite from intense pain. But in the end, they do not and cannot address matters of spirituality. Innate spirituality and natural emotional matters are found in the form of energy. They come out of an energy system, influence an energetic response, and respond to an energetic response. Prescribed pharmacology or self-prescribed medication cannot take away depression or anxiety. Like any analgesic, they buffer the effects, so that the individual can go about the day without the conscious awareness of pain. But the pain is still there. Spiritual issues demand a spiritual response. This may include anything from being in nature to connecting with the unseen spirit of life, listening to music, finding insight, or feeling appreciation in the now moment. These responses are found in practicing M.A.G.I.C. Is this a gift you could give to yourself?

Case note: A young mom goes from reaction to calm

June is a teacher dealing with the everyday issues that teachers face. At the top of her list are the problems presented by disgruntled parents, the challenges presented by "the system," and the complications created by her colleagues. The following is June's story of how she came to know and practice M.A.G.I.C.

"It was a regular school day. There were hundreds of kids talking, laughing, screaming, running, holding hands, and generally filling the air with noise. It was difficult to hear myself think, and I needed to think. In front of me firmly stood an irate parent and an equally irate colleague. The mother of the child in question was defending her parental position to stand up for her ten-year-old. My colleague and I put the child's well-being first and foremost, and so did the parent. The difference was that the parent had some other issues complicating the situation. The voice in my head was nagging, 'There is no chance of getting a win-win outcome here unless something changes quickly.'

"I felt the need rise up for me to scream, 'We all want the best for the child!' But I knew we needed to get past our own stuff first, and the parent needed to vent some of her frustration before we could move forward. Then, like pushing a button on my radio to change radio stations, my brain flipped from problem to solution. The voice said, *Use the M.A.G.I.C. trick—that old M.A.G.I.C. thing that I can engage with anywhere, anytime, for any reason.* Immediately, I began to repeat, *M.A.G.I.C., M.A.G.I.C., M.A.G.I.C.*, over and over in my head. I really didn't think it would change the outcome, but I wanted to calm myself down. Then from those feelings of stress, tension, and pressure, in a few moments came a change in my body. It started in my heart area—a calmness, if you like, that spread outwards like a ripple on a pond through my body.

"The distressed parent and my colleague were changing in front of my eyes. Somehow the conversation was calmer, the faces of my two associates had softened, and there was a slight smile coming from my colleague. Then the parent smiled. The voice in my head was on a loop, continuing to say, M.A.G.I.C., *M.A.G.I.C., M.A.G.I.C.* There was an air of win-win that hadn't been there before, and it was certainly taking me by surprise. Before too long, the conversation had concluded, and we had a win-win outcome. Was this a coincidence? Did my reliving the practice of M.A.G.I.C. influence a change?

"A short time later, I found myself in another situation where my emotional scale was well into anger. I was also aware of a sense of my powerlessness percolating in this situation. I was driving to the shops. I had my three children in the car. It didn't help that the kids were being kids, yelling and finding ways of filling this drive with a sense of 'I don't want to be here.'

"As we were driving, my world changed quickly. With no warning, a car came across in front of me, cutting off my path. I screamed some words that my kids aren't allowed to say as the adrenaline filled my veins and the anger filled my face. I am usually a patient and calm person, but when my kids are at risk, there is a big mama bear that comes out swinging. As I gathered myself and refocused, a little voice went off in my head. It was that radio station thing again. I heard the words, M.A.G.I.C.! *Use the practice!*

"Breathing a little slower and a little deeper, I felt the air being forced out of my chest, and then came the turnaround; as the air came out, the tension went down. As I breathed, I started grounding myself into Mother Earth, deep and strong. I knew I needed to steady myself and calm my mind at the same time, so I breathed my roots deep into the planet until I felt steadiness and reassurance fill my body. This felt good, and it was encouraging. Then I practiced mindfulness of where I was, conscious of my children, and then came appreciation that we were all safe. Before I knew it, I was connecting with my guardian angels saying, 'Thank you!'

"It wasn't over yet. As I drove into the parking lot and got the children out of the car, a man approached me. He was an older man approaching as he waved his hands. 'I am so sorry!' he repeated. 'I am so sorry that I nearly caused an accident. It was all my fault, and I am so sorry.' He went on to explain how his mind was elsewhere and he didn't see my car until it was too late. Again, I could feel sensations in my body—only this time they weren't made up by anger or shock. These feelings were of forgiveness and compassion for this man. I didn't condone the behavior, but I could understand the circumstances.

"I found myself questioning if this was the result of my engaging with M.A.G.I.C. and the practices that make up M.A.G.I.C. Or was this another coincidence? Since then, I have used the practice many times, sometimes in high-pressure situations, and sometimes when I am feeling vulnerable or down. This practice is truly a powerful and empowering tool for me. It has changed my life by allowing me to see events and people with a sense of appreciation and positive expectations. Now my children feel the change, and they act out my sense of M.A.G.I.C.

"This is a note to say thank you for everything you have taught me. In particular, I wanted to tell you how practicing M.A.G.I.C. showed me another way. These are typical examples of situations faced as a teacher and young mom. Before I started practicing M.A.G.I.C., these types of situations had the power to drive me to drink. The worst part was, I would continue to stew over the injustice and disrespect shown by others towards myself and my students for hours, days, and even months. Thank you!

Case note: Lost in a slump

"Nothing was going right in my life. I never seemed to hold down a job for very long. Even though I would do just about anything for work, it was never enough to keep a job any more than six months. Consequently, I never had any more money than the bills I had to pay. Health wasn't a big issue, but at the same time, I was often limited by a sore back or some niggling issue. I didn't have an intimate relationship, while I had many genuine friends. It was as if I were replaying the same day, the same week, the same, same, same, over and over.

"Then I learned about the practice of M.A.G.I.C. and began to practice this in my day. I found it very difficult to begin with, because the day would start okay, but then before I knew it, I would be caught up and forget to practice. One day I was reading about the practice of appreciation, and it really resonated with me. As I thought about my life, as I looked around at where I was living, as I considered what I had in my life, it hit me like a bolt of lightning. I had so much to be appreciative for in my life.

"The practice of appreciation was the first practice of the five that I really deeply connected with. Grounding and meditation were seemingly simple, but this appreciation filled me with feelings of joy and such gratitude that it didn't matter what was going on in my life, or what I had; life was wonderful. Not long after I started practicing, I was offered a job in human services that I absolutely love. As I look back on the past year, there has been so much crisis and pain in the world, and yet my life has been absolutely full of appreciation. This practice—and now I use the greater practice of M.A.G.I.C. —it feels like my life has been supercharged." (A story from J. E.)

CHAPTER 7

Meditation

Meditation

> MEDITATION IS FOR THE MENTAL SELF;
> APPRECIATION IS FOR THE EMOTIONAL SELF;
> GROUNDING IS FOR THE PHYSICAL SELF;
> INSIGHT IS FOR THE INTUITIVE SELF;
> CONNECTION IS FOR THE SPIRITUAL SELF.
> - PAUL DUNNE

Defining Meditation

As an adolescent, I was always fascinated by the traditions of the East, and in particular, the practice of meditation. Growing up on a farm, I spent endless hours going up and down, round and round in circles on a tractor as I cultivated or seeded the soil. I didn't realize it then, but I often spent those hours in a form of meditation. I was actively contemplating and open to insights about life's issues. While I wasn't aware of it at the time, I was actively engaged in a M.A.G.I.C. practice. There was the meditation and mindfulness sitting on machinery; there was the appreciation for the life of a farmer and the connection with nature; there was the visceral experience of being grounded; and finally, there were the copious insights that came with being in this space. With my inexperienced eyes, I recognized that there was more to life than what I could see. It was easy sitting on a machine, carrying out monotonous tasks while I observed nature around me. The questions were many.

So, why wasn't it as easy to meditate when I was older, when I actually wanted to meditate? I had the privilege of undertaking a ten-day vipassana course that was amazing, but which faded after three or four months. I read up on meditation and studied its form so I could find the best way to practice. This may have been a mistake. I gathered a great deal of information and techniques, but this just seemed to push it away. Nothing appeared to work, and the harder I tried, the less successful I was at it, and the less I wanted to practice. I had turned meditation into something I had to "do."

In later years, I came to know that meditation isn't difficult—something I don't remember reading. What I came to realize is that meditation is easy—or at least easier—when we find our own ways of meditating. I found it difficult to let go of the old ways, the old patterns of thinking that reinforced the belief that I had to try harder to succeed. I guess that was a life pattern that related to just about anything. I learned young and I learned well to use my head incessantly. I was taught that this was the way to succeed in life and the way to succeed at anything I wanted. Nowadays, I know this to be just noise in the monkey mind. The need to stay in my head and use my head has been reinforced all of my teenage and adult life. Nowhere did I read or hear that when I set out to meditate like "them," there will be problems. It took me a long time to realize that the only way to meditate is the natural way for me: my way. More importantly, I realized that there would be challenges as I attempted to bridle my noisy mind. Yes, I could adopt one of the many forms offered, but I had to make it my meditation. What was offered to me as I came to accept this became my guide, a form of encouragement, and a great starting place.

As the reader, you may want to research, experiment, and play with different forms of meditation, at least until you find what suits your particular nature and circumstances. You don't need to do it like "them." You don't need forced discipline. In my searching, I found practitioners who were very rigid, if not obsessive about their practice format. The Buddhist nun Pema Chodron puts it best in her book *When Things Fall Apart*: "In practicing meditation, we're not trying to live up to some kind of ideal—quite the opposite. We're just being with our experience, whatever it is ... Awakeness is found in our pain, our confusion, and our wisdom, available in each moment of our weird, unfathomable, ordinary everyday lives ... Meditation is an invitation to notice when we reach our limit and to not get carried away by hope and fear. Through meditation, we're able to see clearly what's going on with our thoughts and emotions, and we can also let them go."[35]

It's helpful to recognize that our minds have been practicing a set of patterns, probably for a long time. The mind may need a little retraining, and we can do this by practicing patience. On this M.A.G.I.C. journey, we begin by looking at the practice of meditation with an emphasis on mindfulness meditation. What we need is the will to commit to our own highest joy by trusting the process. This "process" is the result of our being created in a meditation and by a meditation, and at our very core, we are the presence of an ongoing meditation. Practicing M.A.G.I.C. is being mindful of how we can apply meditation along with the other four individual practices as one practice.

Power pointers

Start with awareness. I have come to the realization that infinite patience is a powerful asset to cultivate. As a have-to-be mechanic, I found myself needing to screw a bolt into the bottom of an engine. I couldn't see the hole where I was supposed to screw the bolt in; I was working in the dark. The harder I tried, the worse things got for me. By the time I skinned my knuckles and tossed the wrench on the ground, it was time to walk away. I did. I walked away, had a drink of water, and after a few minutes, returned to what I now considered a blind monk's trick. Picking up the bolt and bending over, I closed my eyes and trusted my inner knowing to find this path to my goal. The bolt went in immediately—

and I mean *immediately*, with no resistance or complaining. It was all over in moments. What did I learn from this little experience?

One of the biggest challenges experienced by potential meditators is getting their heads around the amount of effort they think needs to go into meditation. There are long-term meditation practitioners who find themselves caught up in the act of meditating. To make it work, many put effort into the act of meditating. This results from a belief that says, "We must engage the head to solve a problem. We think our way through meditating." But the key to meditating is in letting go of effort.

Meditation is not something you "do." See it as something you will be, or something you are. It is an experience we have observing our physical experience from a place of consciousness. Being as one with the bolt and the engine was my way of meditating in that moment. I had stopped resisting any idea that I couldn't get the bolt in and accepted that things were what they were in the moment, and my role was to go with the flow. I had let go of resistance, of trying so hard, along with any thought of failure.

Another common belief is that meditation is difficult. Many students become absorbed in the stubborn thought that their minds just aren't capable of slowing down. When attempting meditation, many hopefuls hold an expectation that the mind will shut down immediately after they cross their legs, close their eyes, and say, "I am meditating." The problem is that most of us have trained the head to stay busy and remain alert. As a result, it is almost impossible to stop thinking. Giving the head a task to focus on provides room for us to slow down and move into a place where we no longer engage the head. This allows us to move into a place of becoming the observer. Closing the eyes and visualizing what is happening at the ends of the fingers gives the head something to do, but the point isn't to make something happen. We can learn to move into an altered state of consciousness, but the head still needs something to do. Sometimes it only needs to believe it is busy. This provides us with the freedom to shift the focus of our consciousness.

Adopting a sense of curiosity about the constant chatter in our head can be the quickest way to deplete the power of that chatter. If we resist, it will persist and grow stronger. Observe it, and it will dissolve. Jon Kabat-Zinn, considered to be the guru of mindfulness meditation, says, "You can't stop the waves but you can learn to surf."[36] Meditation is something we can engage in naturally, but not normally. In M.A.G.I.C. the practice, we emphasize the importance of observing and enjoying what is happening in the moment, allowing mindfulness meditation to be part of our every moment.

One doesn't need to understand the anatomy of a butterfly, or know where it came from, where it is going, or what it is doing, to observe and enjoy the miracle of the butterfly. In mindfulness, we observe the different flavors and textures and the way our body and our mind are reacting. This is being conscious of ourselves in the present moment. Reminding ourselves that there is no need for analysis or judgment is helpful in letting go. Meditation—and in this case, mindfulness meditation—is awareness with curiosity as we consider the miracle of life. This is observation with our heads, feeling in our cells, and appreciation in our hearts, all recognized by our spirit as perfect. "When you are not present with what you are doing, you are not really doing anything. You are wasting your time, because you are reliving or projecting ... If you are ruminating over the past, you are contaminating the eternal now with the past, and you will create a future that looks like your past."[37]

Sometimes I like to sit and people-watch, observing with curiosity. No need for judgment or analysis as I amuse myself with people's expressions, gestures, reactions, and interactions. I think I have always been like this—more interested in what other people are doing or being rather than shining the light on myself. However, there comes a time in everyone's journey when it is time to look within. There is only one trick for this. As I began my journey to get to know myself, I focused on my expressions, gestures, reactions, and interactions—no need to analyze, judge, criticize, defend, or praise. It is an interesting experience to watch or observe oneself as if from an outside place. Watching or simply being aware of the "I" doing something or maybe saying something. Noticing our reactions to certain foods, the flavors and textures, or maybe simply noticing the food itself. Being aware of having a thought such as, *why am I saying this, because it sounds like my mother speaking, and why don't I stop?* is becoming the observer from a place of consciousness. There is no judgment or criticism, expectation, or attachment—only observation with curiosity. There is no problem unless we become caught up in the drama of our stories. When we turn our attention to the story, we inadvertently enter the story and play a role in that story. This is exactly what the ego mind wants us to do. Thoughts become a story, which becomes an episode in an ongoing series. Before long, our inner mind is living the story, believing it to be our truth, our reality, no matter what our conscious mind is seeing.

The essence of meditation lies in its power to help us let go of the stories we play on the screen of the mind. Growing up, we learn to program ourselves to think nonstop (analysis, strategies, planning, problem-solving, problem-seeking, and even creating problems) and replay our stories over and over. When we decide to meditate, it is no wonder that the mind wants to run off and do what we have trained it to do over the years! When we become involved in a story that has taken place in our past, we don't just remember it, we relive it. This now becomes a story that has taken place at least two times in our lives, plus every other time we relive it.

The inner mind has no ability to differentiate between truth and fallacy, nor is there any capacity for it to tell the difference between the past, present, and future. It is no wonder that so many people are saying that they are "stuck." When we engage in thinking about something in the past or something in the future, we bring that memory or vision to life in the now. The reason we appear to be stuck in the same old rut is that we keep creating our future based on our past. We are the ones doing it! We think about, talk about, and act as if the past is real, activating a future based on the illusion of the past. But there is no past, and there is no future, other than in our minds, and nothing can impact us outside of the now unless we believe it can.

Thinking thoughts rooted in past events is a conditioned response most of us have adopted. If there is one thing that has us in a holding pattern—stuck, if you like—it is using old thinking to live our lives.

This is because after the first time we live the story, it is history existing only in our memory, but when we remember it, we are reenergizing it as if it is happening in the now moment. Remember that our inner mind does not know the difference between the past, present, and future. It believes everything is happening in the now moment.

A key point is that every time we relive a story, our physiology changes to accept that the event is happening in the now, and we set our vibrational frequency to that point. We become the result of that story as if it is happening in the now. The outcome of all this is that we succumb to the effects of the original event, while creating our future based on the frequency at which we are currently vibrating. We live life as if this event is always happening. Past thoughts create present conditions; present thoughts create future conditions. But practicing meditation, especially mindfulness meditation, helps us to stay in the present and thus change our future.

We process with our brains; we think with our unconscious minds, which includes our imagination; and we observe with our higher self. We are able to think, process, and observe. The powerful contribution meditation makes is that it allows us to make the unconscious conscious, and it allows us to observe from a distance. The more we can do this, the more we come to know the light and the shadow parts, and we come to know what the world represents. Anything less than this is living shallow. This isn't to suggest that we need to be meditating all day. What we have available is the option to make our day a meditation by practicing mindfulness meditation. This way, we can think about what is happening while remaining open to insights about our "hidden" self.

Thinking isn't a "bad" thing. It is an amazing process that happens without having to turn on a power switch or hit an Enter key. It is the type of thinking and what we think about that can turn into a problem. Over time, we have allowed our thinking to control us. We have come to a place where we accept what the world tells us about who and what we are. Most people live life convinced that this is who and what they are. It is time to challenge this belief by asking ourselves questions like, "Do I, the consciousness, come and go with my thoughts?" Of course, the answer is that we don't; we are not our thoughts. Our thoughts come and go. We are not our thoughts, we are not our feelings, and we are not our bodies. We are consciousness expressed in physical form, experiencing the sensations of what that feels like.

Without really questioning it, most people believe they are their thoughts. Even worse, many of us judge, criticize, condemn, and punish ourselves as a result of our thoughts. All of our unhappiness comes from our thinking based on the beliefs we have about the circumstances, persons, places, or events in our lives. It is never the actual subject of our thinking that causes the discomfort, but our perception of that subject. One hundred people can be aware of the same experience, and yet they can have one hundred different reactions. Everything in our experience is neutral until we layer a belief on top of it; then it becomes our reality.

As humans, we use many props to help us feel secure, safe, lucky, looked after, and so on. These props have no meaning in themselves; we give any meaning these props hold. Consider how two individuals can view a circumstance from two different perspectives. One might see it as positive, and the other might see it as negative. Mindfulness provides a viewing platform that allows us to see a bigger picture—more of a cosmic interpretation.

Meditation is not difficult. It is not even letting go of our old ways, the old patterns of behaving and thinking, that is most difficult. It is letting go of the resistance to letting go of these habits that cause most of our resistance and difficulty. Mention the word *meditation*, and for many people, the very mention of the word can bring about a personality change. Rupert Spira says we often think of meditation as a function of the mind, an activity,[38] as opposed to seeing it as an activity undertaken by the mind. It is being in the presence of awareness. To know ourselves as awareness is to be awareness, and it is not something that needs to be done by the mind. Awareness is consciousness of our greater being, the natural part of us observing our thoughts and feelings, our sensations and happenings. Spira says, "Are you not present seeing these words? Whatever it is that is 'present' and 'seeing' is what we call 'I.' Do you have to do anything special in order to be the one who is seeing or who is aware of these words? If the eyes close, these words disappear, but does the one who is aware of them cease to be? No, it remains present and aware, experiencing the next perception. You are simply this present awareness without having to do anything about it."[39]

The difference between awareness and thought, Spira says, is that thought focuses on objects and sees us as separate from all there is, while awareness is simply being aware. So, meditation is not about seeking, or focusing on an object in time, it is just "to be as you are." This doesn't require the mind to be in any particular condition. In other words, simply allow your thoughts to do their own thing. Let go of any resistance or control and allow them to do what they do. Observe with a knowingness. We cannot stop thinking, but we can learn or train ourselves to observe our thoughts rather than ride them into the ground.

The challenge comes when we allow our ego, via our head, to manage the experience. The head analyzes, while the heart experiences. Our heads do not experience. The head can only judge, analyze, problem-solve, strategize, and continually compare the information coming in with its own history. What most of us do very well is use our head to think thoughts. After all, we are thinking beings; it is just what we do. We are so efficient at using our heads to make things appear real that we can convince ourselves we are going to die—or worse, that we are unworthy of love. It is the paradox of the ego, using our most powerful tool against us.

Meditation has a far greater purpose than quieting the head. It is through meditation that we can connect to our hearts. And why is that important? Because the heart is the communication portal between us and all life in this universe. The heart is the communication portal between us and our inner being, our spiritual self. Our heart is the communication portal between us and our trillions of cells. When we spend a great deal of time in our heads, we fail to recognize and respond to the messages from our hearts. Most people most of the time allocate priority to thinking over feeling—head over heart. While we do function as thinking beings, we also operate as emotional beings; we feel things. When we experience emotion in our bodies, we are receiving something akin to a text message coming from our hearts. First, there is a thought; then there is an emotional response; then there is a thought about the emotional response and another emotional response; and before you know it, the entire response has a life of its own. It is energy moving through the body, bringing about physiological and chemical changes noticed by the brain and reacted to by the inner mind. It is one of the heart's roles to inform us when we are thinking something that is out of alignment with our authentic self.

Past thinking is likely to elicit feelings of anger, depression, sadness, or guilt, while future thinking has us feeling anxious, fearful, depressed, angry, or powerless. The effect is an activation of a vibrational frequency reaction in the present moment relative to these emotions. When we do this, we re member with these emotionally charged memories, reconnecting with them and reliving them all over again. Reliving these old, outdated memories reenergizes them as if we are living them in the present moment. The problem with this is that they become our now reality, and our now reality decides our future experience. It is exactly this that our hearts are trying to tell us.

In his masterpiece, *The Disappearance of the Universe*, Gary Renard explains it like this: "As far as the ego's plan is concerned, your seemingly multiple problems show up in this world in an attempt to get you to react—to feel bad, guilty, mad, defeated, bored, scared, inferior, self-conscious, annoyed, lonely, or superior and condescending. It's all some kind of judgment, regardless of the form. As soon as you make that judgment, you give validity to the ego's world and reinforce the seeming reality of the separation and everything that goes with it."[40]

Past and future thinking based on appreciation will elicit feelings of appreciation, hope, joy, excitement, and acceptance. We can make conscious choices about which thoughts we entertain. Our greatest gift is the freedom to choose our thoughts, which then create who we are, which creates our life experience. While it does contribute, our past does not make us who we are. Who we want to become is revealed in the choices we make in the 3,600 seconds of every hour in every day. Any of us can make a different choice in this now moment in relation to the choices made in the past, and this will contribute to defining who we are. This doesn't make us a different person; it simply highlights different choices made by the same person. Choices are neither good nor bad; they are momentary decisions made because we want to be happy. They don't change who we are or what we are; they simply change our experience and how we present in this world.

Sometimes, it is difficult to manage our choices because they have been repeated so often. Here, the programming is at the core of our belief. In this case, it can be helpful to adopt a different approach and reverse the thought-word-deed process. When we change our behavior, it has a direct effect on our words and thoughts. Dr. Joe Dispenza gives this advice: "... when feelings become the means of thinking, or if we cannot think greater than how we feel, we can never change. To change is to think greater than how we feel. To change is to act greater than the familiar feelings of the memorized self."[41]

M.A.G.I.C. supports this concept by allowing us to be aware of the now moment. We notice the emotional state; reframe our circumstances to find and accept the gift; dissipate the emotional charge through grounding; and find insight, support, and guidance through connection. Through the practice of mindfulness combined with appreciation, we can "act greater than we feel". This is an inside-out job made easier by practicing M.A.G.I.C.

An example found in Neale Donald Walsch's *Conversations with God*: "The trick is to change Sponsoring Thought ... The first thing to do is reverse the thought-word-deed paradigm. Do you remember the old adage, 'Think before you act'? Well, forget it. If you want to change a root thought, you have to act before you think.

"Example: you're walking down the street and come across an old lady begging for quarters. You realize she's a bag lady and is living day-to-day. You instantly know that as little money as you have, you surely have enough to share with her. Your first impulse is to give her some change. There's even a part of you that's ready to reach in your pocket for a little folding money—a one, or even a five. What the heck, make it a grand moment for her. Light her up. Then, thought comes in. *What, are you crazy? We've only got seven dollars to get us through the day! You want to give her a five?*

"So, you start fumbling around for that one. Thought again: *Hey, hey, c'mon. You don't have that many of these that you can just give them away! Give her some coins, for heaven's sake, and let's get out of here.* Quickly you reach into the other pocket to try to come up with some quarters. Your fingers feel only nickels and dimes. You're embarrassed. Here you are, fully clothed, fully fed, and you're going to nickel-and-dime this poor woman who has nothing. You try in vain to find a quarter or two. Oh, there's one, deep in the fold of your pocket. But by now you've walked past her, smiling wanly, and it's too late to go back. She gets nothing. You get nothing, either.

"Instead of the joy of knowing your abundance and sharing, you now feel as poor as the woman. Why didn't you just give her the paper money! It was your first impute, but your thought got in the way. Next time, decide to act before you think. Give the money. Go ahead! You've got it, and there's more where that came from. That's the only thought which separates you from the bag lady. You're clear there's more where that came from, and she doesn't know that.

"When you want to change a root thought, act in accordance with the new idea you have. But you must act quickly, or your mind will kill the idea before you know it. I mean that literally. The idea, the new truth, will be dead in you before you've had a chance to know it. So, act quickly when the opportunity arises, and, if you do this often enough, your mind will soon get the idea. It will be your new thought."[42]

We think we are unhappy because of what is happening to us. In reality, we are unhappy because we don't like not liking what is happening to us. We can't feel good because we have just given away our power to what it is we don't like. Now we are caring more about what is happening outside of us (circumstances) than what is happening inside (state of being). A critical point here is that when we give away our energy to anything outside the present moment, we are opening ourselves up to the agenda of the world around us. If we are not giving our attention to the present moment experience, then chances are that someone in our lives, or on the news, or at the other end of the phone is influencing our life experience.

Some scientific findings

It is a personal observation that people who are serious about meditation never really need any scientific evidence to support their decision to practice. That being said, it is worthwhile knowing some of the amazing benefits that come from practicing meditation. The following is a brief summary of some of these benefits.

Accumulating evidence highlights the many powerful and positive effects that come from practicing meditation. The specific evidence supporting mindfulness meditation continues to expand into areas of commerce, education, personal development, prisons, and many other populations. This is a pleasant reminder of the truth often ignored in a materialistic world. Our indigenous cultures have always practiced meditation as a way of life. It is truly a natural—but maybe not so normal— practice for each of us. Some would argue that it was letting go of such practices that led to so much disharmony and fractured energy in our modern world.

Most of the formal research on meditation and mindfulness has focused on the physiological and mental benefits of the individual. That's interesting, considering that meditation has always been known, acknowledged, and taught for its spiritual benefits. It's also interesting because it highlights our scientific community's need to show quantifiable, physical benefits before considering the unseen benefits. Practices such as Mindfulness-Based Stress Reduction (MBSR) and Mindfulness-Based Cognitive Therapy (MBCT) have served to help many individuals.

With the refinement of measuring instruments such as magnetic resonance imaging (MRI) studies[43] and functional MRI (fMRI) studies,[44] science has recorded physiological changes taking place in the brain during meditation. Research shows that meditation leads to activation in brain areas involved in processing self-relevant information, self-regulation, focused problem-solving, adaptive behavior, and our felt experience of the internal workings of the body, such as digestion, breath regulation, and heart rate. Not to mention, meditation practice induces functional and structural brain modifications.[45]

There are many studies focusing on the reported benefits of meditation and mindfulness meditation. Studies have reported benefits such as the following:

- Anxiety and depression may decrease after meditation training.[46]
- Immune function may improve after meditation training.[47]
- Meditation training may protect your brain from decline due to aging and stress.[48]
- Mental clarity and focus improve after meditation training.
- Your heart health may improve after meditation training.[49]
- Meditation training enhances treatment of mental health.
- Meditation training can improve your mood.
- Sleep may improve after meditation training.
- Mindfulness meditation can be effective as an intervention for binge eating, emotional eating, and weight loss.
- Meditation may help the self-regulation of chronic pain[50] and recovery, and aid with chronic pain and prescription opioid misuse.[51]
- Meditation has successfully been used in interventions for youth in school settings with a focus on a new direction for improving childhood education.[52]

In recent times, the focus of research has expanded to include what science has considered in the past to be impractical or too obscure for research. In a 2018 study, a task force of investigators containing meditation researchers and teachers considered the impact of meditation on people's psychological and spiritual enhancement. The Future of Meditation Research[53] working group reported on their findings of research carried out over a four-year period with 1,120 subjects. The report frequently acknowledged mystical and extraordinary experiences among the meditators.

Points to note

It is important to know why. Much depends on the purpose of our meditation. If we recognize just one thing, we will find clarity in our meditation: knowing why we want to meditate. Knowing why gives purpose, direction, and clarity. Asking other questions—what, how, when—causes the ego mind to engage an all-stops-out approach to answering the questions. Meditation can relax the body, calm the mind, and tune the spirit to the ends of time, or any combination of these outcomes. All three come about with time and practice, so it doesn't matter which one you choose as your purpose for meditating.

One of our today's leading spiritual teachers, Thich Nhat Hanh, is an amazing individual who has some powerful advice for us. When people ask how they can stop their agitation, fear, despair, anger, or craving, Thich Nhat Hanh says we can use mindful breathing, mindful talking, and mindful smiling. "We are always running, and it has become a habit. We struggle all the time, even during our sleep. We are at war within ourselves, and we can easily start a war with others."[54]

Rather than trying to do something in meditation, allow yourself to become the observer and know why you are practicing. If there were one single reason why you would choose to practice meditation, what would that be? Another way to look at this is to ask, "What is the desired outcome?" What do you want to accomplish by practicing meditation? In the M.A.G.I.C. practice, meditation—and in particular, mindfulness—provides a space for practicing appreciation, grounding, insight, and connection. "Providing a space" here refers to staying in the now moment by letting go of past and future stories. This results in a relaxed body, a calm mind, and a spirit tuned to the ends of time.

There are many forms of meditation. Mindfulness meditation[55] is a simple form of meditation for beginners. In different ways, the practice of mindfulness is a component of different forms of meditation. We see mindfulness meditation as the go-to meditation for many people today because of its practical application in everyday life matters. We have widely acknowledged it as a powerful tool in the workplace and in the classroom. Russ Harris, author of *The Happiness Trap*, defines mindfulness as "paying attention to something in a particular way, with openness with curiosity and flexibility."[56]

Jon Kabat-Zinn is considered the guru of mindfulness, particularly because of his scientific research into it. He says, "Mindfulness means moment-to-moment, non-judgmental awareness. It is cultivated by refining our capacity to pay attention, intentionally, in the present moment, then sustaining that attention over time as best you can."[57] The key is to allow and observe without attachment or expectation. Recognize that it is all happening in the now moment, and we really don't have to do anything about it.

Be aware and be comfortable with some resistance. I find it surprising when someone says to me that they have been meditating for years, and yet they still find it difficult. The reason I find this to be surprising is that I often think I am the only one who suffers from this condition. I realize that this is really because of what I do when I am not meditating: thinking, thinking, thinking. This is one reason I like to meditate. I can do it for a short period of time, anywhere, anytime, and not worry about distractions. That being said, when I lock in a regular meditation period for sitting, it works well. Commitment, consistency, no pressure, no worries, and no expectations is my answer, along with practicing mindfulness throughout my waking hours.

What if you knew a meditation practice could happen in one minute, or even thirty seconds? Would this make it more interesting—maybe even inviting? Well, meditation can happen in under one minute, or it can be for hours. You can meditate many times throughout your day, or you can make your day a meditation. One vulnerability in the traditional approach to meditating one or two times each day, especially for the beginner, is that it leaves a sizeable gap between practices. In this gap, the ego mind runs rampant. So, making our day a meditation has much value. In addition, many people can accept practicing mindfulness throughout their day, but they find it difficult to set aside forty mins for sitting in practice. But it is strongly advised, based on the evidence, that engaging in a sitting practice each day has enormous benefits.

Note that resistance will often show up when we decide to meditate. The resistance comes because the ego mind feels threatened when we cease to give it our full attention and full control. The ego mind depends on us to play a power-and-control game. Our ego needs to be the one to call the shots, to decide, to push the red button of emergency, crisis, and catastrophe. Sometimes it seems like it does this just because it can. But ultimately, the ego will accept our choice to meditate, and resistance will dissipate, but it usually requires a change in mindset.

By observing the resistance that arises without judgment, by simply noting the irritation, the agitation, the racing thoughts, the random pain or itch, or "the voice," we give our heads something to do without resistance. As Eckhart Tolle explains in his book *The Power of Now*, whenever you become the observer of your ego, it will withdraw because it doesn't enjoy being looked at.[58] With this approach, you will notice the level of resistance or pain you are experiencing decrease. It helps to remember that while we may not calm the waves of thought in the mind, we don't have to block them, either. We don't even have to ride those waves. Rather than interacting with the waves, meditation invites us to sit in a relaxed state and just observe. This is about becoming the observer, watching the reactive body, the desperado head, and the loving heart. It becomes a meditation as we observe who we become when we practice meditation and how our ego minds cause resistance in our stillness. It is helpful to consider this, whether in a sitting meditation or during mindfulness activities.

Without becoming involved in the drama, we can become curious about the form and the cunning way in which the ego mind attempts to control. With curiosity, we can notice how when you challenge the ego coming in the front door, it will find another way in through the back door. The ego mind loves using the back door and is skilled at coming up with sly ways of doing this. Stepping out of the driver's seat of the ego mind into a meditative state allows us to observe the ego's tricks as intriguing, if not amusing. The skill is to accept this and get on with the practice of meditating. Note to self: avoid becoming caught up in the antics of the ego, and become the observer of being the observer.

When practicing M.A.G.I.C., meditation is the doorway to reconnecting with your authentic self, while mindfulness is the door used for entering the place of meditation. When I first began practicing mindfulness, I was convinced it would be a breeze. What could be so difficult about staying in the now moment and observing what was happening around and within me? I had taken clients through the process of practicing mindfulness, and I had practiced mindfulness in moments of focus. But to allow this practice to become part of my day was another thing. The first real test came when I committed to practicing mindfulness in the shower. Try it, and see how far you get. There were many showers where I would step into the cubicle, focused on the practice, and then step out with the thought, "*two seconds of mindfulness, and then out of the cubicle it went. Next time it will be better.*" Numerous showers later, after placing reminders in the cubicle, I was no further advanced. It wasn't until I said, "I am not going to practice mindfulness in the shower!" that things started to change. I came to realize there are certain circumstances and situations when my mind wanted to run all over the place, and other places where it was easy to be mindful.

Practicing Meditation

Practice: Set out with the intention for your meditation to be enjoyable, and remember why you are practicing. After all, in these moments of calm, you are letting go of the illusion of the ego and reconnecting with your truth. If the practice is painful, then you are taking it too seriously, trying too hard, or choosing a less-than-suitable style for you. Chances are you will walk away disappointed in yourself and the practice. It is sometimes helpful to remember that what you resist will persist and that what frustrates you will isolate you. Let go of your attachment to a particular outcome, and instead play, experiment, investigate, and allow your natural curiosity to guide you into a new wonderland. Knowing your "why" isn't about becoming caught up in or attached to an outcome. Meditation is not "the song;" it is what happens in your being when you feel the song. Listen and enjoy with the heart rather than the head, or observe with the head and feel with the heart.

Practice: Weave the practice of mindfulness into your everyday activities. Go about your day and braid the practice into different activities and situations. If you are in the shower, be completely in the shower and not off at work in your mind. If you think this sounds too easy, play a little, and notice your response. Funny enough, it is only when I am finishing my shower that I become aware that I had my shower while my mind was out in the world—and now I am practicing mindfulness. It is almost like when I relax, my mind goes out the window—or shower, in this case.

When you are having a drink, actually be there observing what you are doing, how you are doing it, and why you are doing what you do. Be present in the now moment, observing without judgment or attachment your movements and how you react to any outcome.

In your conversations, become the observer, witnessing your interactions, reactions, and contribution. The key, of course, is to become the observer of yourself as the observer. Notice how you are interacting, how you are thinking, what you are thinking about, the feelings in your body, and the movement of your body.

Practice: During your day, as you perform your normal tasks, speak with yourself in a way that brings you into the moment. For example, "Here I am having a shower, and I am practicing mindfulness." "Here I am having a shower, and I have not been practicing mindfulness. I have been thinking about..." "Here I am driving my car, practicing mindfulness."

Practice: Practice observing the resistance you have to practice. Meditation is a natural experience, but it threatens the ego's authority. When you meditate, consider any resistance you notice to be a prop—a thing that is neither good nor bad, it just is—and you can watch it with curiosity. Notice the characteristics of your resistance, how it feels in your body, and where it is in your body. The ironic thing is that when you give yourself permission to let go of any resistance and accept that it's okay not to be practicing mindfulness, you are practicing mindfulness.

Again, no judgment; something is happening, and it is to be observed, not judged. If the resistance presents as a distraction, a pain, an itch, or a sense of urgency, rather than getting caught up in a war with the ego, use this moment as an opportunity to remind yourself that this is what the ego does. The ego draws you into a fight like a bored little brother, always poking you, talking at you, and sneaking around behind you.

The ego wants to carry out its role to the best of its ability, and the way it does this is by instilling fear in your thoughts, moving you into a state of self-defense. The cunning rationale behind this is that once the ego has you feeling threatened, it knows you will go to it for help. That is what you do. Notice how you go straight to the head for problem-solving and solutions. When you ask for help, the ego jumps in, promising to save you from all threats if you just follow its instructions. It will offer solutions, questions, answers, past stories, and proof of its loyalty, demonstrating how committed it is to your well-being.

Note to self: accept the ego self as a part of yourself living in this physical reality. If you can come to a place where you neither resist the ego nor follow it, you will find peace. It is neither good nor bad; it only exists because you live in a dualistic experience. Remember, the ego does not like being observed, and so it will retreat whenever you observe it, and eventually, it will give up on the fight.

Practice: Plan a meeting with your resistance until you actually know the feeling, the location in your body, the intensity, how it changes as you meet with it, or how it might change. Observe it over a few days. See resistance as your friend. If meditation is a major problem for you, rather than setting aside time each day to meditate, give yourself permission not to meditate. Then use those fifteen to twenty minutes to come to know your resistance to meditation. Make this time an opportunity for coming to know the shape, location, color, and intensity of your resistance. Is your head racing? What is the primary focus? Simply observe... Is it an itch? Simply observe... Is it a pain? Simply observe... You may need to get up and walk around, in which case, practice mindfulness. Several meditation forms require you to stay with the interruption, but not get caught up in it.

Practice: Recognize mindfulness as part of your everyday experience. Are there activities in your day when your thoughts are focused in the now moment? It might be when you are cooking, playing a sport, performing a work-related task, or even watching a screen, driving a tractor, or sitting on a surfboard. See if you can catch the moment. It is different from daydreaming; mindfulness is a conscious choice. By making this a conscious moment, you make it a mindfulness meditation. Curiosity is the key here. Become curious about when you might be mindful and what is happening when you are mindful. Note: daydreaming isn't a bad thing unless you need to be focused and attentive.

Practice: A big part of practiced meditation is timing. Remove any time pressures, and make meditation a part of your life. Use everyday triggers to become conscious, practicing conscious thinking and engaging in the practice of mindfulness. For example, with some smartphone apps, you have the option of scheduling a text to be received by you in the future. First thing in the morning, send yourself five or six texts at hourly intervals, as reminders to yourself to take notes and become mindful at that moment. Alternatively, set an alarm, or have a M.A.G.I.C. buddy call or text you as a reminder to practice mindfulness—whatever it takes.

Practice: Focus on any sounds you can hear, any colors you can see, or shapes you notice. Make it a part of your day to notice aspects and qualities of your environment that are often missed. Taking advantage of waiting time means noticing what is happening for you rather than noticing what is happening for those around you. When waiting in line, notice the feeling in your body, the sounds you hear, and the surrounding colors.

Practice: Breathing is one of the most powerful activities you can engage in because it not only requires mindfulness, it facilitates change in your physical, mental, emotional, and energetic quadrants. Practicing this for a few minutes will endear you to a mindfulness practice. Take three or four deep, slow breaths, holding each breath for a short time (maybe five seconds). It's helpful to breathe in for the count of four, hold for the count of four, and breathe out for the count of four.

Practice: Focus on a physical part of your body, like your chest. Notice any movement associated with your chest. Follow this movement and appreciate the miracle of what is happening as you breathe. Become aware of how this and the intelligence of your cells sustain life—your life. Try focusing on different parts of your body until you find the part that is calling you. You might focus on your left foot and imagine breathing into it. Visualize or pretend to draw a liquid light down through the top of your head all the way into your foot, noticing your foot becoming brighter and lighter, dissolving all tension, anxiety, and stress. Notice how your foot changes in different ways. After you have done this for a short time, move your focus to your right foot, and notice any differences between your left and right foot. Now give your right foot some of the same loving attention. Continue breathing liquid light into your right foot as you did with your left foot. Watch how your entire body wants to follow suit. The aim here is to observe with curiosity how your body changes and responds to a loving act.

Practice: Use this exercise if you are carrying an overwhelming emotion in your physical body. Notice the feeling, the sensation, the emotion in your body, and recognize where it sits. These changes are taking place to let you know there is something happening because of your thinking. Observe this feeling without judgment. As you observe this emotion, watch how it changes. It might move to different points in your body, it might intensify, or it may dissolve.

Focus on the location in your body where you recognize the uncomfortable emotion and speak to it directly. Say something like, "Thanks for coming. It is time to go. Soften and flow. I want you to soften up and flow out of my body." Repeat "soften and flow" over and over as you observe the feeling in your body. Continue this until the painful emotion has dissipated or left your body. Allow your sense of curiosity to be enriched as you observe without judgment.[59]

Practice: Using mindfulness as a practice throughout your day is a reeducation program. The more you do it, the stronger your practice will become. While extended periods of meditation each day for fifteen minutes (or longer) are the goal, you will benefit enormously from any practice of mindfulness in your day. There are many apps and websites where you can access guidance on meditation and mindfulness. Investigate until you find something that resonates with you and fits your needs. Choosing times when there is calm and a sense of peace is beneficial for practicing so that when it is needed, you can respond intuitively.

Note to self: meditation will relax the body, calm the mind, and tune the spirit to the ends of time.

Some helpful questions

- Am I able to bring my attention to the now moment?
- What are some things I do that bring me into the now moment without trying?
- Are there any hooks or anchors I can use to automatically bring me into a place of mindfulness, such as using a word like "M.A.G.I.C.," or touching my forehead with my finger?
- Are there activities I already engage in that provide me with the opportunity to practice mindfulness or meditation, such as yoga, Tai Chi, martial arts, arts and crafts, music, etc.?
- Do I already do this in my life, just maybe not every day?
- Am I becoming more aware of changes in my physical, mental, emotional, or spiritual worlds from using this practice?

Case note: From anxious carpenter to meditating biker

Peter was a carpenter by trade, and his understanding of the world was a long way off from what the M.A.G.I.C. practice advances. The way Peter understood how this world works conflicted with the principles and essence of the practice. The principles underpinning M.A.G.I.C. did not fit into his perceptions. Most of what the practice promoted was foreign to Peter's world, and yet when he stepped up and engaged with the practice, his world turned around. Soon, his anxiety and panic attacks, along with the anger he didn't really acknowledge, all changed over two to three weeks.

"When I was first introduced to this practice, I walked away thinking, *What the...? What have I gotten myself into?* I had been to see psychologists before, and while they were nice enough, it never seemed to make any difference. I continued to be anxious and angry all the time. While you were way out there, and I had serious doubts about my sanity, I figured, *What have I got to lose?* So, I tried it—and what do you know, things changed pretty well overnight!"

Peter went from a place of living on the edge, always being anxious, working long days, worrying about what was happening to him, and questioning his sanity and ability to live in this world, to going home every day after work and sitting in the garden for fifteen minutes, practicing mindfulness.

"Go figure!" he said, "I'm using the M.A.G.I.C. practice regularly." He was now feeling in control of his life. His anxiety had dissolved, and he had insight into his anger, which allowed him to address some significant issues in his life.

CHAPTER 8

Appreciation

Appreciation

> **APPRECIATION IS FEEDBACK**
> **I AM THINKING THOUGHTS OF LOVE.**
> **IT IS ACCEPTANCE WITH THE MIND,**
> **FELT AS JOY IN THE HEART,**
> **EXPRESSED IN THE CELLS,**
> **AS FEEDBACK FOR THE MIND.**
> **- PAUL DUNNE**

Defining Appreciation

When using words like *appreciation* and *gratitude*, confusion can arise. It makes no difference what word is used to describe the essence of what we are referring to here, but we need to be on the same page. Bottom line: use whatever works for you. Saying, "Thank you!" as a simple acknowledgment can also work. Again, it really depends on what resonates with you. Within M.A.G.I.C., we use the word *appreciation*, and what follows is an attempt to define the spirit that is intended.

When all is said and done, we are looking to emphasize the spirit of appreciation.

The most common word used in and outside of the research is *gratitude*. When people think about gratitude, it conjures up images of thankfulness, gratitude journals, blessings, and the idea of "Just be grateful for what you have, because there are many people out there who have less." From the perspective of M.A.G.I.C., gratitude seems a little like hard work, and that is because it often presents as a contradiction. Consider the following explanation.

In her book *Thank and Grow Rich*, Pam Grout defines what she calls gratitude as "shameless gratitude, ferocious gratitude, in-your-face gratitude."[60] Within M.A.G.I.C. this represents the practice of appreciation. Pam stresses that this isn't allowed to be any "namby-pamby, sunshine-and-lollipops crap." For Pam, this is a way of life, a way of living out each day where we "forget thinking and start thanking everything." This is what she refers to in her book as "the extreme sport of gratitude," and by doing so, she provides us with insight into the depth, wisdom, and unconditional love that are the universal energy force, the potential of energy surrounding and saturating us. Appreciation awakens an emotion deep in the heart and has more of a spirit or lighter feel compared with gratitude. Expressing appreciation has a different feel to it, and that feel aligns with practicing M.A.G.I.C.

Pam Grout highlights how the simple practice of shameless gratitude allows this "organizing intelligence of the universe"—the Source, the God force—to present in our life experience. This is the "essence" of the M.A.G.I.C. practice that we refer to here. This essence underpins M.A.G.I.C. the practice, as it acknowledges the energy supply source we access for living. The guidance from Pam is to "Stop the incessant thinking, and start some gentle recognizing of the thousands of things going on in your life."[61]

The invitation within M.A.G.I.C. is to connect with the essence of appreciation and let go of the words as much as possible by focusing on the experience. That being said, it is important to use the words that best resonate with the core beliefs each of us holds—words that come from the heart, and not necessarily those that come from the head or this book. In the following pages, we use the word *appreciation* when referring to the M.A.G.I.C. practice, and the term *gratitude* when referring to research findings. What words would you choose to describe the essence of what we are talking about?

Writing about his research findings on gratitude, Robert Emmons promotes two essential characteristics. "First, it's an affirmation of goodness," he says. "We affirm that there are good things in the world, gifts and benefits we've received." In acknowledging that the world isn't a perfect place, he highlights that the act of gratitude allows us to see the goodness in life. But where does this goodness come from? He suggests that "We recognize the sources of this goodness as being outside of ourselves … gratitude involves a humble dependence on others: we acknowledge that other people—or even higher powers, if you're of a spiritual mindset—gave us many gifts, big and small, to help us achieve the goodness in our lives."[62]

The question that arises with this approach is, "Does the reason for feeling gratitude come from outside us as individuals?" Maybe we can attribute gratitude to external sources, but appreciation does not come from outside us, because appreciation is who we are. It is what makes us. Attributing the power to outside influences as our source of appreciation is what we do when we aren't playing that "I am less than" game. In its truest form, appreciation acknowledges that we are part of Source energy. When we feel appreciation, it is because we are acknowledging the goodness, the divinity in ourselves and in all things. We see past people, things, and events to recognize that it is our own divinity being reflected back to us.

The M.A.G.I.C. practice highlights that mindfulness and appreciation (rather than gratitude) celebrate the present moment, no matter what the circumstances. Appreciation within the M.A.G.I.C. practice is a state of celebration for all that we have as individuals and as a collective, and all we think we don't have. It comes with an inner knowing that all is as it should be for our highest good and expansion. Here, appreciation is akin to abundance and acceptance, recognizing the opportunity of a gift in every circumstance. It is not focusing on the good or the bad. In fact, it is not making any judgment of good or bad. Rather, it is recognizing the opportunity to accept without conditions and love without attachment.

This is an important point, because it highlights that the practice of appreciation has no connection with the problem or the lack, unlike gratitude, which continues to recognize the problem by holding onto a small facet of that problem. For example, "I am grateful she dropped in to see me. She is a kind person, but I really find her to be too much sometimes." Appreciation is an internal process focusing on the real self, while gratitude focuses on the outside or external world. Most of all, appreciation acknowledges all circumstances for what they are: neutral. *C'est la vie.* It is just amazing to be alive.

It helps to connect with the essence of practicing appreciation by understanding how we judge circumstances in our lives. We judge because this helps us make decisions while living in a dualistic world presenting in physical form. After all, we need to at least judge distance and time in this 3D world. The problem is that we use this same judgment to label people, places, events, and objects, all based on our limited perceptions. It is important to understand that circumstances are neutral until we place a judgment on them. It is our perception or interpretation that allocates a circumstance to either "good" or "bad." How we perceive something regulates how we feel, and how we feel is parallel to our state of being.

We create our reality with our perceptions, which come from our core beliefs. These we project out into our world. It comes down to the state or current vibration of our being. Our state of being is relative to the vibrational frequency of the state of our energetic life force. A simpler explanation is that it is how we are feeling at any moment. It is our state of being that is important in all circumstances, rather than the circumstances themselves. Darryl Anka is a channel for a group of loving beings referred to as Bashar. Bashar teaches that "Circumstances don't matter, and only our state of being matters."[63] Practicing appreciation allows us to see circumstances in a different light, which simultaneously raises our vibrational frequency. It is in this state that we can appreciate that how we feel is more important than the circumstances in our lives.

One of the nice things about working in and with nature is the constant reminder to accept things as they are, for what they are. One can chose to feel good about what is happening, or one can chose to feel like a victim. Farming is what it is, whether we acknowledge the drought or the rain for any good it does. As a farmer, I spent many hours contemplating the role "good luck" and "bad luck" played in farming. I spent much of this time wondering why Evan up on the hill always got good rain when we always seemed to miss out. Was this good luck or bad luck? I never did work that one out. These days I see things differently. I can look at what someone else has and look at what I have and appreciate both for what they are. I appreciate the rain for what it does, and I like it when it stops, because I can go outside. Gratitude says, "The rain is nice, but I am grateful it has gone. It stops me from doing so much."

Appreciation is "thanks for the experience," while gratitude is "thanks, but no thanks." This is the act of recognizing the gift, the opportunity, the blessing, the situation without judgment, to feel a "thank you!" as we appreciate who we are in this world along with the world within. We may not understand what is good about a situation, experience, or event, yet we can accept it without as much judgment and without as much attachment. Again, circumstances don't matter; only the state of our being matters.

Focusing on the circumstances in our lives with a less than appreciative attitude only serves to direct the same limited energy into those circumstances. If the dominant emotion we carry around is anger, then our chances of perceiving anything other than anger in any circumstance are remote. This is something I have tested many times, and always with the same outcome. When I focus on an experience in my life and find the value, the gift in it for me, things always work out for the good. Alternatively, when I have stubbornly stuck to playing the victim, my circumstances continue to reflect victimhood back to me.

Practicing appreciation does not mean that everything is going to be wonderful all the time. What it can teach us is that when we learn to look for something good in all circumstances, we will begin to find good in all circumstances. It may not be the way we would have planned it, but it always works out for the good, if only in hindsight. Sometimes, of course, it is way too difficult to find something "good" in a circumstance, or even to look for something "good." In these times, we are better off adopting the attitude of watching a movie, going to sleep, and focusing on something we can do for ourselves.

Using the practice of appreciation in less challenging times is also valuable for the challenging times. When we are in a place of appreciation or heart-focused gratitude, the universal principle operating in all life guarantees that we will not only find a reason to appreciate, but we will attract more of the same into our life experience. I have observed that angry people attract more angry people, places, and events into their life experience. The same is true for appreciative people. Appreciation attracts more people, places, and events that represent the energy of appreciation.

It can be insightful to consider, are we practicing full appreciation, or are we convincing ourselves it is appreciation when it is only gratitude? Appreciation not only opens the heart portal to feeling the energy of hope, it also opens the connection we have with the all-pervasive life force. When we want to know if we are closed off to the all-pervasive life force, all we need to do is look at our appreciation practice. We can ask ourselves, "Am I practicing appreciation, or focusing on the lack of something?"

As part of the M.A.G.I.C. practice, appreciation holds a distinct vibration that differs from the gratitude most people talk about. While appreciation may include an aspect of gratitude, gratitude does not always include an aspect of appreciation. Appreciation feels complete. It is acceptance without judgment, while gratitude can be half-hearted, holding onto some judgment or attachment. Within the context of M.A.G.I.C. appreciation focuses on the feeling coming from the heart, while gratitude focuses on a thought that comes from the mind. The heart is a feeling instrument, always looking to guide us where we need to go for our highest good and expansion. The mind is a cognitive processing unit (CPU, or ego), programmed with thousands of stories and experiences stored for comparison and prediction. While the head has a valuable role to play in our survival, it has no valuable part to play in higher-level spiritual decision making. It was a wise person who said, "Listen to your heart, your head is desperate."[64]

Appreciation is acceptance with the mind, felt as joy in the heart, expressed in the cells as feedback for the mind. But appreciation does not happen in the mind; it happens in each of the trillions of cells making up the community called the body. Remember, each of those cells is like a miniature representation of who we are as beings, except there are upwards of fifty trillion little ones looking back at us in the mirror. So, appreciation happens in the cells of our body, communicated through the heart. This is because the heart is the part of the physical body that interprets emotions, the feelings taking place in the cells and between the cells, and it is the heart that provides this information to the brain. Again, it begins in the mind as a choice with our thoughts and ends up being feedback for the mind.

The act of appreciation is feedback that we are believing something, thinking thoughts of acceptance and nonattachment and thoughts that acknowledge that everything is okay. As a cause and an effect, one function of appreciation is to bring about a desire for more of the same. It is complete, aligning the physical, mental, emotional, and spiritual aspects into one unit, the Divine as we were created. This concept gathers momentum when we realize how impossible it is to feel anxious, depressed, or angry at the same time that we are feeling appreciation. It is a way of thinking and a way of feeling! Most of all, it is a choice we make between what we think we have or are and what we truly have or are.

As the communication portal between our conscious minds, our inner minds, our cells, and our hearts serve as a gauge for what we are believing and consistently thinking. When we believe something that contradicts what our authentic self believes about us, it is our heart's role to inform us of this contradiction. Therefore, we experience emotions such as anxiety, anger, depression, powerlessness, or despair, as well as joy, love, passion, eagerness, happiness, hope, and appreciation. Our heart is continually sending us text messages about what we are believing about ourselves in any moment. From another perspective, we could say our ego mind is also sending us a message. By causing us to have an emotional response or feeling, our ego mind is letting us know what we are thinking about ourselves in this world, but not for good reasons.

On a physical level, physiological and chemical changes take place in our cell community as a direct result of practicing appreciation. Dopamine is a neurotransmitter well known for its role in reward, movement, motivation, and addiction. It doesn't give us a high so much as a signal pointing towards a reward. The resulting pleasant feeling motivates us to repeat the behavior, and so we show more compassion and express feelings of appreciation. We can, if we choose, intentionally cause chemicals like dopamine to be released by our brains into our bodies by practicing appreciation.

The thing about appreciation is that it lifts us up by the heartstrings. When this happens, the overwhelming feeling is that we are okay, looked after, safe, blessed. We feel lighter somehow, knowing there is always a gift of love offered that is an acknowledgment of our efforts and/or our pain. When we understand the collaboration taking place within the M.A.G.I.C. practice, it becomes a natural progression to recognize the power appreciation plays in our lives. This power results from several characteristics essential to the practice of appreciation. These include, but are not exclusive to, the following:

- Appreciation is energy that we generate as emotion.
- We interpret appreciation as feelings.
- Appreciation is the cause and the effect, as it causes more of the same thoughts and more of the same emotions.
- When we have thoughts, emotions, and beliefs combined as appreciation, we have the ingredients for more of the same.
- What we put out is what we get back.

- Appreciation attracts more appreciation, while raising the vibrational frequency of our cells.
- Appreciation is simple physics operating on a quantum scale.

Sometimes it is difficult to find the gift in our current situation or circumstances. This is how our lives on planet Earth work. We face all forms of challenges as we evolve. Some are painful to the point of securing our full attention. In these times, it is almost impossible to find a gift in the moment, to practice appreciation for the experience. Sometimes we cannot see the gift because it is hidden, and sometimes we won't see it because we cannot allow ourselves to see it. There are times for most people when we will not allow ourselves to consider any gift in the circumstances because we "need" to be in hurting mode. It is only in hindsight that we can consider any possibility that we could appreciate what has occurred.

We may not understand everything that happens to us or why, but we have a choice of how we look at anything. So, we acknowledge the event, acknowledge our pain, and respect our pain, allowing the natural process of loss and grief to play out, and when and only when we are ready, we can look to reframe our circumstances.

It seems there are three options available to us when we are challenged by life matters. The first option is to resist, to stand up and fight with all of our strength, all of our resources, and fight until we are drained of energy. Funny enough, this is often the first port of call for many people, and yet it is the most painful. Somewhere along the way, we learned to use our brute strength, and forcing a situation to change was the way to go. Resisting a set of circumstances can also take a passive approach. Some people will attempt to ignore it, in the hope that it will go away. This option can work, if—and that is a critical "if"—you can completely let it go. No attachment, attention, or expectations, just complete detachment and release.

The second option is to manage our reactions to the circumstances by numbing them. Our society has sanctioned the use of medications, alcohol, drugs, sports, adrenaline-seeking adventures, and social immersion as a means for numbing the emotional charge of circumstances in our lives. The result is that we waste an opportunity to address an ill-informed belief system and/or fail to evolve with strength and wisdom. The reality with this approach is that the force that orchestrates the circumstances and situations in our lives will continue to present us with the same issue, in different forms, until we eventually have no choice other than to face it.

The third approach is the appreciation approach. We must look the issue in the eyes. Look at it, acknowledge it, accept it, and find a way to appreciate it coming into our lives. Ask yourself, "What possible reason would a loving universe have for presenting this in my life?" or "What gift could I get from addressing this issue that has presented in my life?" By practicing appreciation, we can accept all circumstances that are present in our life as meaningful and beneficial. This is not to suggest there will not be any pain or discomfort. Instead, it suggests that we always have an opportunity to receive the best outcome for our highest good. It is an attitude that suggests, "Things are always working out for me, even when I cannot see it or believe it."

Sometimes we may want to hold onto our drama, our pain. We may feel a need for acknowledgment of and justification for the pain we endured. This is because reframing our circumstances means giving up our right to feel victimized. It is still our freedom to choose, and until we have released all charged emotions or reframed our thinking, we will look for relief on the way to hope. Sometimes holding onto the pain can be a way of finding some small relief, but this is transitory. Sooner or later, we need to move on from powerlessness to depression, to anger, then to hope, and on up to appreciation.

This concept of "reframing our circumstances" could do with a brief explanation. First, our brains do not understand the workings of the universe. Think about it: most people don't understand how a cell phone works, but this doesn't stop anyone from using them. How many people switch on a light without knowing or even wanting to know about the workings of electricity? The nice thing is that we don't have to understand some things, and it is still okay to appreciate them for their everyday value. Reframing isn't about ignoring the events in our lives. The purpose of reframing is to acknowledge our experience, while being open to the proverbial light at the end of the tunnel. This is a way of separating consciousness from our emotions and thoughts. This separates the triggers from who we are. By seeing ourselves as separate from the triggers and emotional reactions, we can acknowledge our worth and find appreciation.

Amie Gordon is a social personality psychologist, and in an article called "Five Ways Giving Thanks Can Backfire," she says, "Most of the time, gratitude is good. But research finds that there are situations when 'thank you,' may be the wrong response ... If you mistake feelings of gratitude for indebtedness, you may find yourself working hard to repay a favor not to express your appreciation but to take the weight of a debt off your shoulders. In close relationships, this need to repay tit-for-tat can actually lead to negative feelings between partners."[65] The point here is that gratitude usually has some sense of guilt or resentment or frustration within it, whereas appreciation is unconditional. Essentially, the practice of appreciation backfires when it becomes something less than appreciation. There are no conditions placed on appreciation, and when we attach conditions, there is no true appreciation. Here again, we can distinguish between appreciation and gratitude while considering Amie's comments related to "backfiring." In this scenario, the concept of gratitude and indebtedness go hand in hand, and the underlying implications for gratitude are not nice. This is not an example of practicing appreciation or in-your-face gratitude. Remember, there is no debt associated with appreciation. There is only acceptance with love and nonattachment. Appreciation lets go of the problem entirely and focuses on a gift in the moment—any gift.

It is a common approach when starting the practice of appreciation to push the limits. After reading the books, watching the videos, and listening to the podcasts, many seekers push so hard to appreciate everything in their lives that they end up pushing the essence of appreciation back out the door. It is important to understand that the practice of appreciation, at least within the M.A.G.I.C. practice, is about nonattachment to outcomes, nonattachment to anything. It is acceptance of what is in the moment. As Yoda says in *Star Wars III: Revenge of the Sith*, "Train yourself to let go of everything you fear to lose."[66] Appreciation is acknowledgment that things are always working out, and that an all-pervasive benevolent energy has our back. May the Force be with us as we go about our day searching for the gift offered in all circumstances and situations.

Appreciation allows us to recognize our challenges and problems for what they are in our lives. This isn't ever about ignoring our problems. It is important to recognize, acknowledge, appreciate, and address our challenges the same way we would all our experiences. That being said, there is no need to analyze our circumstances from a place of powerlessness. Circumstances are props with no meaning until our ego mind comes along with a set of beliefs and morphs these circumstances into life dramas. It is our thinking that makes it so. There is no need for analysis, nor is there a need to understand every issue, but this is often what we like to do, right? In many ways, we do enjoy the drama, and that is okay. What isn't okay is deciding to stay in the drama while we think "victim." In his book *Dialogue on Awakening: Communion with a Loving Brother*, Tom Carpenter provides this powerful message for those of us who find ourselves caught up in living the drama. The statement he suggests we use is, "I know I'm doing this and I know it's not going to bring me peace, and for whatever reason, I'm going to do it anyway, and it's OK."[67] Repeating this statement to ourselves will help dissolve the emotion.

It is important to allow insight and understanding to come as a natural process of life, while practicing appreciation for our circumstances. Liking something and appreciating it are two different things. Liking a thing comes from our preferences and what we believe we want and deserve in life. Appreciation allows us to accept responsibility for our own choices and facilitates empowerment without blaming or shaming. We cannot blame and shame when we appreciate. Appreciation guides us to see problems as opportunities, and the invitation is for us to accept the opportunities and address the issue at hand. It is never about ignoring what presents in our lives. In fact, it is the opposite: it is a declaration of recognizing our personal power to change what is materializing in our experience, as well as what is occurring in the world. We heal the world from the inside out with the practice of appreciation.

Underpinning the practice of M.A.G.I.C. is a set of principles. Innate to these principles is an acknowledgment that we are "powerful beyond measure." As Marianne Williamson writes, "As we let our light shine, we unconsciously give other people permission to do the same. As we are liberated from our own fear, our presence actually liberates others."[68] The practice of appreciation begins and ends as an internal personal practice. When we appreciate as an expression of our essence, and nothing less, we can't help but change the world.

Some scientific findings

Old-guard psychologists and mental health practitioners still debate the role (if any) of the mind-body connection in emotional reactivity. A Newtonian perspective held by many practitioners promotes a degree of confusion as to whether emotions are the cause or result of the way we interpret the world. While ancient wisdom teaches that the heart is the center through which we can reach an awakened state and expanded awareness, current conventions promulgate more of a focus on cognitive and behavioral processing.

There is a very special group of scientists and researchers exploring the human heart and its connection, its influence, and the role it plays in life on this planet. The following information comes from the HeartMath Institute (HMI). It is not common knowledge that the heart sends more signals to the brain than the brain sends to the heart. In their investigations, HMI scientists found that the signals from the heart affect brain functioning along with the physiology of the body. These signals influence our emotional processing and higher cognitive faculties, such as attention, perception, memory, and problem-solving.

The part of the nervous system that regulates most of the body's internal functions is the autonomic nervous system (ANS). We call it "autonomic" because it doesn't need our input; it has its own intelligence. There are two branches of the ANS: sympathetic and parasympathetic. The sympathetic has the role of raising the heart rate in times of need, while the parasympathetic has the role of slowing down the heart. When the sympathetic nerves and parasympathetic nerves are working collaboratively, we experience a normal heart rate variability (HRV). The HRV is the changing time lapse between heartbeats, not the heartbeats alone. It is the time between heartbeats.

When we experience uplifting emotions such as appreciation, joy, and love, our heart rhythm becomes highly ordered, looking like a smooth, harmonious wave, i.e., it becomes coherent. When we are generating a coherent heart rhythm, the body's systems operate with increased efficiency and harmony. It's no wonder that positive emotions feel so good; they help our bodies' systems to synchronize and work better. Scientists at HMI have found that the heart not only responds to emotion but that the signals generated by its rhythmic activity actually play a major part in determining the quality of our emotional experience from moment to moment. In short, it appears that the heart recognizes when we are practicing appreciation. It in turn informs the brain and the cells, as well as adjusting its influence on the body.

In an article written for the UC Davis Health Medical Center, Robert Emmons, a leading expert on the science of gratitude, reports on the measurable effects of practicing gratitude. He writes, "[Gratitude] can lower blood pressure, improve immune function and facilitate more efficient sleep. Gratitude reduces lifetime risk for depression, anxiety, and substance abuse disorders, and is a key resiliency factor in the prevention of suicide."[69] One of the surprising findings that Emmons and his colleagues highlight is the function of gratitude in reducing levels of "excessive entitlement."[70] In an article written in *Greater Good* magazine, Emmons says of gratitude in the workplace, "A person who feels entitled to everything will be grateful for nothing; gratitude is the antidote to entitlement, and to other aspects of toxic workplace culture."[71] Note the words, "gratitude is the antidote to entitlement."

In a study called "Counting Blessings vs. Burdens"[72] carried out in 2003, researchers required ill patients to keep a gratitude journal. Keeping this gratitude journal resulted in sixteen percent of subjects reporting reduced symptoms, and ten percent of subjects reporting a decrease in pain. It also showed that subjects were more willing to exercise and were far more motivated in their recovery.

The world as we know it is mental. This is not to say that it is crazy (even though perhaps this could be argued with some conviction). It can be said that the world is mental insofar as our experience comes directly from our mental processing. Even when we are picking up on the surrounding energies, for example, from a partner or in a shopping center, we explain this with our mental processes. If someone doesn't know that other people's energies can influence how they feel, they will not consider this an option. If someone doesn't know that a person's emotional state is encoded into the heart's magnetic field and is communicated throughout the body and into the external environment, they can only attempt to explain this with a physical explanation.

Many studies on the benefits of gratitude practices have shown that keeping a gratitude journal or sending a thank-you note can increase our long-term happiness by more than ten percent. A 2005 study[73] reported that keeping a gratitude journal decreased depression by more than thirty percent for the duration of the study. In a 2012 study on gratitude, Chinese researchers noticed that gratitude had a profound effect on sleep, but they took it a step further. Controlling the quality of sleep in their subjects produced the following results and gratitude benefits: in subjects with depression,[74] the amount and quality of sleep was unrelated to lower depression scores, meaning that gratitude eased their depressive symptoms regardless of how much or how well the patient slept. This suggests that one benefit of gratitude may be to decrease symptoms related to depression.

Sleep is a time of realignment. From a spiritual perspective, it is during sleep that we realign the vibrational frequency of our cells, the very atoms that make up our cellular structure, with our energetic self. This corrects the misalignment that occurs because of emotional stress during our waking state. During the waking state, we have the tendency to become intricately involved in the ego's fear-based stories. During sleep, we detach from the dramas and storytelling, which allows us to realign with our true self. In light of this, it would be beneficial to consider spending a little time prior to sleep practicing appreciation.

Many scientific studies on gratitude have yielded the same result: gratitude increases the quality of sleep, while decreasing the time needed to fall asleep and lengthening the duration of sleep. Several studies have shown that gratitude promotes physiologically restorative behaviors, the chief among which is better sleep. Robert Emmons asserts, "Grateful thinking and grateful moods help us sleep better and longer. In one study, people keeping a gratitude journal slept on average 30 minutes more per night, woke up feeling more refreshed, and had an easier time staying awake during the day compared to those who didn't practice gratitude."[75]

In a study focused on the quality of pre-sleep cognition,[76] researchers found that gratitude predicted greater subjective sleep quality and sleep duration, and less sleep latency and daytime dysfunction. The researchers reported a relationship between gratitude and sleep variables. Any pre-sleep thoughts influenced this relationship, whether these thoughts were positive or distressing. In essence, a few minutes spent in appreciation prior to sleep improves the quality of sleep.

The quality of our well-being, when we fight everyday stressors compared with practicing appreciation, can be measured by our blood pressure. In a 2007 study that speaks to the benefits of gratitude,[77] researchers had patients with hypertension count their blessings once a week. Results showed a significant decrease in the pressure of blood in their arteries during the contraction of the heart muscle (systolic blood pressure). This gratitude research also revealed that writing in a gratitude journal (often) can reduce blood pressure by ten percent.

In a different research study on gratitude,[78] subjects showed a significant reduction in the effects of stress after cultivating appreciation. Twenty-three percent showed a decrease in cortisol, the most prominent stress hormone. We also associate high levels of cortisol with excessive weight gain. The question arises, would practicing gratitude assist in the reduction of excess weight for some individuals? Even more impressive from this study was the finding that eighty percent of participants showed changes in heart rate variability—a direct result of reduced stress levels.

A summary of the research undertaken on the science of gratitude shows us the following:

- Keeping a gratitude diary for two weeks produced sustained reductions in perceived stress (28 percent) and depression (16 percent) in healthcare practitioners.
- Gratitude is related to 23 percent lower levels of stress hormones (cortisol).
- Practicing gratitude led to a 7 percent reduction in biomarkers of inflammation in patients with congestive heart failure.
- Two gratitude activities (counting blessings and gratitude letter writing) reduced the risk of depression in at-risk patients by 41 percent over a six-month period.
- Dietary fat intake was reduced by as much as 25 percent when people were keeping a gratitude journal.
- A daily gratitude practice can decelerate the effects of neurodegeneration (as measured by a 9 percent increase in verbal fluency) that occurs with increasing age.
- Grateful people have 16 percent lower diastolic blood pressure and 10 percent lower systolic blood pressure compared to those less grateful.
- Grateful patients with Stage B asymptomatic heart failure were 16 percent less depressed, 20 percent less fatigued, and 18 percent more likely to believe they could control the symptoms of their illness compared to those less grateful.
- Older adults administered the neuropeptide oxytocin showed a 12 percent increase in gratitude compared to those given a placebo.

- Writing a letter of gratitude reduced feelings of hopelessness in 88 percent of suicidal inpatients and increased levels of optimism in 94 percent of them.
- Grateful people (including people grateful to God) have between 9 and 13 percent lower levels of hemoglobin A1c, a key marker of glucose control that plays a significant role in the diagnosis of diabetes.
- Gratitude is related to a 10 percent improvement in sleep quality in patients with chronic pain (76 percent whom had insomnia) and 19 percent lower depression levels.

Practicing appreciation: some thoughts

Practice: Here is a suggestion for when you are practicing or attempting to practice appreciation, and you find it difficult to actually get the feeling of complete appreciation. Move back from the specifics and start general. Start by appreciating the bigger-picture gifts, such as how this planet is spinning at just the right speed while orbiting around the sun that appears to rise and set every day—all without us having to do anything except enjoy. And we don't even have to do that! Appreciate how the plant and animal life on this planet has sustained us and continues to sustain us with no questions asked. Recognize that your heart beats even when you are asleep, and that it knows when to beat faster or slower depending on what your cells need in that moment.

Practice: At the beginning of your day, say YES. Then as you go about your day, practice saying YES. "When an enlightened being speaks, every word is YES. When they think, every thought is YES. When they act, every action is YES."[79] In this statement, James Twyman captures the essence of who we are and what we are. While it takes a little while to grasp this truth, by starting out with a commitment to YES during your day, the flavor of your day will move in the direction of your happiness and contentment. Hint: you do not have to understand this. It is only necessary to act on it throughout your day and observe the change.

Practice: The ego focuses on lack and therefore creates it. The Spirit concentrates on the endless stream of gifts we give ourselves and thus creates that. This is because the greatest blessing the Divine gives to us is the ability to create more of what we focus on. Pay attention to all that you give yourself, and you get more; focus on lack, and you get less. Thank your spirit self throughout the day, and you will be blessed with abundance. Offer gratitude for being alive, for the opportunities at hand, and for your challenges and the ability to find solutions. Give thanks for your health, your life, your family, and your friends. Show appreciation for your blessings before they even arrive. Thank your Creator out loud for absolutely everything in your life, because it is all a gift from you, to you. Remind yourself that it is not about believing this statement; it is about saying it, pondering it, and letting the energy of life take you where you need to go.

The ego forgets to be thankful. Sometimes it goes so far as to feel deprived and entitled, resentful for the lack it's actually creating. It's all so ridiculous. The ego doesn't like to be bothered with thanking your Godly self—it's too preoccupied with feeling sorry for itself—but it will enjoy the benefits that come from doing so. Tell your ego to be quiet, and learn what thanking your spirit self can do.[80]

Practice: In her book *Thank and Grow Rich*, Pam Grout provides twenty-seven "Party Games." The games are essentially activities we can use to speed up the practice of appreciation in our everyday life. Party Game number one is called AA 2.0, where AA stands for "Amazing Awesomeness." Here is an activity in the words of Pam Grout: "If you want to override your brain's unfortunate habit of leafing through your past and creating a present hologram to match, forget thinking. And start thanking. And I mean thanking everything.[81] … First thing every morning, before you throw off your covers, before you leap out of bed, proclaim to the world that something unexpected, exciting, and amazingly awesome is headed your way today. Step two: Come to believe in blessings and miracles, and go about your day looking, searching, expecting for that Amazing Awesomeness to present somewhere, somehow, in an unexpected form."

Practice: You can choose. Wayne Dyer shares a powerful philosophy with these words: "With everything that has happened to you, you can either feel sorry for yourself or treat what has happened as a gift. Everything is an opportunity to grow or an obstacle to keep you from growing. You get to choose."[82] As with everything we do, we need to practice, to train our bodies, minds, and hearts to follow the script. This is often the first step in exercising appreciation: making a choice.

Here is a training process for receiving your gift from any experience. Think of just one person, circumstance, or event that has caused you some form of pain. Now stay focused on that one person, circumstance, or event throughout the day while asking yourself the question, "What was the gift I received from that experience?" Repeating the question throughout your day is important for retraining your brain and allowing you to gain insight. Repeat the process on different days with different experiences in your life that have caused pain. Note: your focus is on the gift in the experience, not on the drama or lack of something.

Practice: Anthony Robbins has a powerful and simple process that captures the essence of appreciation. He says, "Change your expectations, for appreciation, and the entire world changes for you in an instant."[83]

Practice: Here is a quick technique for feeling appreciation[84] developed by the HeartMath Institute.

Step 1: Heart Focus – Shift your attention to the area of your heart, or the center of your chest. Placing your hand on your heart area makes a physical connection. Breathe slowly and deeply. Breathing for the count of five in and five out is a good baseline. Imagine the air entering and leaving through the heart area, or the center of your chest.

Step 2: Heart Feeling – Remember a time when you felt deep appreciation. Reexperience that feeling. Focus on this feeling as you continue to breathe through the area of your heart. Stay with this as long as it takes to feel a change.

Practice: Keep a journal where you document your appreciation arising from the day. Writing about your appreciation is more powerful than keeping it in your head. When you write down at least five positive experiences (people, places, events, circumstances) you have during your day, it activates more of your senses and consequently creates a stronger vibration in the quantum field. There is no wrong way to keep your journal; it is really up to you and what resonates within your heart. Be creative about this.

Practice: Acceptance of what is, even with associated pain or trauma, is practicing appreciation. Again, we don't have to appreciate something to appreciate its value. But seeing the gift or value in any situation and recognizing it as a blessing, even if in disguise, can be impossible. You would have to be an enlightened being to move from powerlessness or anger to appreciation in one jump. Then again, if you were an enlightened being, you wouldn't be feeling powerless. Part of the trick is to find the smallest amount of value in your circumstances. When you see just the smallest amount of value in any experience, the pain level lowers in association with the level of resistance you have. This won't stop it from hurting, but it gives some purpose to the experience while reducing the hurt.

Rather than trying to stop the pain or find the gift, or even move up the emotion scale, look for ways of moving your attention. The aim here is to recognize that you are having trouble with the pain, you are having trouble finding the gift, and you are having trouble finding any appreciation, and then move to another subject. This is like sticking your head in the sand, but it is also a more loving thing to do for yourself than staying stuck in the pain. Remaining stuck in the pain won't do anything other than keep you stuck. Moving your attention will allow you the space to ask, "What is good about this?"

Practice knowing there is a gift, even when it is hidden from your immediate view. Practicing this when things are good allows you to find a hint of hope when things are not so good. Relief, no matter how small, is the turning point. It is here that feelings of victimhood morph into feelings of appreciation. Lao Tzu is said to have been a mystic philosopher of ancient China, best known as the author of the *Tao Te Ching*. A simple and yet powerful philosophy attributed to Lao Tzu says, "Life is a series of natural and spontaneous changes. Don't resist them—that only creates sorrow. Let reality be reality. Let things flow naturally forward in whatever way they like."[85] Sticking your head in the sand is sometimes the only way to let things flow naturally. The appreciation in this is knowing that on another level, the universal laws are at work, and you have the freedom and power to influence these laws for your own expansion and inner peace.

Practice: "Wouldn't it be good if this happened...?" Make this statement with no need to make it happen, and with no feeling of loss if it doesn't happen. Feel the change in your energy as you contemplate this statement.

Practice: Say the word *YES*. Say it many times. Feel it and recognize the changes taking place in your body. In his book *The Art of Spiritual Peacemaking: Secret Teachings from Jeshua ben Joseph* by James Twyman,[86] there comes a point when Jeshua guides the reader to connect with the wholistic concept of YES. "Be aware of the ways you are currently saying NO to the universe. Allow a new vision to take hold; one where YES is the only reality you embrace. Chant the word over and over. Clap your hands together, or pat all over your body in order to ground the experience."

Practice: Give to others what you can without doubting your actions. In his book *Gene Keys*, Richard Rudd connects the science, the emotion, and the spiritual when he writes, "When you give to another unconditionally, you actually stimulate the secretion of serotonin. This not only makes you feel happy but also induces a deep state of trust that you are in harmony with the entire universe."[87]

Practice: Focus on a person, place, or event you totally appreciate, and hold this image in your mind. Focus on one aspect of this person, place, or event that you can appreciate without resistance. Hold this in your heart. Choose easy ones to begin with, then move on to the hard-to-appreciate ones later. This is giving to another while giving to oneself. As you give, so do you receive.

Practice: Accept the opportunity to make use of the contrast in your life, because it is the contrast in life that causes you to want something better, and subsequently you set in place circumstances that support what you want to come about.

Practice: In their works on the Law of Attraction, Esther and Jerry Hicks continually promote the freedom to choose appreciation as a tool for experiencing abundance in life. One of the processes provided in the book *Money and the Law of Attraction* provides a simple yet powerful way of nurturing appreciation: "Make lists of positive aspects. Make lists of things you love—and never complain about anything. And as you use those things that shine bright and make you feel good as your excuse to give your attention and be who-you-are, you will tune to who-you-are, and the entire world will transform before your eyes. It is not your job to transform the world for others—but it is your job to transform it for you. A state of appreciation is pure Connection to Source where there is no perception of lack."[88]

Practice: We know with certainty that what we focus on, we create more of in life. If it feels better, call it a self-fulfilling prophecy. Whatever the emotion, goal, event, experience, or memory, when we give our attention to it, there is a universal response that magnifies the object of our attention. This is based on universal law. It exists, it operates, and it does not judge; it simply responds to our intention and attention. Even if our intention is on receiving one thing, but our attention is on not receiving it, the law states that the energy goes where our attention goes. Our attention, conscious or unconscious, is what directs the focus of our request. The universe or the law doesn't respond to what we say we want; it responds to what we *feel* we want. Practicing appreciation is an emotional or energetic response. This is the language of the universe and the language that directs universal laws. The practice of appreciation has its own built-in mechanism for cause and effect, and adding more appreciation to what already exists will nourish any minor aspect of appreciation you hold. Begin with a small appreciation. Feel it. Recognize it. Stay with it as you watch it grow. It will build upon itself as it causes its own effect to grow. Note: this works for any feeling or constant thought you hold.

Practice: When in a place of feeling "the problem"—AKA the contrast—it's difficult to move to a place of appreciation. Jumping from a negative, feel-bad place straight into a place of appreciation may not be the easiest thing, nor the best thing. When you can philosophize that a problem has a hidden purpose for guiding you towards insight, this is a part of healing. We need the problems and challenges and stress as a natural part of our expansion. It comes down to knowing which aspect of your circumstances to direct attention toward. At any moment, you can focus on the lack of what you want or the potential of what you want. A quote often attributed to Tony Robbins says, "Where attention goes, energy flows."[89] One doesn't have to believe this to be scientifically correct for it to operate in your life. We can measure quantum entanglement and the influence of thoughts on electrons, atoms, cells, and even people. But how would we measure this statement? While the rules of (quantum) physics and more specifically the rules of electromagnetics give credence to the idea, the best way to check out the authenticity of this statement is to experiment for yourself.

Go about your day and intentionally focus on something that you appreciate working well in your life. Maintain the focus, attention, and intention on this particular aspect of your life. Notice what changes in relation to this aspect of your life. Your freedom lies in the choice to focus your thoughts. Remember to play with this. Let go of the trying and thinking and just play!

Practice: Let go of the uncontrollable. You cannot change certain circumstances, but you can change how you feel about them. If you can move forward step-by-step into feeling a little better and a little better until you reach appreciation, then you will find peace in all experiences.

Note to self: appreciation is a M.A.G.I.C. wand in this physical world.

CHAPTER 9

Grounding

Grounding

> PLACING ONESELF IN THE ARMS OF NATURE
> IS PLACING ONESELF IN THE ARMS OF MOTHER EARTH.
> HERE WE ARE NURTURED AND SUPPORTED.
> FOR IT IS MOTHER EARTH'S DESIRE TO CARE FOR HER
> CHILDREN.
> PAUL DUNNE

Defining Grounding

Within the context of the M.A.G.I.C. practice, we use the term *grounding* to infer a connection between our energy system and the energy system of the earth. The words *grounding* and *earthing* are used interchangeably, even though the term *earthing* can be seen more as a mechanical, electrical, or scientific reference. Each suggests a connection and an exchange of electrons between our bodies and the Earth's energy field. Hopefully, our use of grounding recognizes and promotes more of a relationship with Mother Earth, a oneness if you like, within our electromagnetic status and that of the planet. When we are earthed, we are electrically connected, which brings about its own changes. When we are grounded, no matter what the circumstances around us, we are supported and reassured in ways unexpected.

Another word often confused with grounding is *centering*. Centering relates to coming back into the present moment. Irrespective of how much chaos is around us, if we can center ourselves, we realign our thinking and subsequent emotional response to the present moment, where we are safe. To do this, make a statement such as, "I align my physical, mental, emotional, and energetic aspects with my higher self, now!" Breathe as you visualize your four quadrants lining up.

Our connection with the earth is unseen. Like gravity, electricity, magnetism, and wind, we do not see this connection with our physical eyes. We recognize the effects, and we assume we know the cause, but we don't see what actually causes the effects. Feeling the effects of gravity when we jump in the air, fall out of a tree, or drop onto our bed, we recognize different effects of this unseen force. What this force is, where it comes from, and what sustains it are questions for our exploration as we observe the world. Here we will explore the practice of connecting or grounding our energy with that of Earth.

As stated in *A Course in Miracles*, "Miracles demonstrate that learning has occurred under the right guidance, for learning is invisible and what has been learned can be recognized only by its results. Its generalization is demonstrated as you use it in more and more situations. You cannot see the invisible. Yet if you see its effects, you know it must be there."[90]

Science—at least, that which comes from a Newtonian approach—attempts to show that everything can be reduced to its smallest particle, and then some. This approach looks for an explanation of how things work by breaking everything down into parts. The problem is that things aren't always that straightforward. While we measure everything, from our sun to a light photon, as pure energy held together by an unseen force, science hasn't yet been able to measure the "unseen force" in a way that fosters a sense of credibility.

Isaac Newton, famous for his apple-and-tree trick, deduced that there must be a force acting between our earth, the planets, and the sun. Newton then came up with an equation to explain the phenomenon. This equation says that any two or more objects with mass will exert a force on each other simply because they have mass. It is the mass in relation to the distance between each object that determines the strength of the force, or gravitational pull. This is true for objects as big as our sun down to objects as small as a proton. But what is this force? Where does it come from, and what determines its strength?

A great deal of what we believe to be "real" and "true" in this physical reality is unseen by the physical eyes. The ability to perceive through our eyes, ears, nose, etc. is limited to a narrow band of vibrational frequencies. For example, the human eye can see about 0.0035 percent of the electromagnetic spectrum (which includes gamma rays, radio waves, x-rays, infrared, ultraviolet, microwaves, etc.). Sound travels in waves through the air and other substances. Humans cannot see sound; rather, it is perceived through vibration at different frequencies, just like light. Everything is vibration. The vibrations are translated into data for our brains. Then, based on what we have experienced before, our brains will decode the vibrations into meaning.

Even if one doesn't believe in gravity, electricity, magnetism, or for that matter the wind, it is difficult to ignore the effects caused by these influences. Unseen causes provide observable effects. Fall out of a tree, and there has to be an explanation for why we don't "fall" upward into the sky. Stick a fork in an electric socket, and we learn about a power that can throw us against the wall—something we call electricity. Watching a windmill operate, we can observe the effects of the wind on a set of blades. Of course, every farmer or rancher with a windmill knows about the power of the wind—or do they? The blades move, but what is it that really makes them move? After all, we never see the wind coming or going. We see the effects on the windmill blades, just as we see dust moving in the air, and the crops swaying back and forth. But do we ever see the cause of these effects? There are things unseen, forces and events that take place all the time, but we do not see them. In fact, we are often unconscious of them, even when they are right in front of us. Grounding is one such phenomenon.

Grounding is a natural practice that can happen day in and day out with no conscious effort. The important word here is *can*. Yes, it is true that wearing shoes that insulate us from the earth's energy field impedes our grounding effectiveness. Here is the "but": we don't need to be physically connected with the earth's energy system to be grounded. In reality, most people unconsciously limit the effectiveness of this process by engaging in thinking and activities that disconnect them from the earth's field. The connection does not take place simply because we connect physically with the earth's surface. Grounding also happens because we connect energetically with the energy system of the earth.

The indigenous peoples of the world knew this and practiced it as an everyday experience. They knew our bodies come pre-wired for the job of directing energy through and around the organs and all components that make us what we are. Practitioners of yoga and traditional Chinese medicine and masters of physical arts such as Tai Chi, aikido, and Qigong have taught about the importance and the practice of connecting with the earth's energy system and the movement of energy around the body. They equally understand the relevance of energy allowed to flow through the body. Those who have studied this phenomenon understand that energy stuck or blocked in the body causes dis-ease. They also know about the importance of moving these blocks through such techniques as exercise, massage, meditation, and energy work such as Reiki.

Our bodies absorb free electrons when we are walking barefoot on the earth or swimming in water. It can also happen while sitting, working, or sleeping indoors when connected to a conductive apparatus. These man-made apparatuses facilitate the transfer of energy from the ground to the body. When this happens, there is an exchange of electrons, or an acceptance in the body of free electrons from the earth's surface.[91] Scientific data supports this, just as there is a growing body of evidence to support observations suggesting that grounding into the earth can be a natural event.

When we ground our bodies into the earth, we synchronize our frequency with the frequency of the planet. As Richard Rudd says, "The fact is that when the frequency of your DNA hits the Schumann Resonance, your experience of time stops completely. These are truths that are still experienced and embodied by many of the indigenous cultures alive on our planet today. To live close to the earth's natural rhythms is to experience the wisdom and clarity that comes of moving more slowly through the world."[92]

Spending time in nature, grounding our energy systems with that of the earth's energy system—these are simple ways of tuning our frequency to align with the frequency of the earth, which in itself provides a calming effect. The physics of grounding lie in the fact that the earth's surface is electrically conductive and is maintained at a negative potential by a global electrical circuit. This circuit has three main generators: solar wind entering the magnetosphere, ionospheric wind, and thunderstorms. The earth's surface is an abundant source of free electrons. As soil electrons are conducted into the human body, the grounded body takes on favorable physiologic (normal) and electrophysiologic (electrical) changes.

But there is another side to grounding that isn't talked about in scientific studies: grounding through an energy connection by using our intention.

If someone is looking for scientific evidence for this form of grounding, I don't know if there is any. Scientists don't tend to study things they cannot measure. Consider this, once upon a time, we were not able to measure much of what we can measure today. In fact, we were not able to see a lot of what we can see today with our modern microscopes and quantum measuring instruments. But the question here is, "Is it a real thing, this grounding through intention alone?"

After a great deal of experience with clients who have used the practice of grounding, I would argue that it certainly is a real thing, and it can be measured. Maybe not in mainstream thinking, but if you are prepared to expand your viewpoint a little to consider a few things, then it is very much a real thing. Begin by considering the grounding case previously cited about the twelve-year-old in rage, and the case below about the thirty-four-year-old male with anger issues. In both cases, we were able to measure the individual when ungrounded and grounded. Measurement occurred through observation of behaviors, self-reporting of behavioral and emotional changes, the use muscle testing, and behavior changes reported by family.

Otherwise, why would either individual consider this a thing to do? I always say, "Don't believe anything I tell you. Test it out for yourself. Test it while I support you if you like, but test it for yourself, so you know from experience—not because I told you so."

Next, consider the use and power of your body language (aka kinesiology, or muscle testing), to measure changes in the subtle energy system of a person. If you truly understand kinesiology, then you know that this is a means of connecting with the innate self. Essentially, it is "body language" in its purest form, but it is also a connection with our innate or wiser self, to which we all have access.

Time after time, I have demonstrated to individuals a response in their body language through muscle testing that shows they are grounded, and a different response that shows when they are not grounded. Learn to use their own method of kinesiology, and they can to this for themselves. For example, after the initial muscle testing session with me, young people love to use a pendulum to assess their own responses. This, of course, is empowerment—not something a lot of traditional practitioners like to use here.

Practical use of grounding

When used in a conflict situation, grounding has proven to be a game changer. A teacher referred to me with generalized anxiety and stress. After learning the M.A.G.I.C. practice, she was drawn to grounding herself regularly. (Apparently, practicing grounding reminded her of time spent on the beach.) After two sessions, this young teacher found that after grounding herself in a conflict situation with a staff member or parent, her anxiety dissolved, and her external circumstances changed for the positive. The only thing this tuned-in teacher did was breathe and visualize grounding herself while continuing the conversation. As if this weren't enough, the change in her class as they practiced grounding was the most pleasing outcome. She taught the class how to ground themselves (like trees) and suggested they practice grounding with the earth whenever they were worried, sad, angry, or upset. This is a story—someone else's story. This practice worked for this young teacher. But hearing about it is not enough. Providing you with empirical evidence is not enough. Take this story and make it your own. Experiment in your everyday life with grounding as a practice and measure the results.

Authentic martial arts practitioners of old knew of the power of intention to ground ourselves and practiced it as a central technique for storing chi in the lower Dantian, or the energy center just below the navel in the center of the body. Focusing on building energy in this energy center allowed them to stand with great strength and alignment. There are many reports from clients who tell stories about using grounding as their go-to practice in conflict situations, only to have all tension and blockages diffused. Similarly, there are many client reports attesting to the power of grounding in times of anxiety, with the anxiety-dissolving within minutes. Many of these clients have engaged in the grounding practice through visualization, while others have ventured out to connect physically with the earth. All report that the anxiety, panic, and feelings of overwhelm gently dissolved over a short time.

Young boys are particularly interesting students for grounding. Because many young boys like to think of themselves as strong and able to withstand a little push on the shoulder, they are shocked to realize the difference between a state of being grounded and a state of being disconnected. One of the first tools to give an adolescent is grounding. After they tell their often-sad story, stand them up and seek permission to give them a little push on the shoulder. As this happens, they will generally fall slightly backward. Then, after they have been guided to ground themselves, provide another gentle push, and notice the smile on their face as they stand firm like a post. Then, to demonstrate it in another form, remind them of their sad story and muscle test them. This will result in muscle weakness. Have them ground themselves again, and then muscle test again. Now they will be strong again. Highlight for them the difference between when they are grounded and not grounded.

I worked with a twenty-nine-year-old male with depression, alcohol abuse, and several physical ailments that his general practitioner suggested resulted from his emotional state. I introduced him to a holistic approach to supporting his own well-being. This included changing the physical, mental, emotional, and spiritual quadrants of his life. Along with learning how to clear away his own trapped emotions, he initially used grounding as the go-to mode of defense. For some time, all he did was practice grounding. This worked well, and eventually, he started practicing M.A.G.I.C. throughout his day. This took a little while, but eventually, his depression dissolved, along with the need for substances, and his health improved.

Some scientific findings

Modern society, in its quest for comfort, has built a barrier between what is natural and what is normal. There has been a movement away from our basic needs toward what we think we need. In so many ways, we have become disconnected from that which serves us best. We have become disconnected from the earth and the energies of nature. Does this mean we have to go without shoes or sit on the ground instead of in chairs? No! It does, however, suggest an alternative means to well-being and health, through remembering our natural state.

For some, the conversation around grounding and earthing is a kind of mythical construct made up by the unscientific "woo-woo" crowd. But does one need to have an explanation, an understanding, or a scientific premise before one accepts the benefits of anything? There are many benefits the world experiences without knowing the hidden workings behind those benefits. The insight lies in recognizing, accepting, and using the observed changes to investigate and bring about a change for you.

There is a growing body of scientific evidence highlighting the powerful effects of connecting our energy systems with that of the planet. Work undertaken by such individuals as Dr. Pawel and Dr. Karol Sokal,[93] Gaétan Chevalier,[94] and Dr. Stephen Sinatra[95] provides empirical evidence for the benefits of grounding, or what they refer to as "earthing." Originally, it was Clint Ober[96] who followed up on earthing studies undertaken with animals. He grounded humans while they were asleep, speculating that since this is the primary time when healing and restoration of the body take place, it would be ideal for grounding. His findings started a most important investigative trail for health practitioners.

Clint Ober reported that physically grounding people while they were asleep in bed produced the following results:

- 85% went to sleep quicker.
- 93% reported sleeping better throughout the night.
- 100% reported feeling more rested upon waking.
- 82% experienced a significant reduction in muscle stiffness.
- 74% experienced the elimination or a reduction of chronic back and joint pain.
- 78% reported improved general health.

Several subjects also reported experiencing significant relief from asthmatic and respiratory conditions, rheumatoid arthritis, PMS, sleep apnea, and hypertension.

There is a substantial and growing body of evidence providing indicators for simple, inexpensive, and profound means for better health for all, and this includes grounding. "The research done to date supports the concept that grounding or earthing the human body may be an essential element in the health equation along with sunshine, clean air and water, nutritious food, and physical activity."[97] For the layperson's general interest, there are several documentaries, such as *Down To Earth*[98] and *Grounded*,[99] that focus on grounding/earthing.

Because grounding can help normalize serotonin levels[100] in the brain as it decreases cortisol, people become more aware, chilled out, and centered in themselves. It is known that elevated levels of cortisol induced by stress increase serotonin uptake, under both rest and nerve stimulation, which is overtly expressed in symptoms of depression.[101] Normalizing serotonin levels in the brain results in a reduction has a flow-on effect by reducing the levels of cortisol present in individuals dealing with depression. By adjusting the amount of serotonin available in the brain through grounding, we have a natural means for addressing depression in some cases. Selective serotonin reuptake inhibitors (SSRIs) are the most commonly prescribed antidepressants. More and more individuals are choosing to avoid the use of pharmaceuticals to deal with their symptoms of depression and anxiety. Grounding is a viable option to support an individual in managing symptoms as she or he uses medication to help them over the proverbial mountain.

Tracy Latz, MD, MS, is an integrative psychiatrist in private practice, and in her article "Shifting Lives with Earthing: A Psychiatrist's Perspective," Latz shares her experience with grounding and her clients. Latz says, "I recommend Earthing to anyone with an auto-immune condition. Two patients with systemic lupus erythematosus are feeling much better after they began Earthing."[102]

With advancements in technology, we can now measure, under various conditions, how observable variations that indicate healthy or unhealthy changes take place in our biological, psychological, and energetic systems. As research efforts are expanded to focus on the many implications of grounding, it continues to be demonstrated that grounding significantly contributes to increased health and well-being. Emerging research is revealing that direct physical contact between the human body and the surface of the earth (grounding or earthing) results in positive effects on our physiology and well-being. The study titled "Earthing (Grounding) the Human Body Reduces Blood Viscosity—a Major Factor in Cardiovascular Disease" found that after two hours of grounding, there were changes in the electrical charge (zeta potential) of red blood cells (RBCs) and effects on the extent of RBC clumping. "Grounding to the soil represents yet another intervention that lowers blood viscosity by raising zeta potential, which results in a decrease in RBC (Red Blood Cell) aggregation. Attenuation of the inflammatory response and a favorable impact on blood viscosity and RBC aggregation has been the most recent findings."[103] Note: the data showing decreased clumping of RBC can actually be seen on a screen.

Research reported in the *Journal of Environmental and Public Health*[104] lists some powerful reasons for anybody to consider when assessing the importance of grounding in their life. Using techniques such as infrared medical imaging, blood chemistry, and blood cell counts, they declare that emerging evidence shows that contact with the earth "may be a simple, and yet profoundly effective environmental strategy against chronic stress." The research also highlights the potential benefits for issues of the autonomic nervous system: dysfunction, inflammation, pain, poor sleep, disturbed heart rate variability, hypercoagulable blood, and many common health disorders, including cardiovascular disease.

Practicing grounding: some thoughts

Am I grounded or not? How would I know? Our emotional state at any moment is a good/better/best indicator of what is going on, so if we are wondering whether we are grounded, the best way to know is to learn to recognize our inner guidance. This indicator usually presents as an intuitive feeling that lets us know if we are grounded and centered, or disconnected and fractured. When we are not grounded, there will be feelings of disconnection, a feeling of being out of place, or maybe a feeling of being disconnected from life, flustered, and all over the place. Stuck in the head, never in the heart. When we are grounded, the feeling is more solid, steady, sure of ourselves, and calm, and even when we have some nervousness, there is a certainty.

Within the M.A.G.I.C. practice, there is no right way to ground yourself. While grounding using an electrically conductive wire is fine, within the M.A.G.I.C. practice, we ground without a physical connection by using focused intention. This came out of a need to ground as a practitioner, along with the clients' need to ground themselves while in an office environment. In came the mother of invention; going outside was not a viable option. Practitioners of authentic martial arts, along with the indigenous populations of the world, have for eons taught about the benefits of grounding with the earth. Intention with attention to being grounded is the key!

While there may be a substantial and growing body of evidence supporting the practice of grounding, the question arises, how practical is it to be grounding oneself all the time if we need to have our bare feet touching the earth? Or do we? The M.A.G.I.C. answer is that "It's up to you, grasshopper," and "No, you don't!" But the mainstream scientific answer is that you need to be connected electrically with the earth. What this means is different in different circumstances. Essentially, it means connecting with the electrical properties of the earth via some form of conductive wire. If it is important for you to measure the conductivity or resistance flowing between your body and the earth, you can use a multimeter, or specially designed devices to achieve an electrical connection. It is not incorrect, but it is also not true to say we are not insulated because we are wearing rubber-soled shoes. The common belief says, if we are standing on grass or concrete or a conductive surface, we will be grounded, as measured by a multimeter.

In yoga practice, being grounded connotes being in a place of calm and feeling a sense of safety and security, despite the existing chaos or challenges. There certainly is a physical connection with the earth, but there is also something more holistic happening here. From Yogapedia's article on grounding: "Grounding is connecting with the earth both physically and spiritually. On a physical level, grounding involves practicing yoga poses that facilitate this connection to Earth, including proper techniques to ensure a solid base. For example, making sure we connect all points of the feet to the earth. On a spiritual level, it means tapping into the grounding energy of the earth (and the universe)."[105]

In Tai Chi and Qigong practice, the focus is on the movement of energy in the body. Qi or chi (energy) moves through the meridian system, which is like the electrical wiring of the body. The idea here is that connecting with the earth allows for a practitioner to draw in the free electrons. Life is about energy before it is about what that energy produces. Thoughts are energy. We can measure thoughts. Intention alone guides these packets of information in the form of pure energy. As Dr. Wayne Dyer promulgated in his teachings and books, "When you're connected to the power of intention, everywhere you go, and everyone you meet, will be affected by you and the energy you radiate. As you become the power of intention, you'll see your dreams being fulfilled almost magically, and you'll see yourself creating huge ripples in the energy fields of others by your presence and nothing more."[106]

Practice: Become the tree: a visualization. Stand tall with feet shoulder-width apart, and keep your eyes open. Breathe deeply and slowly, as if you are drawing in the air of life—the prana, the chi, the energy worlds are created from. Draw this breath deep into that area below the navel (Dantian), visualizing it being stored there like filling up a balloon. As you breathe out, imagine, visualize, pretend, intend that you are now sending this life force from that navel energy center down through your hips, down your legs and feet, and through the floor into the earth. When the energy touches the earth, it forms roots. Continue to imagine that these roots are going deeper and deeper, growing bigger as they go deeper. Each time you breathe in and out, repeat the process until your roots are so deep that they hold the planet firm. You are now stable and grounded.

Practice: The energy way: a visualization. Stand tall with your feet shoulder-width apart, or sit comfortably with your back straight. Recognize that you are being pulled towards the center of the earth by the invisible force we call gravity. As you feel the connection downwards with the earth, breathe deeply and slowly as if you are drawing a liquid light down through the top of your head. Accept this as the energy of life, and allow it to come into the area of your sacral chakra or lower abdomen. Send this down until you connect with the crystal core in the center of the earth.

Then, recognize a responsive flow of energy coming up from the earth's core, up through the floor, through your pelvic bone, and up into your heart area. On the out-breath, allow this energy to radiate out from your heart center like waves moving all around you. Continue to breathe, observing the flow of energy down from the cosmos and up from the crystal core of the earth. When you breathe out, visualize, imagine, or pretend that energy is expanding out like a wave of light from your heart into every cell of your body, filling the room and spreading out into the wider world.

Practice: There are as many ways to ground yourself as there are different imaginations. Play and look for the results. Some people adhere to the practice of sending imagined roots deep into the planet. Others always use the visualization of allowing light to flow. Still, others have imagined being deep in the ocean, with legs in the sand, or hugging a tree. It is your choice.

Practice: Some of us need to use a more tactile or solid means to connect with the earth other than visualization. If you are one of these physical-touch individuals, try the following: Notice the physical connection you have with Earth. Where is the strongest connection between your body and the earth? If seated, this connection point may be your bottom or your feet. If you are standing, walking, or running, it would be your feet connecting with the earth as you touch down with each alternate foot. For some, it will happen as they move in the water. Even remembering being in the water is usually enough to establish a connection with the earth.

So, again, move your focus onto the connection point. For example, notice each time you place a foot down on the ground as you walk. Next, recognize this connection as gravity holds you on the surface of the planet by pulling you towards the center of the earth. You cannot see gravity working, but it is happening, and you know it. Similarly, as you connect a part of your body with the earth, there is an unseen process taking place. Continue this practice until you feel a strong sense of being grounded.

Practice: Physically connect yourself with the earth by placing your bare feet on the earth. Spend fifteen mins doing this as your practice of M.A.G.I.C., feeling your connection with the earth by touching or lying on the ground or being in a body of water. This has been promoted as an effective way of clearing jet lag after a long flight.

Practice: Physically connect yourself with the earth by investing in an earthing apparatus. There are several developers and outlets found through online stores.

Practice: You may choose to imagine a place where you have previously been inside the crust of the earth, like in a cave or digging. Breathe into this as you re-member with this memory and the associated experience. Connect with the earth's core through intention, imagination, and visualization, or by pretending to feel the caress of the earth's energy all around you.

Case note: Grounding for anger

A thirty-four-year-old male presented with anger issues (domestic and family violence), alcohol abuse/dependency, and relationship problems. After clearing some outdated core beliefs about self-worth, he went away and committed to grounding himself no matter what.

In the second session, he reported being calm, with no incidents of anger outbursts or abuse (evidence supported by his partner). A combination of dissolving old, outdated stored emotions and associated core beliefs, along with grounding, had changed something. The indication was that this combination had allowed the anger to dissolve, the dependency to disappear, and a sense of worth to return.

The relationship ended in separation, but he and his partner remained friends.

CHAPTER 10

Insight

Insight

> ALWAYS AND ALL WAYS, THERE IS GUIDANCE.
> WE ARE PROVIDED WITH INSIGHTS TO SHOW US THE WAY.
> LOOK FOR THE SIGNS, LISTEN FOR THE SONG;
> THE INSIGHT IS YOURS WHEN YOU ARE OPEN.
> PAUL DUNNE

Defining Insight

This is one practice many newbies to M.A.G.I.C. often misunderstand and pass over for what they consider to be a more common or practical practice. Everyone knows about meditation or mindfulness, and the benefits that come from practicing. But what is this practice of insight? If insight comes spontaneously when you are in the shower or driving down the highway, how can it be a practice? And if, as I claim, you already use each of these five practices in your life, where is the practice of insight?

There are situations when the emotional turmoil in our heads, hearts, and bodies is overwhelming. In these times, very few individuals would—or could—hear you say, "What about practicing mindfulness? Grounding? Appreciation? Or connection?" In times of overwhelm, it is difficult, if not impossible, to move from despair and powerlessness into practicing anything. In such times, the practice of insight checks all the boxes. This is because as a practice, insight opens up an opportunity to access the resources and intuitive wisdom of another individual. This might be a friend or family member, but it could also be—and often is—a professional or practitioner. (It might also be a case of having a session with yourself.) We are in fact practicing insight with connection. This is a way of integrating the practice of insight with connection. So, what do we do when we need support, guidance, or an attentive ear?

Some years ago, I was in one of those dark holes, feeling sad and sorry for myself. A friend commented on my demeanor and suggested that I needed to have a session with myself. I followed up on this not-so-silly suggestion, and with a pen and pad, I went to the water. After writing out what I thought was the problem at the top of the page, I allowed my wiser self to provide me with some guidance by communicating through my written word. The result was powerful and more than helpful. This was exactly what I had always wanted to do for other people: teach them how to access their own therapist within.

"I knew it! I knew it! But I didn't listen," or "I always listen to my gut feeling, my intuition, but this time I ignored it because my head told me something else"—these are the statements people make when they have pushed aside an insight, only to find it again in hindsight, on the other side of the pain. Therefore, it is so important to get out of our heads and into silence, into a place where we can hear our hearts speaking. This is a place where we connect with our authentic self, the all-knowing self.

Insight is the combination of inspiration, investigation, intuition, and inner knowing. It is activating our inner sight so that we can realize who we are in this world. Insight within the M.A.G.I.C. practice is a combination and assimilation of different modes of looking within for answers. It helps us explain who we are in this world, and to communicate with that part of us known as the innate or innocence, which is our true essence. This is our conscious spirit self, the unseen part of us. This part of us never judges, criticizes, or condemns us for our choices. It watches, guides, and loves us unconditionally.

Everyone has access to insight all the time. We carry around with us an instrument that allows us to know at any moment what we are thinking and believing about ourselves living in this world. Our emotions are our most active and accurate indicators of our state of being at any moment. It is our hearts in collaboration and cooperation with our trillions of cells, our organs, our chakras, our energetic being, and our inner being that provide us with insight, intuition, inner knowing, and inspiration.

Most of us know insight as that light bulb moment when we realize the uselessness of banging our heads against the proverbial wall, recognizing that it achieves nothing except giving us a headache. Until the moment we stop banging our heads, we are convinced there is value in persisting, stubbornly fighting for what we want to achieve, resisting any chance of not reaching our goal. There is a sense of relief when it is all over, when we let go. It is here, in this moment, that insight may enter. It is in the moment that we stop fighting and open up to the possibility of an alternative answer that insightful answers often present themselves. It is also the time when our spirit team has a clear/er communication channel to speak through.

As we let go of the resistance to failure, the first insight is something like, *This isn't getting me anywhere*. Then there is an opportunity for a second insight. This second insight leads us to the solution, the answer to what we had been wrestling with up to this moment. Interestingly enough, the first insight that comes softens our ego's inflexibility. This is probably the most significant insight, as it opens us up to personal growth. The second insight is usually the solution to the problem, which is ultimately less important.

This ability to move from controlling the problem to allowing the problem to find resolution is not taught well in our society. We are taught to control the people, events, objects, and experiences in our lives so that we can ultimately control how we feel. We learn to hold onto the problem or the effect because we believe the effect (problem) causes our discomfort. Children are great at letting us know when we are being too rational in our response to their needs; when we use a cognitive-rational approach, what is already a tense situation will often escalate. This is because rationalizing an issue, depending on logic, and intellectualizing the situation is about meeting our needs as adults, and this does not acknowledge the emotional needs of the child.

The emotional component of the situation is what is important here. It doesn't matter so much that someone has called the child a name; it only matters that he or she feels hurt, and that this hurt is acknowledged. The child will get on with finding a solution once his or her feelings are acknowledged and valued. The clue for adults is to move out of the ego-based frame of mind into a heart-based feeling state, where we are open to insight while supporting the child. Recognizing and activating the internal state of an individual is an empowering experience. Adults are not any different from children, except adults tend to go into a cognitive response rather than a heart-based response. True insight comes when we listen through the heart rather than through the head. Only when the heart has been heard can the head come on board for processing and problem-solving.

"Everything you'll ever need to know is within you; the secrets of the universe are imprinted on the cells of your body."[107] The practice of insight in M.A.G.I.C. will highlight the programs or core beliefs you hold about yourself; how these operate (react, respond) to circumstances; their uniqueness, gifts, and purpose in this life; and guidance for expanding, expressing, and enjoying life. Here, insight incorporates the inner voice of intuition and the outer voice of inspiration through music, books, movies, and art. This can come while walking, sitting, or talking. We are each at different times a teacher, a practitioner, or a student. When we are alone, insight can come through meditation, and most often through a grounded connection with nature and life as we know it.

Changemakers such as Richard Rudd and Dr. Bruce Lipton have described that we are not victims of our DNA. Neither can we be a victim of fate. As Dr. Lipton said, "Suddenly I realized that a cell's life is controlled by the physical and energetic environment and not by its genes. Genes are simply molecular blueprints used in the construction of cells, tissues, and organs. The environment serves as a 'contractor' who reads and engages those genetic blueprints and is ultimately responsible for the character of a cell's life. It is a single cell's 'awareness' of the environment, not its genes, that sets into motion the mechanisms of life."[108]

Richard Rudd says, "You can only be a victim of your attitude."[109] Insight, as it is used in the M.A.G.I.C. practice, is a combination of personal inquiry, contemplation, reflection, and questioning, and finally quieting the mind in meditation or with distraction. For many, this process needs the cooperation of a teacher, counselor, or practitioner. This is not to say that insight must come from one of these sources; it presents in many forms, anywhere, anytime.

Insight is a little different from inspiration. While each comes like a light bulb moment, inspiration is insight plus a surge of energy and an inner knowing that surpasses insight. Insight turns on your inner light, and you may choose to leave it there. On the other hand, inspiration draws you to the light, causing you to follow the call, filling you with an energy of movement and fulfillment. It is light filling you up: "inspirited." People often speak of insight coming to them while in the shower. The fact that it happens in the shower or similar "time-out" situations shows how important it is to just let go, to surrender into the moment.

Have you ever had the experience of trying to remember someone's name, only to become frustrated? Then, once you let it go, the once elusive name pops into your brain. We can prompt insight while going for a walk, exercising in the gym, sleeping, in the shower, listening to music, or in meditation. This will vary with the individual and the circumstances, but it will more than likely come when there is no need, when the resistance has stopped, when we are more open to the possibility of a result.

When we stop the struggle against our stubborn, mind-based, egotistical demand to come up with a solution, resistance softens, and insight is allowed to flow. Not that a little head banging is unhelpful. We resist and struggle against an outcome, only to arrive at a place where we can let go and watch circumstances change for the better. The classical term "artist's block" is an example of this process.

Most individuals attending counseling or therapy are looking for insight. With insight often comes relief. They have been so engrossed in their stories, their dramas, their "what is" experience that they have not allowed themselves the opportunity to pick up on their insights, their inner guidance. When individuals present to a practitioner, I believe they are looking for guidance and support in accessing this inner knowing, their insight. Practicing insight, as suggested within the M.A.G.I.C. practice, increases the speed and efficiency with which one arrives at a solution.

Some scientific findings

Insight, as defined in the dictionary, is "the capacity to gain an accurate and deep understanding of someone or something." The origin of the word *intuition* is the Latin verb *intueri*, which is usually translated as "to look inside or contemplate." Intuition is defined as "the ability to understand something instinctively, with no conscious reasoning." Note those words: "with no conscious reasoning".

Gary Klein, PhD, has studied the subject of insight and has developed what he calls the Insight Stance (In/Stance).[110] This is a mindset we adopt when we encounter new ideas and events, for nurturing insight. Klein affirms that we can adopt an active, curious mindset, preparing to be delighted by our discoveries. He argues that promoting curiosity and exploration is a much more powerful technique than engaging the traditionally adopted meditative and skeptical stances. This makes a great deal of sense, as it is a much more positive and exciting approach than the traditional approaches, which adopt a laborious and less-than-inspiring attitude. This In/Stance opens the mind and the heart to intuition by short-circuiting our cognition.

As previously mentioned, the words insight and intuition can be interchangeable. Scientific research at the HeartMath Institute[111] suggests that there are three types of intuitive processes. The first type of intuition refers to information and knowledge that we have assimilated into our life experience. This is called "implicit knowledge" or "implicit learning." This type of intuition aligns with the neuroscience view of the brain as a proficient pattern-matching device. It is always looking for patterns in our environment and matching them with our experience, providing insight into how we might meet the current problem.

The second type of intuition HMI refers to is "energetic sensitivity." This is the ability of an individual animal or plant to detect and respond to electromagnetic signals in its environment. While many humans have this ability, we often meet it with an attitude of mistrust, at least compared to what we see in animals. One example of energetic sensitivity is when you sense that someone is staring at you. Children, women, young people on the autism spectrum, animals, spiritual masters, and teachers display this marvel best.

The third type of intuition referred to in HMI's research is "nonlocal intuition," which moves into what many would refer to as the unexplainable. Some suggest that everyone can receive signals from nonlocal sources and register information about nonlocal events. Demonstration of this comes from work undertaken by R. T. Bradley[112] and S. Rezaei et al[113] and investigative research by Lynne McTaggart.[114] Examples of this type of intuition would be a parent sensing that something is happening to their child, who is many miles away. A personal experience of this is the time I sat up in bed from a deep sleep in the middle of the night and yelled, "Dad, your feet are on fire!" He had been reading with his feet propped up against the wood stove to keep them warm. They were smoldering when he woke up. I had no recollection of this incident and only came to know what transpired the next morning, when he thanked me!

Intuition plays out in different forms. It is not a simple light bulb moment; it often presents as an inner knowing. Take for example the sensitive young people we have coming into the world these days. For many young people, what goes on in school or at home is confusing and can be overwhelming. The energetics of their environment impact their state of being, and this is reported in counseling. They do not understand what is happening or how other people's energetic signals are impacting them. Many have adopted the attitude that they are "broken," because they have no explanation for what they are feeling or observing. There is an expectation that they should be stronger and more resilient. This is the message society puts out to them through counselors, parents, authority, and practitioners alike. These young people are far more sensitive than most. They are what we might call Highly Sensitive People (HSPs), but this isn't taken into account. A classic example of this is in the family environment, where kids act out the emotional energetics they are absorbing from a parent or caregiver, only to then be reprimanded for their behavior.

In her book *The Empath's Survival Guide: Life Strategies for Sensitive People*, Judith Orloff, MD, describes these individuals as "empaths." Dr. Orloff explains how empaths take the experience of the Highly Sensitive Person much further: "We can sense subtle energy (called shakti or prana in Eastern healing traditions) and actually absorb it from other people and different environments into our own bodies."[115] Based on this premise, it is easy to see how, depending on the type of energy absorbed—or to be more scientific, the vibrational frequency of that energy—the recipient will experience an equivalent physiological response. Heavy energy will give a heavy feeling, while the absorption of a higher frequency will give a higher feeling. This is why it feels good to be around some people and not so good to be around others.

In the practice of M.A.G.I.C., insight relates to more than a light bulb moment. Here, insight as a practice is tantamount to intuition, inspiration, investigation, inner knowing, self-inquiry, and awareness. Insight here is our process as we come to understand and appreciate the questions, "Who am I in this world?" and "How do I see myself fitting into this world?"

The daily practice of insight is a journey. It is not a destination, focusing on a place at which to arrive. Make a conscious choice every day whether you take part in this journey. Like any journey we embark upon, it entails many paths, amazing scenery, and an increasing number of nonphysical experiences. The result of practicing insight in M.A.G.I.C. often turns out to be what Zen Buddhists might refer to as *satori*. While this may not be the purpose of the practice, it can be the inspiration, the ultimate experience. In the Zen Buddhist tradition, *satori* refers to the experience an aspirant has on the way to *kenshō*, "seeing into one's true nature."

Again, the result is not the destination. When an integration of many micro-practices (intuition, inspiration, investigation, intuition, inner knowing, self-inquiry) takes place, the destination can be a single yet complex insight. The answers are accessible to everybody.

We do not practice insight in a vacuum. While insight is a personal and internal process, it offers an opportunity for us to accept the messages that come from the people, places, events, and circumstances in our lives. We have the opportunity most days to engage with these things and accept the feedback offered. The combination of subtle inferences, in-your-face challenges, and loving reflections provides "insight" into what we are thinking and believing about ourselves in this world. Insight is available in any moment that we are conscious, and then some. Using the practice of insight is recognizing and accepting the many messages provided by the world we live in as reflections of who we are and what we carry within ourselves.

Insight comes from within while we are communicating with ourselves, life on this planet, and the unseen Spirit. One amazing practitioner who has contributed significantly to change in this world is Silvia Hartmann, PhD. EmoTrance[116] is a technique that views all emotions in our bodies as simply energy, and as Hartmann describes it, we are essentially energy balls living in a sea of energy. Energy flows, and when it becomes stuck, it cannot act as it needs to in its natural state. By recognizing all emotional states as energy in the body, one can intend for this energy to soften and flow. All it needs is focused attention to have it respond, along with a focused intention to have it dissolve. Repeating the words "soften and flow" over and over as you observe the emotional tension, without judgment, allows the stuck energy called pain to start flowing again.

The following is a powerful example of an EmoTrance practitioner (ETP) working with a client.

Client (crying on the telephone): "My husband has left me! I'm all alone! My heart is broken, and all is lost!"

ETP: "Where do you feel that in your body?"

C: "In my stomach. It's so horrible!" (Sobs out loud.)

ETP: "It's only an energy. Soften it and allow it to move."

C: "But it only wants to protect me!"

ETP: "It's only an energy. It can't want anything. Let it move."

C (surprised): "Oh, alright, then. Yes, it's moving into my back, into my spine and down my legs."

ETP: "How do you feel now?"

C (amazed): "Much better! My goodness, that was so easy... Thank you!"

Because we think a lot, and we are used to thinking a lot with our conscious minds, we literally anthropomorphize energetic occurrences, giving them a will where none exists. "It only wants to protect me"; "It's only an energy—it can't want anything!" is an example of this.[117] The insight here is seen in the client's reaction to the sensations in her body in response to her thoughts. Further insights follow from this. Of course, some practitioners are more skilled with this—or maybe more connected—than others. To have skills in finding our own insights is empowering. Practicing M.A.G.I.C. will assist in this process.

Case note: The user and abuser allowed love to take over

"It was cool. I was everyone's friend—until I realized I wasn't. I had it all sorted, and I was kicking goals like you wouldn't believe. Then one day, I found myself in court, served with an apprehended violence order. Now I wasn't so cool, and I knew I had screwed up, but I didn't mean to. I couldn't help it!"

These were the words of a thirty-four-year-old male presenting with anger issues (domestic violence), alcohol abuse/dependency, and relationship problems. After clearing some outdated core beliefs that impacted his sense of self and diminished his self-worth, he committed to going home and grounding himself no matter what.

During the second session, he reported being calm with no incidents of anger outbursts or abuse (verified by his partner). After having left the first session, he had grounded himself every hour, on the hour, using his phone alarm, as we had agreed. A combination of dissolving some old, outdated stored emotions and associated core beliefs along with the consistent grounding allowed this man to let go of any purpose for the anger. Soon he was using the M.A.G.I.C. practice every day.

His partner supported this commitment to change, and along with his own realization that there was another way, he became determined to do anything to improve his life. His dependency lessened and then disappeared. A sense of self-worth returned. The relationship ended in separation, but he and his partner remained friends.

Practicing Insight

Practice: A simple yet valuable way to begin the practice of insight is to establish communication with your inner being. This wiser self or personal therapist is always available and always authentic, because this is where your authentic guidance comes from. Notice if you have any resistance to this statement. If you notice resistance, accept this as an insight in itself knocking on your door. An insight rarely presents with flashing lights or ringing bells, but it is always calling for your attention.

The easiest way to establish this link with your inner being in order to establish a flow of insight is to communicate through your heart. This is because communicating through your heart is communicating with your inner being. Starting with the head invites the ego to interfere—and we know what the ego uses fictional stories and false promises for. The process needs to be heart-head-hand or inspiration-thought-deed.

Again, notice if you have any resistance to this statement. If you have noticed any resistance to anything I've just said, this may very well be your first insight. The trick now is to take this insight and use it for your benefit. Remember what we said about the heart being the communication portal? It is the heart, not the head, that is involved in the processing[118] and decoding of intuitive information. Your brain might think it's the communication manager, but science and experience show us this is not the case. How you choose to go about this is your choice. Meditation is, of course, a powerful means of establishing and nurturing this communication portal. Part of the purpose behind M.A.G.I.C. is to provide a simple practice that allows newcomers an opportunity to establish this communication connection without jumping into the deep end of meditation, meditation, meditation.

Practice: If there is one technique above all that I would recommend, it is one you already have. Ultimately, you are consciousness having a physical experience. It means you can watch yourself, observe yourself, and become the witness of your every experience and how you react to those experiences. This technique is mindfulness meditation.

This is because when you quiet your mind and calm your body, you allow insight to flow. Practicing mindfulness throughout your day will strengthen your connection with the body, mind, heart, and spirit.

That being said, for those who want a more hands-on approach, there is a simple way to establish this communication process using your body language, in the form of kinesiology. If children and young people can learn to use this technique, as has been my experience, then any committed individual can. Different terms are used when we talk about what in most circles is known as body language. Labels such as "muscle testing," "mind-body connection," "kinesthetic testing," or "applied kinesiology"[119] are all used. Ultimately, we are talking about using the muscles of the body to communicate with our innate self through the intelligence of the heart.

If you wonder why scientific research does not support the use of kinesiology as a reliable tool, as I have, it may come down to this: The heart, not the head or hand, is the communication portal between our trillions of cells, our inner being, life around us, the unseen spirit, and our conscious minds. When communicating with the heart rather than the head, our level of proficiency, efficiency, reliability, and validity increases. It reminds me of the experiments undertaken with individuals who claim to be able to find water underground by using a stick or piece of wire. From personal experience—and the experience of my father, his father, and several individuals I know personally—the ability to find a water source underground with a forked stick or a piece of wire is a definite "yes." The integrity of this water-divining practice does not depend on scientific research, and yet measurement can help some to find acceptance for this. Until we develop measuring tools for phenomena such as water divining, there will be unbelievers and intellectual skeptics. The point here is to trust your own findings, and your own inner knowing to seek answers.

Practice: Check out chapter five in Dr. Bradley Nelson's book *The Emotion Code*,[120] where you will find an excellent explanation and demonstration of using your body language to connect with your inner mind/heart. As a practitioner, I have successfully used muscle testing, but I choose to teach people how to use a pendulum[121] as their go-to technique. This is because it is easy for most people's rational minds to dismiss any suggestion that they can connect intuitively with their bodies through the use of body language. A pendulum sometimes called a Chevreul[122] pendulum, is simply a tool. As an indicator of micro-movements in the muscles, the pendulum moves as directed by the inner mind through the muscles. Many clients will doubt their own abilities when using muscle testing, but the pendulum acts like an external source to be trusted, as opposed to an individual trusting his or her mind-body connection.[123]

Using our own body language is a technique for seeking insight—at least, insight about what is going on for us at that moment, as well as providing insight into past experiences. This is because our innate self has access to every experience we have ever had in this lifetime, plus a lot more. There is an endless list of ways to use a pendulum, each for different reasons. For me, simple is best. Originally, I used a crystal swinging on a chain, mainly because someone had given me one and it seemed like the right thing to do. But what I came to realize, especially in working with young people, was that they interpreted this as "spiritual" or "magical" and thus attributed the power to me. Big mistake!

I found an old rusty nut on the road one day when I was speaking with a client. I added a little string, and wham, we had a pendulum! The client used it and felt empowered to do this for himself. And so, the nut and the string technique became a thing. In other situations, I have been without my trusty nut and have instead used a tea bag, a set of keys, or an old fishing sinker I found by the water, and in one case I made a pendulum from a stone and a piece of string.

It doesn't matter what you use. It can be fancy, but it can also be a tea bag. The practice is the same. Hold the pendulum out in front of you. You may wish to rest your elbow on your leg or on a table. Approach this as though you are speaking with your heart or innate self. You are asking for support as you access information within your subconscious mind to share with your conscious mind. The aim is to access answers to your questions by using your body language or the movement of your muscles, asking yes-or-no questions.

The process should be something like the following, but develop your own style and be flexible. While holding the pendulum out in front of you, ask what is to be the signal for "yes" whenever you ask a question of your inner mind. The micro-movements of your muscles will cause the pendulum to move at the end of the string. It may swing sideways or forwards and backwards, or it may move around in circles, and sometimes it may even stay still. When you have a movement as a "yes" signal, find one for the "no" signal. Now you have a direct communication portal with your innate self.

Once you have a signal for "yes" and one for "no," test it by making a statement you know to be true, such as, "My name is…" Once confirmed, say something false, such as, "My name is Peter Pan." Accept the truthful answer and movement as a signal for the answer "yes," and do the same with the "no" answer.

Once you have asked a question, trust and breathe slowly as you wait for a response. Take a deep breath and relax. Do not to ask other questions while you await a response. Often, people ask a question and then quickly follow up by asking other questions in their head. This confuses the answer because the heart doesn't know which question to answer and ends up trying to answer all the questions at the same time. The trick is to do this with a sense of curiosity and wonderment. Being respectful of yourself and your heart is an underlying principle, so after you have asked a question, be quiet in your mind, as if you were speaking with your very best friend in the world, or to a god.

When there is an inconsistency in answers, or there is an inconsistency in the pendulum's movement, check the following. First, are you dehydrated? You can go from no response to big swings after just drinking some water. Next, set aside all electronic devices, such as mobile phones. Some people find phones can be a total disaster for this process if they have it on their person. The third point here is this: if neither of these efforts corrects the inconsistent response, ground yourself as described in the section on grounding. This seems especially important for young people. After they ground themselves, the pendulum or muscle testing works beautifully.

Grounding is especially important when an individual is focused on a traumatic experience. Simply talking about the event can cause a disconnection from the energy system of the earth. If you are still not able to gain a clear response, it's useful to put it away and try again later. (Note: interruptions can also be caused by a misalignment of the neck or the ingestion of certain chemicals that confuse the body's capacity to respond.)

Finally, there are some individuals who resist the use of a pendulum or muscle testing. What is written here isn't intended to convince anyone to do anything against their will. If you do have problems with muscle testing or using a pendulum, have someone test you for the reasons for your inconsistency.

Practice: Here is a little profound guidance from Eckhart Tolle. In his book *The Power of Now: A Guide to Spiritual Enlightenment,* Tolle writes, "Watching the thinker—start listening to the voice in your head as often as you can. Pay particular attention to any repetitive thought patterns, those old audiotapes that have been playing in your head, perhaps for many years. This is what I mean by 'watching the thinker,' which is another way of saying: Listen to the voice in your head, be there as the witnessing presence. When you listen to that voice, listen to it impartially. Do not judge. Do not judge or condemn what you hear, for doing so would mean that the same voice has come in again through the back door. You'll soon realize: There is the voice, and here I am listening to it, watching it. This I AM realization, this sense of your own presence, is not a thought."[124]

Practice: Rubert Spira[125] is a therapist and yoga teacher in the non-dual tradition of Kashmir Shaivism. When asked about self-inquiry, an inner process for personal insight, Spira provides a practical and simple technique anyone can use anywhere. He advises that you ask yourself who is the "I" who is unhappy, anxious, depressed, angry, happy, and so on. Your thoughts are always coming and going, and in fact, you can watch these thoughts come and go. Similarly, your feelings come and go, so you are not your thoughts or your feelings. The same applies to sensations and images; all sensory experiences come and go. Spira explains how the "I" is separate from these things, while the "I" is always present, aware of your experiences and the world. So, what is your happiness or unhappiness? It is the combination of your experiences at the moment. The cause of your happiness or unhappiness is your mistaking yourself for the collection of your feelings and thoughts. Notice how you are becoming caught up in the drama story of your ego mind, by way of your thoughts. It so happens that the more we become aware of our emotional response to our thoughts, the more insight we gain into the cause of our un/happiness.

Practice: Play with trusting your intuition every day when it comes to the people, places, events, and choices in your life. Listen to and follow your intuition, always trusting your heart of hearts to provide guidance. Ask, "What would my heart say to me now?" or "What is my heart telling me right now with this emotion?" One of the most powerful, simplest built-in devices you have is your intuition. The best way to practice insight is to notice and listen to your intuition. That being said, it can be difficult in this world to put aside the logical mind and listen to a part of ourselves that we are neither encouraged nor taught to use. It is because of this that we need to train ourselves to use and trust our intuition.

Your intuition is a communication from the "wiser" part of you, and your emotional responses or feelings are a way of reminding you of what you already know. As with anything you are not used to, this requires practice and retraining your mind. To be clear, there are your emotional indicators, and there is your intuition. Your emotional indicators will tell you what you are believing (thinking) about you living in this world. Alternatively, your intuition is a direct communication from your inner being, your higher self, or your spirit team. Using your intuition is the obvious choice, but until you are comfortable with this, at least use your emotional response as an indicator of whether you are on track. You may come to recognize that your intuitive voice is immediate, soft, and loving, while your ego mind is often calculating, forceful, and judgmental.

Practice: Life is an inside-out job. Change your inside world, and you change your outside world. By practicing insight through meditation, exercise, journaling, talking with a practitioner, or any other way that suits you, you are initiating a change in your inner world. Through insight, you have a choice to do something about any old, outdated program that is not serving you anymore. Practicing insight is the beginning of the healing journey. As you embark on this journey, make it part of your intention to look for the changes in your outer world as healing takes place within.

Whenever pain is recognized, investigate the origin of the dominant emotion using your body language. What is the best word to describe the feeling you are experiencing? Where did it first come from, at what age, and what would you have to believe about yourself to support the underlying belief? Understanding where you first experienced the painful event and recognizing the program set in place by the experience can support the release of that program, or start your reprogramming. A note of interest here: while we don't need to go back and fix things from our past, it is often helpful for our conscious mind's sake to investigate the origins of a program or core belief.

Practice: Working with a practitioner is a common way of accessing insight. Different practitioners have different ways of working, different agendas, and different beliefs about what their role is in supporting you. It is important for you to remind yourself that the practitioner is there for you, not the other way around. Secondly, you go there for the practitioner's skills, information, and knowledge, but mainly you look for one who believes in your ability to change through finding insight. A practitioner's role is to assist you in connecting with your inner being for insight. You don't go there to get "fixed." Insight is equivalent to being in power. The power is within you to become what life designed you to be in this world. Initially, you go seeking insight to find relief from pain, to find a solution to your particular problem, sometimes to find the underlying cause of this pain, and to find out what you can do to avoid repeating this pain. This is a lifelong journey as we travel the road of life.

So often, insight comes when you tell your story in an unconditionally positive environment. With acknowledgment, nonjudgmental acceptance, and encouragement, we provide ourselves with the conditions for insight and inspiration. Choose a practitioner who sees you as the authority on your wellbeing, as a master in dealing with your life matters, and not a victim, but as someone who is looking for insight, encouragement, and inspiration for happiness. Finally, choose a practitioner who will teach you their mode of practice, while not considering it to be the "only" mode of practice for you.

Practice: Use the M.A.G.I.C. practice for a day, focusing on an issue that is important to you. As you go about your day, practice mindfulness while holding the issue in mind. If holding this issue in mind causes you to feel emotional discomfort, ground yourself to dissipate the feeling into the earth. As you ground yourself, it might be helpful to focus on the exact place in your body where you feel the emotion. Next, without judgment, ask this emotion to soften and flow while you ground yourself with the energy of the earth. This is connecting you with your inner being, looking for insight.

Go about your day, remaining mindful of this issue in your life. Seek guidance from your inner being, your spirit team, and all of life. Finally, engage with appreciation for those aspects of the issue that you might consider valuable to your experience. Even appreciating the fact that you are engaged in using M.A.G.I.C. to address this issue in your life is being proactive.

Practice: Automatic writing has been a favorite practice for many seekers of insight. It is a powerful way of accessing answers and insights, especially when we are in one of those black holes, playing "poor me." Take a pad and pencil, sit, and ground yourself. Ask for your team to come in, then just write, without thinking. Ask for a clear and simple explanation; otherwise, your ego will want to analyze, debate, and question what you receive.

Here is one way of going about this. At the top of the page, write a statement that sums up your state of being. It is usually a statement followed by a question. For example, "I am feeling depressed, sad, heavy, for no good reason. I don't know what is wrong with me. What is the cause of my pain, and what do I need to do about it?" Next, take the pencil in your nondominant hand and write whatever comes into your head. The non-dominant hand provides a more direct connection to your intuitive right brain. The trick is to avoid judging, analyzing, and questioning. Simply write whatever comes into your head. After a while, it will flow, and then you can change hands (mainly so you can read it later), because you may need to write faster to get the information down on paper. When there is no more information coming through, say thank you and look over what is usually something very profound and insightful.

Practice: Similar to the automatic writing technique, journaling can be a powerful means of gaining insight. Journaling can provide insight in relation to your present circumstances, and it can provide insight into your life patterns. Journaling, when designed by you for you, can help dissolve stress, anxiety, and all that other "stuff" while inviting you to practice gratitude. If journaling is a tool you want to investigate, this is a powerful means for practicing insight, mindfulness, appreciation, connection, and often grounding. For some down-to-earth tips on journaling, check out "17 Journaling Tips for Beginners (and how to start)"[126] at Vanilla Papers.

Practice: Short and sweet: let go of what other people are thinking about you, and focus on what you are believing about you. How do you know what you are believing about you? Consider everyone in your life as a mirror of what emotional response is active in you. Ask yourself the question, "What could I be believing about myself to allow what someone else is thinking to stir up such an emotion?" Again, you can return to using something like a pendulum if you do not feel you can trust your insight.

Practice: The final comment here is that there are many ways of finding insight. It really comes down to you as an individual and what you relate to. Some people will want to be specific and trust her or his intuition and connect using oracle cards. There are numerous themes and styles of oracle decks focused on connection with the earth or acknowledging oneself as an empath, and decks for working with angles, dreams, animal totems, and wildflowers. This is a personal choice, and the best suggestion I can give is to follow your intuition or inner guidance as you shop around. The internet has much to offer, but nothing beats feeling and holding the deck in your hands before you purchase.

Looks are important for some people, but the feel is what stands out as important for me. Some people will want to go for a walk in the woods, while some use music as a powerful means of allowing insight to present itself. It comes down to turning off the analytical ego mind and opening up to the inner heart-mind. This explains why some people will wake up in the middle of the night and write down their insights in a journal. Do whatever you need to do to get out of your head and into the flow. The insights are always there—always. You just need to be in a place to let them into your awareness.

Case note: Work made me sick

Thomas was a twenty-nine-year-old male referred by his doctor with depression, substance abuse, and physiological indicators of excessive stress. When we met, his words were something like, "My doctor said I would benefit from seeing a psychologist to help with my stomach problems." I introduced Thomas to a holistic approach to help him see his situation from its true perspective. This included changing the physical, mental, emotional, and spiritual quadrants of his life.

In terms of the practice, Thomas started with insight, which allowed him to access and clear away some of his own emotional pain. With the use of a pendulum (which is body language in another form), he learned to focus inward on the underlying cause of some of his pain. He transitioned from blaming and shaming himself (and others) to a recognition and acceptance of the underlying causal factors and a sense of peace. He could continue his own clearing and healing process, along with some intermittent sessions with me. With an immediate positive change in his physical and psychological state of being, Thomas learned as much as he could about becoming his own practitioner.

As a practice, M.A.G.I.C. allowed him to have a blueprint, a road map if you like, for his own journey of healing. Like many others, Thomas associated strongly with meditation, and particularly mindfulness meditation. The benefits were inspirational. This encouraged him to use the entire practice. This took a little while, but in time his depression dissolved, along with the need to use substances. Eventually, his physical health improved. The bonus, as Thomas would describe it, was, "I am now finding I can deal with work stuff, like the jerks on-site as well as that insecure little leading hand."

CHAPTER 11

Connection

Connection

> **LIKE THE THREADS OF A CLOTH,
> WE HAVE BEEN WOVEN INTO THE FABRIC OF THIS UNIVERSE.
> WE ARE ATTACHED TO, DEPENDENT UPON,
> COMPLIMENTARY, AND COMPLEMENTARY WITH
> EACH OTHER AND THE UNIVERSE.**
> *- PAUL DUNNE*

Defining Connection

We, the universe, are connected as one. Connection, as a practice, includes a connection with the self, connection with everyone and everything—all of life—and a connection with the very fabric of this universe (Spirit, God, Source, All There Is). Connection is not optional. Human connection with other humans, the animal, bird, and plant life in this world, the spirit of the unseen, and ultimately with ourselves is not optional. This connection happens whether we like it or not, and whether we believe it or not. It is happening continuously, whether we are asleep or awake, happy or sad, busy or still. We have connections with our parents, with their parents, with our children, family, friends, and fellow travelers. The practice of connecting is at the very foundation of all these relationships.

Most people understand the connections or lack of connections present in their lives—at least, some of the more significant connections. But it may not be until someone points out these particular connections that we fully appreciated the significance of them. It is important for all of us to take time to recognize the connections in our life experience, and even more importantly, to consider the current role these connections play. In so many ways, our connections tell us who we are, what we are, and why we are here. Our connections act as a reminder to us that we are experiencing the world as we believe it to exist, and not the world we see. What we believe about any subject is reflected by everyone and everything we have a relationship with. All relationships reflect an aspect of us, and for this reason, all relationships are holy.

We cannot get away from connection. An agenda is peddled in Western societies that says we are separate and apart; we exist in different groups. We are distinct individuals, making our own way, independent of those around us. In reality, this couldn't be further from the truth. This thinking comes from the premise that we are just our bodies. The argument is that if we are seen as our bodies—if we are seen to be individualized and independent from all other life forms, including other humans—then it is our ego that rules. Within the limitations of a separated, vulnerable world, the ego substantiates itself. The alternative affirms that we are One Energy presenting as individual consciousnesses, having individual experiences that are separate from each other but one with our Source.

On an unconscious level, we are aware of and responsive to all connections. This is because connection happens on an energetic level. We initially connect energetically, and only after this does it appear on the physical plane. Even our communication happens first energetically and only then on a physical level. We take many of these connections for granted; sometimes even the most important connections are taken for granted. We recognize those connections that impact our life experiences and especially our happiness. But most people are not aware of the importance of their everyday connections.

We think our thoughts are private, but in reality, our thoughts go out into the world. Our thoughts impact and affect people, animals, and plant life, and the places we visit. It is a scary concept for many individuals to consider the idea that our thoughts are not private. If magnetism is real, if electromagnetic pulses are real, then we have the basis for what scientists at the HeartMath Institute have researched extensively. This research has focused on the power of the heart, the heart/brain connection, heart intelligence, and practical intuition.[127]

Besides the impact our thoughts and feelings have on life around us, there is ongoing research into the established connection between all living things. The Global Coherence Initiative (GCI) is a science-based co-creative project to unite people in heart-focused care and intention. GCI is working in concert with other initiatives to realize the increased power of collective intention and consciousness.[128] There is acceptance that a "global information field that connects all living systems and consciousness" exists and operates within, throughout, and around all life on this planet.[129]

Support for this thinking that there is a unifying field of consciousness comes from the Global Consciousness Project,[130] which is an international multidisciplinary collaboration of scientists and engineers. This project has a global network of physical random number generators (RNGs) located in up to seventy host sites around the world at any given time. The project describes how RGNs based on quantum tunneling produce completely unpredictable sequences of zeros and ones, but when a significant event synchronizes the feelings of millions of people, the network of RNGs becomes subtly structured. The teaching that we are one continues to emphasize the importance of our connection with all of life.

M.A.G.I.C. is a spiritual practice that affects the physical, mental, emotional, and energetic quadrants of our lives all at once. As energetic beings in a physical form, we change the recipe on an energetic level before there is any change on a physical plane. A thought must always precede the manifestation in a physical form. Change our belief system, and we change our thoughts; change our thoughts, and we change our energetics. When we change our energetics, we are changing our vibrational frequency and the manner in which we influence the energy field around us. We become the change we want to see in the world.

The effects of changing something on the inside can be seen in the physical world as a change in form or behavior. Knowing this, we have the power to change our physical bodies, our relationships, our study or work environment, our finances, or any other part of our experience, in any way we wish to imagine. And we usually do.

The practice of connection has a major part to play in this process. It is through our connection with life around us that we are able to effect change. When we come to understand that our thoughts, along with our emotional state, influence everything and everyone around us all the time, then we can understand the impact we have on the world. This also works in reverse. An angry person will send out a different lot of information than a person who is full of compassion and love. An emotional person will transmit lots of energy, while a neutral person will transmit very little.

Connection is listed as a noun in the dictionary. We see it as a relationship in which a person or thing is linked or associated with something else. It can be people with whom one has social or professional contact, or to whom one is related, especially those with influence and who are able to offer help. As for synonyms, they include link, relationship, relation, relatedness, interrelation, interrelatedness, interconnection, interdependence, association, attachment, and many more. It is interesting that the definition states that a connection is a relationship, link, or contact one has with something or someone. Then, when we search for the definition of *relationship*, we find "how two or more people or things are connected, or the state of being connected." The connection we have with family, pets, friends, and colleagues applies to the relationship we have with those things in our lives. We could say that the quality of connection in any relationship is proportionate to the quality of that relationship. A relationship that provides personal fulfillment in terms of happiness, acceptance, acknowledgment, and self-worth will be a strong connection. Thus, it is logical that the effort focused on those connections is vital to ensure greater meaning in the relationship.

In the M.A.G.I.C. practice, we focus on the connections in our lives. This includes the connection we have with ourselves and the connection we have with other people and life on this planet (and the planet itself), as well as the connection we have with the creative force or energy that creates this experience. M.A.G.I.C. asks that we recognize the existence of these three connections, but more importantly, that we cherish these connections consciously, in a unique and personalized way. We must show up each day and intend to strengthen these connections. We must remind ourselves, even when we are not consciously aware of the connection, that we determine the quality of the connection by the thoughts we choose to entertain. This way, we are determining the quality of our relationships, rather than letting the relationships determine the quality of our experience.

By practicing M.A.G.I.C., we recognize that connection may not be optional, but it is adjustable, and we have the power and freedom to make that adjustment. Another fundamental tenet here is that any connection or relationship we have with anyone or anything only ever changes in its form. It never ends. Every relationship or connection we have or have ever had continues to exist in some form. It may be in a different form, a different quality, or a different place, but it will continue to exist. We judge our connections as good or bad, loving or strained because we have this need to categorize things—or at least, the ego does. If we see our relationships as important, we nurture and care for them, but if we do not see them as important, we ignore or starve them. This is neither good nor bad and certainly not to be judged with our ego minds. Any connection is what it is: a spiritual union we have with another aspect of ourselves.

All connections are divine, and so all relationships are of a divine nature. Even those relationships we see as painful hold a gift for us, even when we don't want to know about it. Any relationship that holds pain, whether current or past, is a sign that we have not acknowledged or taken responsibility for a part of ourselves projected into that relationship. The ego is the only barrier to having a genuine, authentic connection with ourselves, others, and the creative force. The ego kills the joy in relationships. By practicing M.A.G.I.C., we short-circuit the ego's need for power and control so that it lets go of its fear-based beliefs, and we open up to the gifts offered in all relationships.

Note: strictly speaking, the ego isn't our enemy. It is a valuable part of our experience on this planet. The problem is that the ego comes from a place of fear, based on a database of fictional stories, and it uses these stories to make important decisions that impact our lives. The problem starts when we give the ego permission to step beyond its job description and take responsibility for matters of an emotional or spiritual nature. The ego is meant to handle matters relating to physical safety, such as not putting our hand on a hot stove. Meanwhile, it is the job description of the authentic self to look after anything related to emotional and spiritual matters. And since all connections are foremost energetic connections through the heart, they can exist gloriously only through the heart and are diminished through the ego mind.

"The first rule of building heart-to-heart connections is that even though it takes two people to create a relationship, the responsibility for connecting starts with you. The second rule is that everything depends on your level of awareness."[131] This reflection is a clear call for each of us to take responsibility by practicing connection consciously. The divine power we have to influence all connections lies in our freedom to view them as projections or reflections of self, and to love the self.

Connection with self

What does it mean to "connect with the self"? Are we talking about the trillions of cells that make up the body? Is the self in the mind? Do we need to be talking about our emotions and feelings as the real self? Or is the self, something unseen and nonphysical?

Connection with the trillions of cells that make up the body and with the feeling sensations experienced in the body are recognized in the mind. They come and go. Your cells, like your emotions and thoughts, are being replaced while this sentence is being written. Now I am a different body, with different thoughts and slightly different feelings, but I am still the same "I." This means connecting with our cells, our thoughts, or our feelings is not connecting with the self, since all these things come and go, yet the self remains.

If we connect with our cells in a deep and meaningful way, on a personal basis, then we will come to know our cells. We will come to establish a communication based on genuine interest. If we are able to recognize our emotional status in any moment—to know how we feel—then we are listening to our hearts. If we can step outside of our personalities and view our experience without judgment, we come to see ourselves for who and what we really are.

Our innate self, or authentic self, is who and what we are—our very essence. Life made us with the same ingredients, the same energetic formula that worlds are made of. "I am one self, united with my Creator."[132] Love made us with love, for love, and out of love. It made us as an expression of It Self. We are each, or altogether, a thought in the mind of Creation, and a thought never leaves its source. It is true what they say: me, myself, as much as anybody in the entire universe, deserves my love and affection. Looking for love in all the wrong places means not looking in the mirror. In practical terms, we have never left home. What has taken place and is taking place is that we have slipped into a dream state. As happens in what we term a dream state (or nightmare), we have been fooled into believing the dream is real. It is the ego's role to make sure this "dream" becomes a long-lasting series over a lifetime.

Eckhart Tolle, spiritual teacher and best-selling author, explains how the phrase *human being* highlights a human and the action of what the human is doing, or rather being. The term *human being* shows the distinction between you as the physical and mental presentation in this world, while emphasizing the authentic you. Tolle writes, "[Being] ... points to the essence of who you are as timeless, formless, and unconditioned consciousness. Human and being, form and essence, are ultimately not separate, in the same way that a wave or ripple on the surface of the ocean is not separate from the ocean or from any other wave or ripple, although it may appear to be so."[133] Another way of looking at this is to accept that we are a spirit being a human. Each of us is pure consciousness, though often living our lives unconsciously.

If we see ourselves as the body, given the way we compare our body with others we see in the world, it limits our worthiness. If our connection with ourselves is based on a physical construct, then we play small, and this serves no one. Worthiness is a judgment based on the values, opinions, and preferences that we hold in high regard, and these often belong to other people. We don't own most of these things because they come from our parents, teachers, television, and advertisements. Our personal worth and value depend on us and how we see ourselves in this world in relation to what other people say, do, and think. The only way to recognize and appreciate our physical bodies is to see the spirit within. Recognize and appreciate the M.A.G.I.C. and intelligence of our fifty trillion cells.

If we consider the awesomeness that is the trillions of cells making up the community called our body, we realize that each cell has all the same information, data, genetic blueprints, and information as every other cell. Dr. Bruce Lipton says, "It doesn't make a difference if the cell is in a plastic dish or the skin-covered dish. The cell's fate is determined by the composition of the blood, which represents the environment for the cells. As you change the composition of your blood, you change the fate of your cells."[134] This is what we do all day: we change the composition of our blood by thinking the thoughts we think. Our life isn't determined by our genes. Dr. Bruce Lipton's work has revealed that the environment, operating through the cell membrane, controls the behavior and physiology of the cell, turning genes on and off. Our life experience is determined by the environment in which the cells live, which in our case is the blood. What determines the makeup of the blood? It directly results from our perceptions and resultant thinking. As a result of our perceptions, the brain sends various cocktails of chemicals and hormones around the body, influencing each of the trillions of cells to turn genes on or off.

The brain is the engine room, the operational manager of our body. As Dr. Lipton says, it is the chemist distributing all the required chemicals it thinks the body needs. It is the brain in our heads that monitors, assesses, analyzes, and arranges for chemical and physiological changes to come about. The way this plays out, in reality, is that if we perceive ourselves to be of a certain characteristic, it will direct our genes to ensure this becomes our truth. In addition, if we consider how our cells communicate with one another—firstly through electromagnetics, then through chemical and mineral exchanges—it becomes easier to understand how our thoughts and the surrounding energy can influence our experience.

Research,[135] including that from Fritz-Albert Popp,[136] has shown that cells and even animals communicate with each other via electromagnetic waves called biophotons. Popp concluded that biophotons appear to communicate with all the cells of the body instantaneously in a synchronous wave of informational energy. Biophotons may represent a complex cell-to-cell communication that relies upon speed-of-light transmission. This form of communication between cells goes aways towards explaining the near-instantaneous chain reaction seen in biochemistry when we get a fright, or someone goes from calm to rage in a split second. As Dr. Lipton points out, the speed of electromagnetic energy signals is 186,000 miles per second, while the speed of a diffusible chemical is considerably less than one centimeter per second.[137]

We are not our thoughts, feelings, or sensations. These are processes or effects of processes of communications between our cells. They are the experiences we have, but they are not us. From another perspective, our heart continually observes the process and knows what is going on seconds before our brain has any idea of what is happening. Research undertaken by the HeartMath Institute reinforces the importance of trusting our heart for guidance.[138] The heart processes and decodes intuitive information up to six seconds before the brain has any recognition of what is being observed. Results pointed to the heart being the first part of the subject's physiology to react to a perceived stimulus.

It was the heart that sent input to the brain, not the other way around. Sometimes this happened up to six seconds before the stimulus presented itself. In an article in the *Journal of Alternative and Complementary Medicine* in 2004, Dr. Rollin McCraty from the HeartMath Institute said, "What is truly surprising about the result is the fact that the heart appears to play a direct role in the perception of future events, at the very least it implies that the brain does not act alone in this regard."[139]

If we allow our heads to make all the decisions, we will find ourselves stressed, tense, and anxious, always looking to manipulate and control people, places, and events in our lives. Why? Because our head chooses a response based upon its database of trillions of video clips—fictional video clips stored since before we were born. The head can provide us with experiences that feel "good," but which may not be contributing to our highest good. This can act like a placebo effect, the name given to the positive results an individual experiences when they take what they think is a drug, but which in fact is nothing more than a sugar pill.[140] But the placebo doesn't need to be a drug. A placebo is more of a belief that something we are having, being, or doing has benefits, when in fact, there are no tangible benefits known. It draws its power from us believing there is a benefit.

We live in a world based on perception. It is our perceptions that give meaning to everything we see, smell, taste, touch, or hear. Up until this moment, nothing has any meaning. Everything we observe and experience is nothing but a prop standing on the stage of our lives. Therefore, another person can give a different meaning from the one we have for something both of us are observing. They have a different perception based on their own information and data archives. The information our inner minds retrieve from our archives results from experiences and genetic records. Our brains act like a mixer and use the same information to decide which chemicals are to be sent throughout the body.

Perception is the way we give meaning to the world, but it isn't the cause of the world we see. The cause is traced back to what we project onto the world. Project anger, and we get anger back; project compassion, and it is compassion we get back. We are the cause of the effects we experience because of what we project onto the world. As we have previously described, consider the world we see to be similar to a screen onto which we cast images through a projector. There is a light source that passes through a filter or film, which passes through a lens system on its way to the screen. What we see on the screen results from an ongoing adjustment of the film or filter through which the light is passed. If the light source varies, the projection on the screen will vary.

Similarly, if the filter or film varies, so too will the images on the screen. If the lens is dirty, this will show up on the screen. But it is ultimately the person controlling the projector that controls the images on the screen. We operate much the same way. We can vary the intensity of the light source (Source energy). We can change the filter or film through which we project the light (our beliefs and thinking). And it is us who project the light onto the screen through a dirty lens (false stories about yourself, held by the ego mind). Then we see what is on the screen, and we either praise or blame someone for these images. Seeing it convinces us it is real and true.

A powerful insight is provided by the teachings of *A Course in Miracles*: "Projection makes perception. The world you see is what you gave it, nothing more than that. But though it is no more than that, it is not less. Therefore, to you, it is important. It is the witness to your state of mind, the outside picture of an inward condition. As a man thinketh, so does he perceive. Therefore, seek not to change the world, but choose to change your mind about the world. Perception is a result and not a cause."[141]

Simplified, we cause the effects we see in our world, and yet we attribute those effects to someone or something other than ourselves. While we are doing this, we are talking with our cells all day via the thoughts we entertain, the words we use, and the actions we take. Thoughts of appreciation affect our entire being in a way that is the opposite of thoughts of fear. The gift in this statement is this: when we are thinking with appreciation, there is no room for fear.

Our genes do not limit us. It is our perceptions, based on our beliefs, that limit us to the circumstances in which we find ourselves. Change our beliefs, and we change what we project outward. This has the combined effect of changing what we project outward, as well as changing the perception we hold, all leading to changes in the way we experience life. By practicing M.A.G.I.C., we not only change our projection, we change our perception, and consequently, we change our experience.

In summary, it all starts with us. When we consciously and genuinely connect with ourselves by talking with our cells, listening to our hearts, and aligning with our authentic self, the best probable outcomes are allowed to happen. On a physical level, our bodies will change for us as we change for our bodies. On an emotional level, our intuition or communication with our hearts will strengthen as we listen from a place of compassion. And on a spiritual level, our guidance through our authentic self will show up more convincingly, demonstrating that we are never alone. All of this is facilitated through the practice of M.A.G.I.C.

Connection with others

It is often said that communication is the key to having a great relationship. This is true, but not in the way most people mean it. Communication, like connection, happens first energetically, and perhaps ninety percent of communication, like connection, happens on an energetic level. Next, it takes place on an unconscious level through the unconscious observations of body language and voice modulation. Finally, this all comes together at a cognitive level when the brain accepts the perceptions.

We are sending and receiving transmissions continuously into the energy field, the surrounding space, with every thought we entertain and every emotion we express. For example, when we are angry, we are sending arrows of anger out into the world. The best indicators of the messages we are sending out are seen in our relationships.

"Relationships" here refers to the quality of the connections we have with the people, places, objects, and events in our lives. So ultimately, taking responsibility for my feeling and thinking is the key to me having quality relationships. If we depend on words to establish and nurture our connections with others, eventually there will be a better debater, a con artist, someone who has more baggage than us, someone who is a wizard with words and a master manipulator of emotions.

We send out messages at the same time as we receive messages. This is similar to the way a cell phone sends and receives text messages. This is what our kids are picking up on: our parental text messages. As with a mobile phone, we receive only those messages we are tuned to receive. Like having a conversation in a crowded room, we have a choice of which conversation we wish to tune into, and which to ignore, while we are hearing all of them on some level. Kids and animals are known for reflecting this type of energy back at us quickly. Sometimes, we may even blame them for reflecting our state of being.

We have no choice: we connect energetically through the oneness of the indiscriminate energy field surrounding and saturating all that exists in this world. From more of a local perspective, this happens heart-to-heart through electromagnetic communications. Research by the HeartMath Institute scientists reveals that the heart generates an electrical field about sixty times greater in amplitude than the electrical activity generated by the brain. In addition, the heart's magnetic field is one hundred to five thousand times greater in strength than the magnetic field generated by the brain. SQUID-based magnetometers can measure this electromagnetic field up to three meters away. In simple terms, we are connected energetically with everything around us, and as such, we pick up on their messages at the same time that they pick up on our messages.

At the HeartMath Institute, it has been established that there is "a direct relationship between the heart-rhythm patterns and the spectral information encoded in the frequency spectra of the magnetic field radiated by the heart."[142] This means that a person's emotional state, encoded in the heart's magnetic field, communicates throughout the body and into the external environment. So, whether we are angry or happy, our emotional state is being transmitted out 360 degrees to everyone within a three-meter radius (calculated). Ongoing research shows that it is possible for the magnetic signals radiated by the heart of one individual to influence the brain rhythms of another. In addition, it has been observed that individuals who have a close working or living relationship produce true heart-rhythm synchronization. Using signal-averaging techniques, HMI researchers have detected synchronization between a mother's brain waves (EEG-CZ) and her baby's heartbeats (ECG). The pair were not in physical contact, but when the mother focused her attention on the baby, her brain waves synchronized with the baby's heartbeat.[143] "[I]t is a fact that there are no private thoughts."[144]

Probably the most powerful and loving gift we give ourselves through connection with others is the gift of insight into understanding how we operate in this world. It is through this connection with people, places, events, and circumstances that valuable insight is possible. The reasoning behind this is simple. The world around us is a direct reflection on the outside of who we are on the inside. Neale Donald Walsch provides this explanation: "Most people enter into relationships with an eye toward what they can get out of them, rather than what they can put into them. The purpose of a relationship is to decide what part of yourself you'd like to see 'show up,' not what part of another you can capture and hold. There can be only one purpose for relationships—and for all of life: to be and to decide Who You Really Are."[145]

The universal principle "We are all One" has been promulgated since teachers first walked this earth. What was once a philosophical statement has in recent years become an accepted premise within mainstream science, specifically quantum physics. But for those who are not into quantum physics and are not awake to the completeness of life, this concept plays out to be a purely philosophical notion or just "woo-woo." To suggest that all life on this planet (including the planet itself) expresses the One Energy of Creation goes over the heads of many people, and yet it is one of the most fundamental universal principles.

If we want to gain true insight, it is necessary for us to start with ourselves—not him, not her, not them, nor anyone else in this world. The paradox here is that for us to start with ourselves, we need to look at the world outside of ourselves. We need to look at the people, places, objects, and events around us in the world. These things are the reflections of our projections and perceptions. As mentioned earlier, projection makes perception. It is said that we cannot see beyond perception because we cannot see what we don't know and believe.[146] Whatever our belief system, we project it onto the screen of our minds, showing up in the world. This is what we know as our perception of the world.

The truth is that each of us sees what we believe makes up this reality. We see what "we" believe to be reality. This is spawned from past memories of life experiences, including genetic memory. Then we take this further and end up seeing only what we want to see. If you want to know what you believe about someone or something, which is a reflection of your core belief system, observe what is being mirrored to you. Let's look at this another way because it isn't true that just because I have an abusive individual in my life (parent, partner, boss, teacher, colleague) that I am abusive. It may be that I am the opposite of this. What is being reflected has nothing to do with overt behavior as much as it has to do with the underlying belief system that governs the behavior.

Ask yourself, "Why would someone behave in an abusive manner around me or towards me, someone else, or something?" Is it because he/she believes themselves to be a victim, and the only way they know of to feel good about themselves is to make someone else the victim? Is it because he/she believes they have no real power or control over their life and life matters, and as such, they need to have power and control over someone else; this way, they can feel like they have some influence? Is it because this world is a "violent" place to live in, and no matter where I look, there is violence, abuse, disrespect, and hurting, and holding this belief causes it to be continually presented in my awareness? Of course, there are other possibilities, but the point is, the world is a reflection of our individual and collective core beliefs.

As has been stated previously, you don't have to believe this concept and accept it as your truth. The most this book asks of you, the student, is to take the concept and observe it in your own life. No need to prove it or disprove it! In fact, pushing to prove or disprove this—or any principle, for that matter—will cause more resistance. Remember, what you resist does persist and grow stronger. Simply observe and play with the possibilities. Try different ways of looking at people, things, and events in your life, and see if it makes any difference.

It is by using the reflections from relationships—particularly family and intimate relationships—that we are able to undertake self-inquiry and in turn gain insight into the hidden self. This is interesting, if not daunting when we consider how much time we might spend resisting what we see in others. If we like someone, it usually means there is something we recognize in them that we like in ourselves. If there is something we don't like about someone, it is usually because we don't like that aspect of ourselves. And yes, if we are unaware of this little gem, it certainly complicates finding and managing relationships.

The people I have tangled with in my life have been my greatest teachers. Maybe not all of them, because I pushed some of them away before I became more aware. These teachers have lovingly and not so lovingly pushed my buttons and called me out with their words and behavior. As a result, I have experienced many emotional responses such as anger, frustration, anxiety, and insecurity, and the list goes on. As I have become more aware, I have been able to see all interactions as an opportunity to learn more about myself. Does it stop me from getting angry, etc.? No! I still react at times, but it is much briefer, allowing me to recognize and own my stuff.

Without a doubt, appreciating my connections with other people has allowed me to become more of an authentic me. A quote from Abraham Hicks's teachings explains it in down-to-earth language: "Almost no one knows how to love themselves 'cause you're running around trying to find other people to love you. Standing on your head in all kinds of different ways. 'If I'm like this, do you like me?' 'If I give you this, will you like me?' So, you lose track of who you are because the more you're looking to others to love you, the more you're not in sync with who you are."[147]

In his book *The Power of Now*, Eckhart Tolle says, "Give up defining yourself—to yourself or to others. You won't die. You will come to life. And don't be concerned with how others define you. When they define you, they are limiting themselves, so it's their problem. Whenever you interact with people, don't be there primarily as a function or a role, but as the field of conscious presence. You can only lose something that you have, but you cannot lose something that you are."[148]

When we come to see the wholesomeness of every connection we have, it is then that we will find true power and freedom. Our connections with the people who come into our lives are the most powerful tool we have in knowing ourselves. In fact, without our relationships with people, places, and events in this life, we wouldn't exist.

Connection with Spirit

What does "connection with Spirit" really mean? Is connecting with Spirit the same as being spiritual? The quick answer is "yes." The long answer is not absolute. One can be spiritual without a conscious connection with Spirit. The significant word here is "conscious." While we live unconsciously, we let life and other people's agendas take us where they will. The person with the strongest conscious intention will make the path for those around them.

The observational and scientific evidence suggests that it is natural to be spiritual, even though it may not be "normal" to practice spirituality. We are born spiritual with a biological component designed and allocated to our experience and experiencing of spirituality. Lisa J. Miller is a psychologist and researcher on the subject of spirituality. In her book *The Spiritual Child: The New Science on Parenting for Health and Lifelong Thriving*, Dr. Miller writes, "Spirituality is an inner sense of relationship to a higher power that is loving and guiding. The word we give to this higher power might be God, nature, spirit, the universe, the Creator, or other words that represent a divine presence. But spirituality encompasses our relationship and dialogue with this higher presence."[149]

One of the amazing outcomes of Dr. Miller and her colleagues' research is the recognition that this spiritual faculty is innate in every human being. "[Spirituality is] ... part of our inborn nature and heredity: a biologically based, identifiable, measurable, and observable aspect of our development, much like speech or cognitive, physical, social, and emotional development."[150] When it comes down to it, as long as we are alive, we cannot help but be spiritual. This doesn't mean we are practicing a particular quality of spirituality. It simply means we are expressing our spiritual nature by presenting in this physical world. How we choose to do this is up to us. Maybe the significant difference between people in terms of the good, the bad, and the ugly is that those who limit their spirituality from expressing in this world present as disrespectful, abusive, users, and power-and-control personalities, while those who choose to open up to and express their innate potential of spirituality are respectful, compassionate, sensitive, and giving.

Connection with Spirit is always taking place. As previously mentioned, this connection can be adjusted by our approach to how we go about living life on this planet. The innocence of children in nature and the manner in which each child connects with life on this planet is a simple embodiment of what spirituality can mean. This is a connection with the essence, the spirit of All There Is that exists in all life on this planet. For children, this extends across nature's spectrum to include people, dragonflies, horses, pets, trees, and all things in between. Children still have the innocence and knowingness that allows them to notice this presence.

Many people have been seeking a connection with this presence through a physical activity or material ownership, or through religion and ritual, and not through experiencing the nonphysical things in life to which children are innately drawn. One of the byproducts to come from the 2020 pandemic experience is that many more individuals are now (returning to) seeking a connection with the spirit of life through a connection with nature and nurture. It is by nurturing our connection with the earth, with nature, with the spirit of life that we begin to remember the spirit within. This results in a feeling of completeness and oneness that resonates with our origins, and our inner being.

Ever since life became conscious on this planet, we have looked to what we refer to as Spirit for guidance, support, help, and acceptance. As our scientific brains have taken more and more control, we have painted much of what we think we know about early spirituality—and connection with Spirit—with superstition and false gods. The ceremonies and traditions accepted by our ancestors had meaning and purpose intended to establish and strengthen the connection between peoples and the spirit world. In so many ways, this spiritual connection threatens the existence of the ego and what it represents. Perhaps we fear that if we spend much time and energy on our connection with Spirt, the options for the materialistic world to prosper would be too limited.

Often, the key role of establishing this connection with Spirit and the unseen belonged to the shaman. Shamans understood the importance of ritual, meditation, and believing, along with deeds and words, to demonstrate the presence of Spirit being active in our everyday affairs. This was facilitated through lots of ceremonies. A shaman worked with the spirits of the land, animal spirits, tree spirits, the four elements, the ancestors, and future beings, especially the seen and unseen forces, to heal and advise their community. Not only were the shamans aware of this relationship, but the peoples they represented were aware and lived accordingly.

"All of us have a God in us, and that God is the spirit that unites all life, everything that is on this planet."[151] We are Spirit looking through the filter of an ego mind that has limited itself (and us) to the physical experience. In reality, connection with Spirit takes place every day, all day, with every person, place, event, and object we experience, because we are Spirit. Spirit is in all of life. We are life. The very substance that allows us to exist and allows life on this planet to exist—including Mother Earth—is what we refer to as Spirit, and it permeates everything. If it feels more comfortable, replace the word Spirit with the preferred descriptor: God, Allah, Buddha, All There Is, Great Mystery.

This Spirit has taken many names, presented in many forms, been ascribed various powers, and been prayed to in thousands of ways.

Establishing a connection with Spirit is establishing a connection with a deity. What most of us miss is that this deity or Spirit is within each of us and between each of us. When we look past the form and find the essence of an individual, object, or place, we open up to the opportunity for recognizing a life force in all things. It's helpful to remember how we connect with the wind, with magnetism, with gravity, and with "the feeling in the room," then allow this to be an indicator of our ability to connect with Spirit. In his book *The Art of Spiritual Peacemaking: Secret Teachings from Jeshua ben Joseph*, James F. Twyman writes, "Turning toward the Buddha nature within is the same as turning toward your Christ Consciousness. Each is a reference, nothing more, which will link your mind to the eternal movement of Spirit that flows through us all."[152]

Recognizing a connection with the essence of All There Is allows a deep awareness to grow within, which allows the establishment of a genuine connection. Not just any connection, but a connection that highlights the Spirit of self in others, in the planet, in the stars, in the very essence of life. Play with this as you look for the existence of some form of intelligent energy operating behind the scenes, then connect in whatever way you find comfortable. The practice of connection with Spirit is as easy as we want to make it, and as extensive as you become inspired to stretch it.

Practicing connection: some thoughts

In M.A.G.I.C., each individual practice supports and enhances each of the other practices. When you engage in any individual practice, all other practices are activated to some extent. Connection takes place when you practice mindfulness, appreciation, grounding, and insight. This is because each of these practices allows you to come into the present moment while recognizing the potential for connection. The trick to strengthening any connection is providing attention and intention, preferably coming from the heart. Certainly, be aware of what your head is telling you, but adopt a nonjudgmental, nonattachment approach to outcomes. Accept that your connection with all of life is always there. It is up to you to turn the dial up or down for a stronger or weaker connection in a mindful manner.

The connection with self, life on this planet, and Spirit is unbroken. Connection never stops. Of course, the strength of any connection changes, depending on the frequency you hold in the moment relative to that person, place, or object. You activate your freedom to adjust the strength or quality of a connection when you make a conscious choice to accept the connection or judge it.

M.A.G.I.C. the practice allows you to press the reset button and return to a place where you can choose again and again the extent of the connection you wish to practice. In some ways, practicing connection is a paradox, because we are promoting doing something that we are, something that already exists, and something that will always exist: a connection with Spirit. Realistically, we are acknowledging this while opening ourselves to an increased flow of current between us and Spirit.

Connecting with self

Practice: Take a couple minutes to look at one of your hands. Observe the details of your hand. Notice the different colors, shapes, highs and lows, and any characteristics that stand out to you about your hand. Recognize that your hand is a community of trillions of intelligent cells, all doing what they know to do for your well-being. Notice the connection your hand has with your brain, your mind, your heart, and the rest of your body. Appreciate your hand for the amazing living apparatus it is. Even if it isn't moving, it is still alive. Appreciate your hand and the intelligence that created it, how it keeps it alive, and how this energy lives within the trillions of intelligent cells that form your hand.

Practice: As you walk or move today, notice your body's movement. Notice your feet touching the ground (grounding); notice your legs doing what they know how to do; notice your body moving in a particular manner, allowing you to move forward. Notice your trillions of cells collaborating to allow you to function and exist as a physical being in this world. Appreciate the miracle that is your body presenting in this world. Make this connection with yourself as a physical being operating on this planet. Now that you have noticed your body, talk to it by sharing your thoughts about it. Appreciation is the most loving connection we can establish with our being.

Practice: All of life was created by Love, for love, with love. You are included in this creation. Go about your day, stopping on the hour and repeating over and over the following statement: "I am not that which my ego believes. I am free, for I am still as Love created and is continuing to create me."[153] You don't have to believe this statement; just be aware of any insights that might come to mind as you play with this statement.

Practice: A simple and powerful way to connect with the self is to consciously speak with your heart while you imagine breathing in and out of this area of your chest. Focus on your heart (place your hand on your chest), and start up a conversation, like you are speaking with an old friend. It is not about what you "should" say; allow the conversation to flow naturally. This is a private conversation and needs your full attention and respect. It is something very special. After all, you are speaking with your bestest friend in the entire world.

How will you know if it is your heart or your head talking? When the answer comes from your heart, the response will usually come instantly. Sometimes the answer will come before you even finish asking the question. When the answer comes a little slower, this is usually your head analyzing, recalling, assessing, and strategizing an answer. Feel it or simply know it rather than intellectualize it. Note: if you are not familiar with communicating with your heart, it might take a little practice for you to reestablish trust. A lack of any trust isn't from your heart or your authentic self; it comes from the ego mind not wanting to let go of control as the manager.

Practice: Each of the trillions of cells that make up the community called your body is an intelligent being. Each cell has all the operating parts you have as a human person, including intelligence. Cells know what they need to do for optimum health if only you allow them the space to do what they know best. Therese Wade says we can and need to have a conscious conversation with our cells, rather than an unconscious conversation. This probably makes a great deal of sense when you consider some conversations you have had over the years. Most people have these conversations like "I am too skinny, or too fat; I'm too..." Wade promotes speaking with your body, your cells, to access and gain the cooperation of the body. Three steps are suggested:

Approach your body with genuine compassion, understanding that it comprises conscious cells that experience emotions.

Build trust by engaging your body in mental conversations about your desire for the two of you to cooperate and overcome the ailment.

Allow changes in the conversation by using different thoughts and words that elicit spontaneous elevated emotions.[154]

Practice: Connection with the self is the most powerful way to receive love. Of course, we all tend to be hard on ourselves. We find it difficult, if not impossible, to show compassion to, care for, or practice unconditional acceptance of self. One way to short-circuit this is to remind yourself that your ego mind has been making decisions—sometimes important decisions—based on fictional stories collected over a lifetime. Today, you are more aware, and so now you will make different and better decisions. Between your ego self and your authentic self, there is you, the decision maker. The more you consciously decide, the more you will feel empowered. Making decisions is empowering, even if you have to change your decision later. Not making decisions is disempowering. Connecting with and trusting your heart self will encourage trust from your ego self. When all work together, nothing is impossible.

Practice: In any moment of your day, take note of and observe your self-talk, the conversation taking place in your mind. Check this conversation and decide if you are speaking words of support, acceptance, compassion, and care, or words that denigrate, abuse, or belittle your being. Make a choice about your self-talk, then get on with your day. Eventually, your consistent choices will become the new normal.

Practice: Make an appointment with the shaman within. Seek insight, awareness, and guidance from the wise part of yourself. Use this prior to sleep, and then when you awake, write your dreams down. Alternatively, you can use an automatic writing technique. Take a pen and paper and find a place of solitude. Become clear about the information you want relating to any subject. At the top of the page, write a question, seeking a response from your shaman within. Now pick up the pen in your non-dominant hand, take a breath or two, and begin writing. No analysis, no questioning, no judgments—simply write until there is no further information. Wait a few minutes to be sure. Now read what you have written and look for insights.

Practice: Spend two or three minutes (longer if possible) looking in the mirror, deep into your eyes. Say out loud, "I see past my ego mask. I love me as I am from the depths of my soul." Breathe … repeat.

Practice: Formally introduce yourself to yourself, your aware self to your heart. Have a conversation as if you are meeting a soul mate. After all, this is your soul mate. This is the most important and most rewarding friendship you will ever have. This is where love starts: within. When you come from a place of love and friendship, rather than a place of pride or shame, you will love knowing you.

Connection with others

Practice: Practice being aware of what messages you are sending out into the world. Be aware of your thoughts and emotions. This way, you choose to send only those messages you want to send out into the world around you. A hint here: what you send out comes back, often with more force.

Practice: You can be connected with others while not taking on any of their emotional baggage. When you are around other people, make a conscious choice to remain separate from their emotional baggage. Making this conscious choice allows you to be aware of what you take on, and secondly, intending to remain detached from another's energy means you maintain your own power. This is a great time to engage in the practice of grounding by intentionally connecting with the earth.

This will allow any extraneous energies to dissipate into the earth. In addition, use visualization to provide a protective field around your presence (some people use light or bubbles).

Practice: As a personal experiment, next time you notice yourself going into blaming or shaming of another, stop for a moment and consider, "What part of me is this person's behavior reflecting back, and what do I want to do about it?" This is a moment when you have a choice to accept this as an opportunity or a crisis. Refuse to accept it as an opportunity, and it will return in this or another form until you open your arms in acceptance of the gift. Taking ownership of your projection into the world, which is being reflected back at you, ensures that you are honoring yourself through acceptance of yourself—the good, the bad, and the unseen. It is by remaining in or returning to my consciousness that I exercise my innate power, especially amongst those who are living unconsciously. The trick is to remain in my own power by avoiding becoming caught up in another's or others' unconsciousness.

Practice: When you communicate with another, look him or her in the eye. If you can, look deep into their left eye as if looking at a point six inches behind their head. Say something in your mind such as, "I am here for you, and me." Listen with your entire being, not just your ears. Giving your mind this job of listening to the intention of their words while your heart listens to the intuitive message allows you to connect without judgment. A reminder: your heart is a transmitter radiating electromagnetic pulses 360 degrees outwards up to at least three meters, if not further. What you are thinking and what you are feeling is broadcast outward to those around you. The heart's energetic message is direct, while our body language and words can be distorted and certainly misinterpreted.

Practice: Consider as you move through your day the many gifts offered to you through connections. If you aren't recognizing the gifts, become proactive about it and look for them. You will be surprised at how many gift offerings you might be missing. Adopt the attitude that everyone who comes into your life experience has presented there by design. This way, you will be open to the insights and genuineness of connection. While your ego mind might resist this concept, your higher self will identify the gift and guide you to its presence.

Practice: Look for the Divine in people and things, and leave the rest to Love. You can never really see the truth in another until you stop looking for whatever else it is you expect to find. By looking for the Divine in people and things, you allow yourself to see the Divine within yourself.

A neat little experiment to try is one you can use with any person you have an issue with. When you remember that it is always free will operating for both parties, this little trick can influence a change in your connection from a distance. Before you see this specific person, practice thinking about her or him in a way that praises them. You might consider one aspect about this person that you really like, respect, or admire. Focus on this aspect and nothing else. Do this a few times before you meet with this person and repeat this when you meet with them, and see what changes.

Practice: Choose your words with purpose. This applies whether communicating with self or another. Every time we speak, think, or act, we are communicating with our cells. This is not to say that they listen to the words; rather, they listen to the intent, the energy behind the words, thoughts, or actions. Words are powerful and impact the inner mind more than the conscious mind. The inner mind takes words in a literal sense, and your cells respond immediately. Not only do the cells of each individual respond instantly to the dominant energy being broadcast, but if you set your intention for the connection before you start, you keep your power.

Connecting with Spirit

Practice: How one looks at life on this planet and in the universe says a lot about his or her sense of spirituality. M.A.G.I.C. the practice is one way of identifying and nurturing a sense of spirituality. It acknowledges that you are part of the Great Mystery: Spirit. If nothing else, going outside each day and looking around while saying, "thank you!" or grounding yourself will nurture this connection. Saying "thank you!" is an assertion of your oneness and an affirmation of your greatness. You are saying, "I am here during this expression of life, and I am conscious of its magnificence." The active expression of appreciation is the active expression of unconditional love.

Practice: Having a daily practice while seeking a way of living that represents your spiritual journey is important. You may not know what a spiritual life means for you, but this isn't the key. The key is to go searching, proactively exploring a meaningful spiritual connection. When you think you have found it, then go out and live it. Many people live a spiritual life, but they don't call it spiritual. Some don't truly live a spiritual life, but they do call it that. A spiritual life starts with a spiritual practice, and practicing connection is a spiritual practice. This practice will take place for some of us in nature, such as in the forest, in a garden, or around water. For others, it can be playing with children, or with pets. It can start in a place of worship or sitting on a tractor. The trick is to be conscious of your connection and choose to strengthen it.

Practice: To connect with Spirit—whatever you perceive Spirit to be, or even if you do not know what this might mean—is as easy as being in nature, petting your pet, hang gliding, flying a kite, or listening to music. More than anything, we strengthen this connection when we say, "Thank you for the connection!" or "I want to feel more connected now!" Remember, this is all about intention and attention.

Practice: Be conscious that you are connecting with Spirit non-stop. Just because you don't see it happening doesn't mean it isn't. Whether you are connecting with Spirit, life on this planet, or another human being, the connection is first and foremost energetic. This is simple physics and not philosophy. Understanding this basic principle of physics allows you to move past religion and theology into the very essence of life. This connection with Spirit isn't about religion, nor is it about theology; it is about connecting with All of Life, because you are an aspect of Creation. This connection with Spirit can be as big or as small as you feel comfortable making it, and you can determine this by your choice to connect with life. Buddha wasn't Buddhist, Jesus wasn't

Christian, and as Gandhi said, "God has no religion." Ask yourself, "If I am not part of All There Is, what am I?"

Practice: Wake each day and appreciate life. Recognize and appreciate that your trillions of cells are still holding hands; that the sun continues to rise above the horizon, and you don't have to pay anyone for this to happen; that the rain falling is a magical process of nature that nourishes the plants, fills the rivers, and cleanses the earth. This is the recognition of a connection with Spirit. With this recognition, there is an undeniable connection. This recognition and subsequent application adjust your state of being to be in alignment with your authentic self, and when you live the truth, you feel the truth.

Practice: The entire practice of M.A.G.I.C. is spiritual. This is a collection of five practices, the substance of which is a spiritual practice in a physical world made from thought. By practicing M.A.G.I.C. or any of the individual practices, you will strengthen your connection with the Spirit that lives within you and in all life on this planet.

Practice: Some of the most intoxicating ways to connect with Spirit are the simplest. What it comes down to is raising your vibrational frequency. What does this mean? For some, this means listening to a particular type of music to feel better. For another, it might be working in the garden, painting a picture, riding a horse, meditating, or even playing sports. It is not what you do; it is more about why you do it and the place you go to when you do it. A simple rule is that when you get your mind out of the way, the connection with Spirit will stay.

Practice: Meditation has the powerful effect of quieting the chatter in your head. Because your connection with Spirit is always there, even when it seems like it is not, you need a way of allowing this connection to be made tangible. When you quiet the chatter in your head, this connection will show itself in as many forms as you might encounter in your day. Practiced regularly as mindful meditation throughout your day, it will strengthen this connection. You can then get on with your everyday matters while still maintaining a strong connection.

Practice: Actively engaging in or imagining an aspect of nature is a powerful means for connecting with Spirit. The powerful benefits of being in nature or imagining being in nature have been shown scientifically. But perhaps even more important than scientific experiments is the experience and realization of this connection in the lives of millions of people across time. Nature is Spirit, and Spirit is nature. Spend time in nature that suits you and your lifestyle.

Practice: Making a conscious intention to connect through prayer, affirmations, or meditation will help to enhance your connection. Consciously interact with the Spirit you believe in through conversation, internal appreciation, or physical activity that is focused on strengthening this connection. To further this connection, use your imagination and visualization, or simply pretend there is a connection and feel the results. To this end, the use of rituals and ceremonies serve to establish and strengthen the awareness of connection.

Practice: Connect with self, others, and Spirit consciously and with purpose. Show up every day for yourself. Do this by connecting with your physical body, amazing mind, and loving heart. Recognize and connect with all life on the planet, including the planet itself. Finally, look up into the cosmos and connect with all of Creation as you understand it.

Practice: Start small by making a conscious decision to be proactive with the energy that makes up your physical body. Consider the energy that allows the atoms in your body to spin while moving in and out of your body. Consider the energy that allows your cells to communicate and your heart to communicate as you reach out to others. Methodically move outwards to consider the energy that supports this planet as it revolves around the sun in such a precise manner.

Case note: He didn't love me, and I didn't love me

"He didn't love me, and I didn't love me. Then I found a new relationship with my soul through M.A.G.I.C."

It had been coming for some time, and as with many relationships, especially when kids are part of the equation, Pete was aware that the relationship with her husband was destructive for everyone. Tensions had been rising, and psychological, emotional, social, and spiritual abuse was part of her and her husband's everyday game. Now he wanted a divorce, and he was arguing for his right to blame and shame. But regardless of how much intellectualizing, blaming, and shaming either of them engaged in, Pete realized it was an unwinnable situation to maintain a long-term relationship fueled by resentment, anger, victimization, and desperation to "make it work."

When she presented, Pete was tearful, spending much of her time crying, screaming, and releasing rage that seemed to come from her very core. We used the practice of insight to begin her journey of healing. Through the process of insight, we used body language (in this case, applied kinesiology) to investigate any trapped emotions, as defined by Dr. Bradley Nelson. This investigation-intuition combination allowed Pete to reach a place of deep insight. She came to understand her current circumstances in the context of her experiences and belief system. This allowed Pete to let go of the blame and shame, while finding forgiveness for her husband, for other people in her life, and finally for herself.

Pete's belief system had been protecting her during her adult life, concomitant with destroying any hope of true love and happiness. We established that she had developed a powerful and effective protection system. It was preventing anyone from hurting her the way she had been hurt as a child. The problem was that it was doing such a great job, it was also preventing any chance of genuine love entering her heart—or for that matter, coming from her heart.

With insight came a burning desire to find inner peace and the personal freedom to be herself in this world. Pete had children in her care, and it was now her passion to become the person she aspired to become. Underpinning this was the need to provide her children with an example of fulfilling their individual potential and of what was possible, even in the worst of circumstances.

Pete considered M.A.G.I.C. a lifesaver. "This practice literally saves lives. It provides someone in a place of powerlessness and desperation with a sense of self and hope. It provided me with a way to dissipate my rage and find insight into my current place in this world, and a way of reconnecting with myself and Spirit. I always wanted to believe in Spirit, but could never find the practical, everyday way to go about this. M.A.G.I.C. allowed me to do all of this, and within a few weeks, I was feeling compassion for the man who abused me and for the man who rejected me. Most importantly, I found compassion for me."

CHAPTER 12

Applying M.A.G.I.C. the Practice

Applying M.A.G.I.C. the Practice

Words alone do not teach. It is only through practice and experience that we learn. Read the words, then give them their way, and give them away as you play, play, play. Adopting this practice in your everyday life takes a little training or retraining of your mind. It is important to have an intellectual understanding of the conscious mind, followed by a feeling in the heart, and finally, knowing it with the spirit.\

Before you do anything, review the principles underpinning the practice and consider how they might fit into your life.

Take one of the five practices each day (extend it over multiple days, if you choose), allowing yourself to discover the particulars and essence of that practice and what it means for you. Know how and when you might engage with this particular practice. See the section, "Which practice when."

Work out whether you have preferences for any particular practice. Maybe you feel more comfortable practicing mindfulness or grounding before you move into connection or appreciation. Maybe one is easier for you because you are already familiar with its protocol.

There may be times when you find it near impossible to begin your practice of M.A.G.I.C., especially in the beginning of your training. In these cases, it is suggested that you act on your practice by doing something physical, such as doing something for someone or giving someone something as an expression of appreciation. Do some physical exercise and practice mindfulness or grounding, or spend time in the arms of nature, where you can dissipate emotional charge if not feel the unconditional acceptance. Spending time in nature also allows you to practice any of the five practices, as they complement one another. In extremely heavy circumstances, it is helpful to consider sitting with a friend or counselor with whom you can practice insight. Having another listen to your story allows you to open up to insights regarding your current reaction to a situation.

Think about keeping a journal of your journey. The process of writing in a journal can open you up to insights from another part of you. A journal can serve as a reminder of where you have come from and what you have achieved. It might include your doubts and fears, as well as your insights, successes, and flow. There might be comments regarding specific practices that you can share with others or your future self.

Consider the ways you already engage with a particular practice in your life, and whether there is any way you can have it work more effectively for you. Is your practicing appreciation truly appreciation and not more like gratitude? Is your mindfulness practice focused on the lack of something in your life (love, health, finances)? If your mindfulness practice is focused on the lack of something, then consider whether you are engaged in judgment. That is not true mindfulness. Mindfulness has no judgment, simply observation in the moment. It is easy to believe we are practicing mindfulness when in fact we are practicing focused judgement. It is easy to convince ourselves we are practicing appreciation when what we are doing is practicing gratitude. If this is the case, remind yourself that whether you focus your attention on the abundance or the lack of something, the results will provide the evidence.

Contemplate how to assimilate M.A.G.I.C. into your everyday routine. Remember, it fits into your life, not the other way around. So, as you eat your meal, consider how you might practice. If you are working in the garden or washing the dishes, consider how you can practice.

Reflect on any limitations you have in the application of any individual practice and the requirements demanded by that practice. This will allow you to mold the practice to suit your needs and your life. For example, when you do not have the luxury of taking time out for a meditation session, practice mindfulness at distinct moments throughout your day. Because it is about choice, you can practice appreciation just as easily as you choose to practice resentment.

As you move into the next practice and the next, consider how each one balances and complements the others, and how they might work as one practice.

Find someone who practices M.A.G.I.C. and share your experiences with each other.

Read over the information provided in this book, and consider seriously undertaking some of your own research.

Teach kids and young people how to practice M.A.G.I.C.

Power pointers for each practice

While it matters not which practice you begin with, here we will consider each practice in the order they appear in the acronym M.A.G.I.C. beginning with the practice of meditation and proceeding through to connection.

Meditation

Meditation is not something you "do." Meditation is an experience. If you make it something to do, then your head will get in the way. Allow it to become an experience, and your heart will guide you. Play with it until you find the fun in it. Trust your inner being and your spirit team to support and guide you through the mind chatter and distractions as you surrender to a place of calm. Asking for support and guidance is always helpful. Then relax into curiosity. There is no need to worry about your head taking off on a tangent; this will happen to the best of us. Simply and lovingly bring your focus back to your chosen place. Eventually, the time between tangents will expand and the number of tangents will lessen.

Mindfulness meditation is being consciously aware, without judgment, of events in this moment. It is awareness of what is happening, without attachment or resistance to outcomes.

At different times during your day, reflect on how you are practicing mindfulness or not in that moment. Say something to yourself like, "Here I am, having dinner and practicing mindfulness" or "Here I am in the shower practicing mindfulness / not practicing mindfulness." Placing something in the shower to remind you of your practice can be helpful. It was a personal challenge for me to practice mindfulness while I had my shower; I could not believe how difficult this turned out to be. I would always remember to practice just as I was finishing my shower. Eventually, I placed a bottle of shampoo in the way so that it would jog my memory. I am happy to say it worked, but it only lasted for thirty seconds. Eventually, my neuropathways developed enough to allow it to become a routine experience.

Focus your eyes on a point in front of you. While keeping your eyes on this point, ask yourself, "Can I see any red? Can I see the color orange? Can I see the color yellow? Observe the colors you notice and the shades of those colors.

Simply notice: observe, now! The past has gone, and the future hasn't yet come. "I am here now, and that's okay! In this moment, I do not have to deal with anything from the past nor anything that might be in the future." Practice looking for ways that allow you to stay in the here and now. Understand that a mind that has been used for jumping from thought to thought for so long probably needs a little re-educating.

Focus on a part of your body like your chest. Notice any movement associated with your breathing. Follow this movement, and appreciate the miracle of what is happening as you breathe. It keeps you living. Again, simply observe without judgment or analysis. Notice the feeling, the sensation, and the emotion in your body. Recognize it as a part of you, letting you know there is something for you to observe. Watch this feeling without judgment, analysis, or expectation. This feeling could be the sensation of excitement, or it could be anxiety. It doesn't matter.

Relax into curiosity again.

Focus on any sounds you can hear or any colors you can see, even shapes you can see. Observe without judgment. Stay with this focused observation while you breathe a little slower and a little deeper. Practice this while in line at the store, or while you are eating lunch in a quiet place.

Mindfulness meditation will allow you to move into any of the other practices. When you are practicing being in the moment, then appreciation, grounding, insight, and connection come far easier. Practicing mindfulness meditation is like setting the scene for the other practices to ignite.

Relax into curiosity, again.

Appreciation

Sometimes, the easiest route into appreciation is to start general. In other words, step back from the specifics and consider the bigger picture. Can you find appreciation for something that you already have and maybe take for granted? Do you ever appreciate your body and the way it operates to serve you, even when you are negative towards it? There are some things that always operate in this universe, whether we are focused on the abundance of it or the lack of it.

Focusing on a person, place, or event you fully appreciate is a simple and powerful way of beginning the practice. There are no limitations on what subject you place your focus on. Finding a focus where you can use as many of your senses as possible is certainly powerful. Once you have stimulated the feeling of appreciation, allow yourself to move your focus inward so that you appreciate the feeling of appreciation, rather than just the original object of your attention.

Appreciation is seeing the value, joy, love, the gift in a subject or circumstance, without judgment. When you look at something, you frame it in terms of your beliefs about you and that subject. Positive psychology teaches us how to use the technique of reframing. The difference between reframing a circumstance and practicing appreciation is that reframing holds onto a sense of the problem. However, if reframing allows you to move into appreciation, the trick is to use whatever it takes. Use this affirmation often: "Things do always work out for me, even when I can't see it and it seems impossible."

Holding a loving image in your mind will cause a deeper sense of appreciation to develop because practicing appreciation becomes its own generator of appreciation. Not even focusing on the person, place, or event, but focusing on just one aspect of it and holding this in your heart will build on itself. Appreciation is the cause and the effect.

Choose simple images to begin with, then move on to the hard-to-appreciate ones later. This is a journey. Practice appreciation over time to recognize the gentle aspects of your life. Appreciate what you have and keep your mind off what you don't have. Write your story of how you developed a relationship and fell in love with appreciation.

Avoid thinking along the lines of *appreciation is a wonderful practice, and it makes me feel better, I must practice appreciation*, and leaving it at that. Make a commitment to practice appreciation until all resistance you feel has dissolved, or you feel joy in all your cells. Then carry it into your everyday activities. This is not only a way of living; for the masters, this is living The Way.

Practice seeing past the behavior and seeing past the form. Recognize that we are all made from the same essence, and that essence is love. Behavior and form are shells, disguises for the genuine beauty in all things. When one looks for ugliness, it is ugliness one finds. When one looks for the Divine, it is the Divine one finds.

See appreciation as a consequence of being nonjudgmental. You are the cause of an effect called appreciation.

Finding the gift or value in any situation won't stop the hurting immediately, but it gives purpose to the experience and works to dissolve the pain. Practicing appreciation helps to reduce the pain level. This isn't about changing the conditions; this is about changing the purpose you give to the conditions, the way you perceive the conditions. It has been shown in research and bedside observation that appreciation as a practice reduces the level of physical pain.

Sometimes it is a long way from where you are emotionally to being able to feel appreciation, so start small. Here, it can be easier to begin with another practice, such as grounding or mindfulness. This will help to reduce your emotional charge as you move towards appreciation. Likewise, practicing connection where you connect with a friend or practitioner will reduce the emotional charge enough to allow you to move into appreciation more easily.

Grounding

The most common means of grounding is to establish a physical connection between your energy system and the earth's energy system. You can do this by walking with bare feet on the ground or being in the water. As you walk, stand, or sit, notice your feet in connection with the ground. Focus on the connection you make with the earth, breathe into it, and even imagine an exchange of electrons taking place. For those interested or who need to, there are commercial apparatuses available for purchase as a way of grounding (earthing).

While there are many benefits to standing on the earth with bare feet, it is unnecessary for grounding yourself. Grounding through intention is how we do it in the practice of M.A.G.I.C. This allows you to connect even when you are inside a building, or as one client reported, flying at thirty-five thousand feet! Intention is the key here. You can ground your energy deep down into the central core of Mother Earth as simply as walking on the earth with bare feet. Connect with the earth's crystal core using your energy system. Use your intention, imagination, visualization, or simply pretend to connect. Breathe into this image and allow it to develop.

Stand with your feet shoulder-width apart. As you breathe a little deeper and a little slower, you will imagine, visualize, or pretend you are sending roots down through the floor, deep into the earth. First, as you breathe in, imagine you are drawing down the energy of life from the heavens. Fill the area below your navel (Dantian). This is also called "diaphragmatic breathing" and sometimes "belly breathing." As you breathe out, imagine sending down roots through the floor into the earth. Imagine you are an enormous tree, taking hold of the earth with your roots. Breathe into this connection, sending roots down deeper and deeper. Continue this until you feel you have a hold on the entire planet with your roots. Own your connection and feel the strength that comes from this.

You can use your body language (in the form of a pendulum) to establish whether you are grounded. Simply make a statement like, "I am grounded." The pendulum will provide you with a confirmation or denial. If grounded, great; simply recognize the connection, say thank you, and move on. If you are disconnected from the earth, and you want to be connected, use one of the suggested practices and then check in again using your body language.

Sometimes a person who is grounded will become disconnected when they reflect on a traumatic event in their life. Therefore, it is good to check in now and then to make sure you are still grounded.

When you practice grounding as your go-to practice, it establishes a base for the other practices. As you ground yourself energetically, you provide yourself room for moving into any of the other practices. You may even recognize that you are already practicing meditation and connection. This is practicing insight at the same time.

Insight

Insight is your inner knowing, intuition, inspiration, or creative flow. Ask yourself what you do that results in stimulating your creative flow. Then use this to achieve insight, because it will be your key.

Experiment with trusting your intuition, your "gut feeling." Spend time each day asking, "How do I tell the difference between my intuition and the thoughts in my head?"

Avoid turning this into a serious task or hard work. If you play with it, there will be an opportunity to recognize the place for intuition in your life. Do this every day as you interact with the people, places, events, and choices in your life. The more you play and experiment, the more you train that intuition muscle to be strong.

Simply observe and wonder. When you make an intention to observe your intuition, go about playing detective. Find out how your intuition plays out, and as you develop a rapport with your inner being, you will find that the communication grows stronger and clearer. Attention to intuition is the way to grow intuition.

Follow your inner guidance, always trusting your heart of hearts to provide the most loving of guidance. Ask, "What would my heart say to me now?" or "What is my heart telling me right now?" When you feel emotional, know that there is a purpose behind this sensation; it is not just a reaction.

Life is an inside-out job. Change your inside world, and you will change your outside world. Allow your intuition to provide you with insight by practicing. As with any muscle, there is a need to practice and train your insight muscle for peak performance. If you don't use it, it will grow weaker.

Investigate the origins of your dominant emotion using your body language (kinesiology, pendulum, muscle testing). You could use a chart such as Dr. Bradley Nelson's previously mentioned chart of trapped emotions as a reference point to name the dominant emotion you are sensing. Next, establish whether there are underlying charged memories or trapped emotions supporting this dominant emotion. Once you have established that there are underlying charged memories to be cleared, use your technique of choice to clear them.

The number-one practice for supporting your intuition is meditation. This is because meditation (like sleep) will quiet mind chatter, allowing messages of insight to flow through. Consider intuition and insight as your creativity flowing into a piece of art or a project. The piece of art or project is your life. The harder you try, the more you shut down the flow. The more you relax, get on with your project and stay open to inspiration, the more the insights flow.

Similar to meditation, the use of music to stimulate insight is a powerful technique. Music has a way of stimulating memories and allowing them to come to awareness for processing. It is beneficial to use music that is instrumental and has less than sixty beats per minute.

Ask your heart a question like, "Is there something I am believing and thinking that is stopping me from being happy?" Make this your mission over a few days. Establish whether you have a built-in protection mechanism against being hurt or disappointed. It may present as a heart wall,[155] which serves to protect you from being emotionally hurt. While this wall acts as a shield, it simultaneously prevents you from enjoying life because it keeps you from taking chances to live and love. Or it may simply be a protective mechanism/program.

To stimulate insight, consider gentle exercise like walking (particularly in nature); massage; creative writing; classical music; shamanic journeying; praying; drawing; time in nature; playing with your pet, kids, or partner; or simply daydreaming.

Connection

Make your connection practice with self, others, and Spirit conscious and purposeful. Use words like, "I want to connect with ... now!", along with words of appreciation for the awareness of an option to strengthen this connection.

Formally introduce you to you, your aware self to your heart. Have a conversation as you meet this soul mate. This is the most important and most rewarding friendship you will ever have. This is an important daily event. Not a task, not a have-to, not a must, but an event that is part of every day to nurture joy in your life. Take some time to be alone and listen to your inner dialogue. Listen to this part of you as you would listen to a genuine friend. Take part with sensitivity, compassion, and interest, aiming to find out what is going on in the life of you.

Stand in front of a mirror and take a few minutes to look deep into your eyes and establish a sincere connection. You may wish to say something like, "I love you, exactly as you are."

Be open to and aware of the spirit of others, even if you don't like/accept their behavior. Practice distinguishing between the behavior of others and the actual person. You can reject the behavior while still accepting, forgiving, and loving the person. The person isn't the behavior. This behavior shows what is happening for the person.

Every time you meet someone, no matter what their relationship with you, recognize that there is an energetic connection, irrespective of what else is happening. Attempt to send a message that is filled with acceptance and compassion through the connection. You will find that what you send out is what comes back to you.

Consider your connection with others as an opportunity to learn something about yourself. You can do this by recognizing the reflections offered. Ask yourself, "What is it I am projecting into the world considering what is being reflected back to me?"

Make a point to establish a relationship with someone you can connect with whenever you have challenges in your life, or when you are feeling the emotional effects of life. Choose someone like a genuine friend, or if you are wanting a detached perspective, consider connecting with a professional life coach or counsellor.

Be conscious of your impact on the world around you whenever you are experiencing, expressing, and transmitting negative emotions. All your thoughts and emotional responses impact individuals around you, as well as impacting the global collective.

Consciously connect with the Spirit of all life by being open to the unseen forces and energies around you. How you believe it works really doesn't matter. All that is asked of you is that you recognize that energy never dies; it simply changes form. The energy of centuries past, of previous generations, of masters and mutants, is a thought away. Consciously recognize and acknowledge that there are energies you cannot see or observe in the physical world, and choose which one you would want to connect with, as well as how you want to connect with it.

Say thank you and express appreciation for life in your world. Life is life, no matter the form. It is just that some forms are more endearing to us than others. Ask for a stronger connection and bonding.

Spend time communicating with the unseen forces. Speak, pray, ask, say thank you, and express how you are feeling.

Notice the connection you have with people and animals in particular, even those you have not met yet. Notice any connection that takes place without words or gestures.\

Thinking about spirituality in connection

Like the dichotomy between science and spirituality, there exists a gap in explaining what we can't see, but at the same time, we can feel. We are able to recognize a sensation within and between our cells. Something is happening within our physical bodies that we call emotion, and we use feeling words to describe these sensations, but no one has ever seen an emotion. We only see the changes in our chemistry and cells along with the effects as emotional responses. In science, we can see and measure actions, reactions, and interactions. In spirituality, we cannot necessarily see anything, and often we are not able to measure any changes.

Much of what we can measure in spirituality has come about in recent times with the invention and development of measuring instruments. We can measure changes in the brain when a subject is participating in spiritual activities. We can measure the changes in the structure of the brain when a subject has been nurturing his or her spirituality. We can measure the reduction in levels of depression, substance abuse, risk-taking, and self-harm behaviors. But how do you measure spirituality, and how do you measure connection?

The art of connection, as with the art of spirituality, may be best described as an energetic interaction between fifty trillion living, intelligent cells; between friends and family; between pets and owners; between two hearts at a distance or close together; and between each of us and the force field that nourishes and supports us in life. Maybe this isn't necessarily a question that many people talk about as such, while they do think about it in subtle ways. We can talk about the joy and healing qualities of being in nature, of interacting with animals, friends, and loved ones. But this conversation often remains on a surface level, never acknowledging the quintessence of the M.A.G.I.C. of life. And that is okay! In so many ways, practicing connection allows us to experience this M.A.G.I.C. and benefit from it while never becoming bogged down in intellectualizing it. Like the practice of M.A.G.I.C., connection and spirituality are to be experienced, not done. Being spiritual or being connected is far more important than doing.

CHAPTER 13

The Thirty-Second Practice

The Thirty-Second Practice

Begin by choosing one practice you are drawn to engage with from the five individual practices. If you are having difficulty with this, consider "actioning" one practice. For example:

You can action *grounding* yourself by saturating yourself in nature. If you choose grounding, ground yourself in such a way that you know, with certainty, that you are grounded. Stay with this a little longer than you think you need to, and then a moment longer. Stay with it until you are certain of your connection with the earth. Some people report that they know when they are absolutely grounded when they feel a little shudder in their body or notice a little gasp for air.

You can action *insight* by talking with someone you trust for guidance, a friend, family, or practitioner. Insight is a practice many people stumble over. This is because many people turn insight into a "doing" thing rather than allowing. If insight is the chosen practice for you, it would serve you to recognize that this is already an insight. As you listen to your intuition, or as you sit with someone, recognize the inner guidance for what it is and be open to insights. Insight is often pushed aside as "just a thought that popped into my head." Follow the clues if you want insight as a practice. Many people practice insight by choosing to speak with a friend, family member, or practitioner. Others will go outdoors and contemplate[156] the issue, finding inspiration within the arms of nature. Intuition may be specific to an issue, your reaction, or your heart's choice to use insight as your first practice. Stick with this until another practice calls to you intuitively.

Action *appreciation* by doing something for somebody, or a pet — anybody, anything. At this point, you may come to the realization that you are engaging a number of practices at the same time. This may even allow you to feel appreciation for your progress doing this thing called M.A.G.I.C. Choose one thing and find many reasons for your appreciation. Starting general is often an effective route to travel. General referring to the many things we take for granted such as the stars in the sky, gravity, the earth spinning consistently and just at the right speed, and so on.

Consider as many appreciative thoughts as you can for this one subject until you can notice the sensation of appreciation in your physical body. Studies show that giving your attention or appreciation to one subject for a period is far more effective than appreciating many subjects at once. Again, start by stepping back from the subject and noticing the aspects you appreciate, then slowly focus in on a particular aspect you truly appreciate. Finish by observing and acknowledging the appreciation active within your cells. Smile while you practice this.

You can action *mindfulness* by placing one hand on top of your other hand and noticing the feel of touch, the look of touch, and the changes in touch. Focus your attention on what is happening in the moment. Observe your thoughts focused on the ever-present now, and know that you are in this moment without judgment or attachment. Start general and slowly adjust your focus from the big picture down to what is happening within your physical body. Observe with curiosity and non-attachment. Stay with this long enough to recognize the result.

If you wanted to action *connection* with yourself, how would you go about this? Maybe simply by saying thank you to your trillions of intelligent cells for being there and working as a unit to mold your physical body into what you see in the mirror.

Connection with others or other life forces on the planet can happen with a smile, a word, a gesture. You may choose to begin your connection practice by focusing on the unseen. For this you may remember your ancestors (those who have gone before you), the endless options for the presence of spirit in your everyday events. It is easy if you have a particular deity to connect with, and yet, spirit is not restricted to anything less than The One.

Again, follow your intuition and begin where you begin. Decide which is the easiest to connect with in this moment and focus there. For some individuals, it always begins with connecting with Spirit, and for others, it is connecting with all of life. It is whatever works for you.

Connection is a practice that often results in an all-consuming experience. As you acknowledge your practice of connection, notice that you are mindfully meditative, universally appreciative, and grounded in the cosmos and the earth, all at the same time. This is insight, and all of this comes from a genuine connection.

Notice how you can practice and are practicing five different practices all at the same time. Also, recognize how you are practicing this in a short period. As you play with this, the time needed will decrease. That being said, you may choose to extend the time to longer periods. Just know you can practice in thirty seconds when push comes to shove, or you can practice for an hour in a sitting practice.

The last note here is to observe the process and enjoy the experience. Play with this over and over throughout your day. Make it fun in whatever way you feel is beneficial. Remember, this is you practicing your highest joy and excitement in any circumstance. Engaging with M.A.G.I.C. allows you to be in any circumstance, any situation, and maintain a sense of inner peace about where to go next. You can't do it too much. You can't get it wrong. You can't not benefit from the intention and attention given in M.A.G.I.C. the practice.

CHAPTER 14

Challenges You May Encounter

Challenges You May Encounter

M.A.G.I.C. IS THE MUSIC, IT'S NOT THE SONG.
IT WILL GET YOU IN THE GROOVE FOR THE SONG.
- PAUL DUNNE

Most people are familiar with the experience of having plans sabotaged by an unknown source. We often blame some internal aspect of the self without really knowing what that means. Practicing M.A.G.I.C. is no different from any other activity we might engage in. Considering this, it might be helpful to talk about some of the potential challenges known to arise as we begin this practice. It is helpful to start by reminding ourselves that this practice does not differ from any other practice or training activity. This is retraining our brains to think differently. It acknowledges the realities of living in a physical world while highlighting our personal power to create the life we want.

The following are not to be seen as expected challenges, but as potential challenges that some people—may be not you, but some people—will encounter. As human beings, our ego will insist that it needs to be in control of all our affairs, and when we make decisions that align with the authentic self, there is likely to be trouble. There is an ongoing battle waged by the ego to maintain control, not just of our physical safety, but of all our physical, emotional, and spiritual matters. The following are some possible sabotage-thinking strategies used by our ego in the event of starting a new practice.

Most days, most people show up for work, study, or play. We will show up to support a friend or love a pet. But when it comes to showing up for our own expansion, our own growth, being our bestest friend in the entire world, we often fail to show up. As has been mentioned previously, our ego minds are not necessarily into doing the best thing for our highest good and spiritual growth. It is because the ego mind is not into experiencing pain, and it is certainly not into spiritual growth. It will lead us in ways that avoid pain, even if it means not giving ourselves the most loving and empowering experience. The ego mind is more into disempowerment and background-trauma-related pain. This leaves us with a sense of vulnerability that can cause most of us to retreat from what we need to do most for our own well-being. Vulnerability often presents as the sense of being in danger of physical, mental, emotional, or spiritual attack. The ego believes that we are alone and separate in this world, and it says, "I am open to attack by just about anything and anybody—and I'm not wearing any protection!"

Veteran social researcher, storyteller, and vulnerability advocate Brené Brown[157] says, "Vulnerability is having the courage to show up when you can't control the outcome. And, sometimes the bravest and most important thing you can do is just show up." M.A.G.I.C. has a loving and gentle way of allowing us to show up. It does this by opening us up to inner guidance so that we can courageously acknowledge our vulnerability and move through it with dignity and integrity. We are reassured through the practice of connection of the presence of a spiritual self, a connection with the One Energy of all of life, and the connection we recognize between us and our Creator. Through the practice of mindfulness, we are able to let go of past and future fear-based thinking while we enjoy the present.

Sabotage is a setup

We provide the ego mind with ammunition for sabotaging our plans as we hold onto attachments and expectations. This applies to you practicing M.A.G.I.C. What often happens is that we will set up expectations for our practice, then lock our sights on reaching those expectations. This is not a "bad" thing, and in fact, it can even prove beneficial. The problem develops when we become so attached to one or more of these outcomes that we focus all our energy on realizing these outcomes, no matter what. As we do this, we are increasing the level of resistance to any chance of failing in our mission. It is this resistance to failing that provides energy and momentum in the opposite direction from our desired outcome.

By focusing on what we don't want rather than what we do want, we end up activating what we don't want. Remember what Carl Jung alluded to and what is so eloquently expressed by Neale Donald Walsch, "What you resist, persists. What you look at disappears. It ceases to have its illusory form. You see it for what it is."[158] The trick, then, is to let go of all attachment to expectations we might have regarding our practice. We know the "why"; now we need to trust it as the driving force to reach our goal point. When we allow the practice to take us where we need to go, the flow will be as it should. Experiment, explore, and play with the practice with a mindset of wonderment, and see what comes out of it. There is no "must," "should," "have to," or "or else" in this practice. Only play and see, play and see.

The evolution and expansion

An adapted Zen proverb says, "Before enlightenment, chop wood, carry water. After enlightenment, chop wood, carry water." The wisdom drawn from this proverb might read, "Before I practiced M.A.G.I.C., there was lots of dedicated effort, and then when I practiced M.A.G.I.C., there was more dedication and effort." After practicing M.A.G.I.C. for a while, it will become clear. We notice the dedication is sweeter; we want to practice, and the effort comes out of inspiration rather than motivation.

One individual who practices M.A.G.I.C. told how he moved past a sense of hopelessness and helplessness. "As I practiced, I was aware of the change. Initially, the feelings of hopelessness and helplessness went away. Altogether! But one day, to my astonishment and disappointment, I noticed a sense of helplessness and hopelessness, but now it was different. It was different because now the pain was different. Sounds weird, but it was like I had visited an old friend. Somehow, I learned to appreciate these experiences. Now I understand that chopping wood and carrying water is the destination and the journey in one. Life is perfect as it is." And from a Zen student: "Before I had studied Zen for thirty years, I saw mountains as mountains and waters as waters. When I arrived at a more intimate knowledge, I came to the point where I saw mountains are not mountains, and waters are not waters. But now that I have got its very substance, I am at rest. For it's just that I see mountains once again as mountains, and waters once again as waters."[159]

Need for conscious living

Becoming aware that we have returned to an old pattern of thinking or behaving that doesn't serve us can come as a surprise. *Conscious living* is a term to describe our awareness of the events happening around us, along with our thinking at any moment. Our feeling in these moments, and the manner in which we are responding or reacting, are our clues to what we are believing about ourselves living in this world. Conscious living allows us to notice our emotional state and the triggers responsible for activating these emotions. Being in an emotional state is our state of being. When we are aware of our current state of being, there is real-time conscious awareness of our capacity and power to choose the way we react to triggers. Choosing to live more consciously in any moment is really about choosing to use our free will. It is a benefit of practicing M.A.G.I.C. that we retrain ourselves to choose more consciously while raising the frequency of our state of being.

A favorite quote of mine comes from Viktor E. Frankl: "Between stimulus and response, there is a space. In that space is our power to choose our response. In our response lies our growth and our freedom."[160] It is in this space that we find our greatest gift: the gift of choice, the gift of free will. As freedom-seeking beings, this then becomes the moment of opportunity for becoming aware, conscious creators. It is in this place that we have the opportunity to choose whether we want to play the victim or play the god. It is the combination of these individual spaces which creates our life experience. Practice conscious living by being present using M.A.G.I.C.

Engage the heart before the head

"The soul conceives, the mind creates the body's experiences. The circle is complete. The soul then knows itself in its own experience." Also, "The function of the soul is to indicate its desire, not impose it. The function of the mind is to choose from its alternatives. The function of the body is to act out that choice."[161]

Practicing M.A.G.I.C. allows the natural process of flow to occur while not supporting what is often considered the normal process. For most of us, the normal process involves using our heads to think our way through, over, and around problems. We learn to ignore our inner knowing, our intuition, and our wiser self, which is the natural way. The natural process is when there is flow in life when the painting is evolving into a masterpiece when the game is played by instinct through the head and hands. It is important to engage the heart first, then allow our heads to support the process by working out strategies and solving problems. This way, we are following our hearts and allowing our onboard computer, our heads, to support the process, rather than the other way around. This is a good blueprint for life. M.A.G.I.C. is exactly this: an experience our body has after our mind has created a practice that our soul conceived. Our mind needed inspiration, guidance, a concept before it could begin the process of creating something that our body could experience.

Nonattachment

Holding expectations of ourselves, or of something we want to be, do, or have, can easily grow into an attachment. Some would argue this is a good thing because it keeps us focused on the outcome. If it reminds us of the feeling, then we know when we reach this goal, and this is a good thing. The problem arises when we are energized toward the outcome with resistance to failure. When this happens—when we develop this resistance to failure—our energy is in resisting, not in reaching the outcome. And what we resist will persist and grow stronger. Our energy is now going in the opposite direction from what we want. It is taking us towards what we don't want rather than what we do want.

Being attached to these expectations rather than flowing with the music of life limits our options, along with our chances for true happiness. This is important as we practice M.A.G.I.C., because as with any practice when we resist (failure), we limit ourselves from receiving the complete essence of the practice. Do the practice for its benefit, and let go of the ego's expectations. So, we say, play, play, play. When we play, we let go of the need to achieve. Siddhartha Gautama, the Lord Buddha, is credited with the philosophical truth that attachment (acquisition) is the root of all suffering. M.A.G.I.C. is meant to be fun. Life is meant to be fun. Let go of attachments and feel the freedom of the ride.

Way of living

M.A.G.I.C. is to be designed by you for your life. It is to be lived and practiced by you in your everyday routine. While practicing once a day for an extended period is a powerful option, it is not the main focus of this practice. In some ways, it limits the effect of the practice to use it once each day, like a meditation or yoga practice. It is designed to be a part of your all-day, everyday affairs. This practice is a way of living.

It may surprise some to find that in so many ways, each of us already exercises the individual practices in some form or another. Everyone practices mindfulness, whether it be listening to music or as a form of meditation. We each practice appreciation at different times, even if this appreciation is practiced only in relation to a pet, or music, or nature. It would be safe to say that everyone feels the effects of grounding when in a nature setting, whether this presents a sense of connection or oneness with nature or simply a nice feeling that doesn't need to be explained. With the addition of a little focus and awareness, you will find you are practicing some if not all of these practices in your life. By all means, practice M.A.G.I.C. as a concentrated meditation at a focused time, but more than this, allow the practice to be integrated into the hours of your day. Even better still, allow your day to be integrated into your practice.

Let go of ego

Life is a type of dance. The ego is unwavering with its need to make sure everything is tangible, explainable, practical, logical, and rational, based on our life experiences and a collection of fictional stories gathered over time. Because the ego mind grows out of our life experiences and the stories we have formed from those experiences, it has a database of made-up stories—fictional stories that have come from science, religion, politics, school, government authorities, and loving or not-so-loving parents. The ego is a fictional work, a work in progress from before birth to death. We are not our egos, but we can represent the result of our ego's limited belief system. The M.A.G.I.C. practice engages the authentic self while respecting the ego's role in our physical experience. The dance comes out of managing our ego mind and following the guidance of our authentic self. This way, we live as a creation in the mind of universal Love.

Allow yourself to experience

When engaged as a practice, M.A.G.I.C. is an experience and needs to be experienced; it is not something to be "done." Rather than attempting to understand, analyze, or judge this practice, the seeker needs to allow him or herself to engage with the practice and experience the results. Words cannot teach! We can tell someone what it was like to walk across hot coals, zone out at a music festival, or sit on a tractor for twelve hours a day, but until they experience it for themselves, they can't fully appreciate the essence of the event. After all, it is the journey, the exhilaration of the ride we are chasing. M.A.G.I.C. is an experience unique to our individual journeys, and letting go of our ego's illusion allows us to recognize the journey.

This is not to say that it is not okay or beneficial to question and experiment with any practice we engage with, like yoga, Tai Chi, meditation, or any regularly engaged in activity that integrates our physical, mental, emotional, and spiritual aspects. However, it is unhelpful to debate and intellectualize the practice while looking for its benefits. If we hope to investigate, understand, or historicize this practice, there is certainly a wide scope of information out there to fill the most skeptical and intellectual of minds.

Because each of the individual practices comes from a spiritual base, promoting spiritual awareness, M.A.G.I.C. is open to contemplation, meditation, introspection, deep and meaningful discussion, and most of all, experiencing. For those who enjoy (do not depend on) science, there is plenty of research and evidence available to nourish the mind. Taste it and play with it, at least until you have some sense of its potential in your life, and then feel free to analyze, intellectualize, and debate it, if that is your thing.

Skeptical is good

This isn't about believing everything written here. Rather, it is about taking what you, the seeker, feel comfortable with and developing your own practice. Remaining skeptical about everything here isn't about being narrow-minded or biased to the point where you cut off your nose to spite your face or the other way around. Skepticism is good, but there comes a point where skepticism can become an arrogant, ego-based fear that closes us off from the essence of life and our full potential as spiritual beings in physical form.

CHAPTER 15

Daily Maintenance

Daily Maintenance

> *"I hear and I forget.*
> *I see and I remember.*
> *I do and I understand."*
> *—Confucius*

Probably the most important thing you can do for yourself in practicing M.A.G.I.C. is to make a commitment to daily personal upkeep with the practice. With some consistent, focused playing, M.A.G.I.C. will become a way of living. This will influence the way you think and what you think about. When you change the way you think, you change your life. Like using a fresh pair of spectacles, you will see the world differently. Commit to using this practice as part of your everyday activities. Play with it until the practice is a way of living. Aim to practice this and hold it for thirty seconds. Get out of your head and into your heart.

Commit to the practice by setting your watch, smartphone, alarm, or anything you can use to remind you to stop and engage with the practice. It may be beneficial to set your alarm for every hour for the first one or two days, extending the gap to every three hours after. Also, sharing or choosing to engage with this practice within a group serves to energize your own commitment while supporting those around you.

Set your intention

It is important for us to set our intention before we do anything, especially anything that has the potential of influencing our holistic self. Decide to change a particular aspect of your life by using this practice as a change agent. By setting your intention to change an aspect of your life while practicing M.A.G.I.C., you will summon the universal energies in support. These are the same energies that make up the universe, and of which worlds are made. Using the M.A.G.I.C. practice every time you consider this aspect of your life will enable change from the inside out.

This is because when practicing m.a.g.i.c, there is little or no resistance. Begin by considering, visualizing, and documenting what your life will feel like after you have manifested the desired change. Now use M.A.G.I.C. to help overcome any obstacles to this change. Using the practice every time you consider this aspect of your life—today, tomorrow, next Sunday—will place you in the driver's seat to bring about change.

Decide to play, play, play

Make a commitment to play with the practice in a way that best suits your lifestyle, until it is your lifestyle. Play is a powerful formula for learning. Play until you have incorporated the practice as a way of living, such that your day becomes the practice. When you can complete the practice in less than thirty seconds, recognize the ease with which you achieved this. Choose to have fun with the practice and allow it to flow into your daily activities, knowing that you become what you practice.

Get out of your head

Remember, M.A.G.I.C. is a spirituality-based practice. The heart instigates it for spiritual reasons. Choosing to stay out of your head and remaining connected with your heart, you will limit the amount of resistance that your head will want to conjure up. One of life's greatest challenges—probably the greatest challenge—is to accept the ego mind for what it is while not giving up your power to it. Put another way, you are accepting that your ego mind has a role to play, while not allowing yourself to become caught up in the games that say you are your ego mind. You are not! We often see the ego as an evil aspect of human nature. By itself, the ego is not evil. In our evolution, we have made the ego what it is in our lives. Rather than being fueled by "evil," the ego is fueled by fear. Fear is the lack of love, and love is where the heart is. The problem has come about because we have handed over to the ego our power and freedom to choose our destiny. And who convinced us to do this? Nobody but the ego.

The ego serves to provide an experience in physical reality. It is from this experience of yourself as a physical being that an ego-dependency is established. In this way, the ego has evolved as a very creative, fear-based, worldly guide. The ego has set itself up as the god aspect. It has created a place for itself separate from who we truly are in spirit. Everything that Love/Creator/God created is like itself: Love. Life is a continual game, which we call "reality." In this game, there is a protagonist and an antagonist in an oscillating play of contrast. In this play, the hero is your authentic self, and she or he sees you as perfect. The antagonist is your ego self, always doubting, always afraid, always looking for a creative solution to justify your dependence on and addiction to its presence. One way the ego cleverly directs your behavior and thinking is by sabotaging your good intentions.

The more you get out of your head and align with your authentic self, the more your life will reflect authenticity and integrity. The more you practice M.A.G.I.C., the more you free yourself of the ego's fear-based control. To help with your practice, set up reminders, indicators, or reset points in your day. Have a friend text you, call you, or otherwise remind you to engage in the practice. Most of all, have a reminder of why you engaged the practice in the first place.

Reflect on the principles

Review the principles of the practice to remind your conscious mind of what your heart already knows. The principles underpinning M.A.G.I.C. the practice serve as a blueprint for life. They are not intended to stand as the only principles for living life. Rather, they are here to guide your practice and help you return to why you have engaged with the practice. It is important for each of us to establish our own principles for practicing. If your only principle is to focus on being happy and following your bliss, then use the M.A.G.I.C. practice for exactly this. By knowing what you believe in and starting the practice from this place, the principles you set will serve as a reset button in times of crisis.

Intensify the results in a group

Sharing or choosing to engage in this practice with one or more individuals will energize your own commitment, and it also serves to support those you interact with. As with the practice of yoga, Tai Chi, or meditation, you significantly multiply the benefits by joining with others as you practice. Sharing or choosing to engage in this practice with friends, family, colleagues, or even enemies will energize your own commitment and provide mutual support for anyone on the team. Have your kids remind you; then you will have an invitation to remind them. Throughout history, many of our teachers have talked about the power of the collective. When more than two are gathered to focus with a single intent, this multiplies the power of that intent. The form really doesn't matter. It can be a group of individuals coming together for a formal practice session, a group of individuals practicing in a virtual group, or two or three people acting as supports for each other.

Affirmations are powerful

Many people report that they simply spell out M-A-G-I-C in their heads, and the results are immediate. Others speak of the extra push they receive when they speak the letters out aloud. This effect flows from practicing. Then, when they need to realign, spelling the acronym in their minds has the desired effect. "M.A.G.I.C." has become an affirmation or a personal mantra, replacing old, outdated self-talk with confirmation and inspiration.

Play with one piece at a time

Just start! Choose a practice out of the five and begin. Focus your attention on engaging with this one practice fully. It is important to focus on one practice until you know it intimately. Take it slowly, building on each practice until the five individual practices integrate into one. Remember, you are in charge of this game, and it is you who benefits. The guidance is to take baby steps until you can walk; then you can choose to run.

Case note: The children reflect M.A.G.I.C. back at me

Referred by her general practitioner with generalized anxiety and stress, June was a twenty-five-year-old teacher. The anxiety and stress were now impacting her physical health. June had enjoyed teaching until this year. With a new class came a new "class" of parents, and a new class of challenges. These children were wonderful at the beginning of the year, but now they were disrespectful to one another and to her as a teacher.

"It doesn't matter how many times I pull them up on their behavior, how many lectures I give them about respect, or how many times I send them to the office. Nothing seems to work. The worst part of this job is dealing with the parents and admin. Parents treat you like crap, and admin treats you like you are dumb. I go home every day exhausted and wanting to drink. I spend nights checking my emails in case a parent has complained."

After learning about the M.A.G.I.C. practice, June took it into the classroom. She reasoned that if she could use it for her own sense of calm and peace, she might just be able to introduce parts of it to her students. In the beginning, June always started with grounding herself, and so she introduced her students to the idea of sending their roots deep into the earth. June told me how a five-minute pause at the beginning of the period, having her class send their roots deep into the earth, had an immediate and powerful effect for the entire period. June and her children were calmer and more focused, and there was definitely more respect shown. No more lectures and no more reason for lectures.

June taught the class how to ground themselves, use mindfulness to calm themselves, and practice appreciation when worried, sad, angry, or scared. Now to deal with those parents!

CHAPTER 16

Which practice, when?

Which practice, when?

In this section, we will consider which practice to use in which circumstances. There is no golden rule here. Follow your inner knowing.

Meditation

When there is continuous noise in my head, and I want to soften or clear this noise.

When I want to allow my head to trust my inner knowing for managing life choices.

To focus attention on an experience in the here and now, I practice mindfulness.

When I am thinking too much, I cannot hear my inner knowing, so I make biased choices.

When I am feeling overwhelming emotions, this is a sign to turn off my thinking.

When I want to stop focusing on the past, always thinking about what could have been— "if only."

When I want to be focused on the present moment, with no concern about the future— "What if."

When looking at my life as a block of time, and I want to appreciate every moment's gift from Spirit.

When experiencing physical, mental, or emotional pain, and I want to stop resisting and find acceptance.

When I want to improve my capacity to focus during the day and sleep during the night.

Accepting that life is an inside-out process, and meditation allows me to go within to change without.

To recognize that the power of now is the only true power I have.

Appreciation

Practicing appreciation, because it allows joy to flow.

When I want to experience rather than "do" joy in my life.

When I want to recognize an experience in my life with love, I can sit in appreciation and say thank you.

When I want to look back over my life and see the value in all my experiences, I can reflect so that I can gain insight and find appreciation.

Practicing being appreciative ensures that I value all emotional responses as messages from my inner being.

To accept that all things, people, and events come into my life for a purpose.

When I want to go with the flow, practicing appreciation opens the way.

When I want to change how I feel in any moment by changing the vibrational frequency of my cells.

When I understand that I am always in the creation process, because that is what I do, appreciation allows me to create with deliberate intention.

When I accept that I am to be my bestest friend in the entire world, practicing appreciation allows me to recognize the love.

When I want to be a role model, a shining light in this world, I can use the practice of appreciation.

Grounding

When I want to change my current state of feeling, grounding helps dissipate negativity and provides healing.

When I am feeling fractured, confused, and all over the place, practicing grounding helps steady me.

When I want to feel settled, I become aware of the magnetic pull of Mother Earth.

Grounding is an effective way of practicing mindfulness.

To access the healing potential of the earth for my physical, mental, emotional, and spiritual quadrants.

When my intuition says, "Go into the arms of nature."

When I want to replenish negative electrons in my body from the earth's surplus.

When I want to stop and come into the now moment, grounding supports this while helping me reconnect.

When I want to release my stored emotional charge, I can do this through grounding with the earth.

To improve my holistic sense of well-being when I am not able to go out into a place in nature.

To improve my sense of connection and steadiness through grounding with the earth.

To increase my sense of confidence and self-awareness, I will connect with the earth.

To enhance my sense of mindfulness and connection by grounding with the earth.

Insight

When I feel stuck and unable to move forward.

When I have emotional turmoil happening, and I want to find some clarity for healing.

When I am lost and looking for guidance and support, I can connect with a practitioner.

When I am too caught up in the drama to see the possibilities and potential.

When I am feeling helpless and hopeless, caught up in blaming and shaming.

When I am listening to my head that is caught up in the drama.

When I am looking for any reasons that I am not manifesting what I want.

When I am looking for reasons why I am manifesting what I am manifesting.

When I want to make a direct connection with my inner child and its innocence.

When I want to know why I feel certain feelings in certain circumstances.

To investigate why I keep doing something, even when I don't want to.

To assist in my physical, mental, emotional, and spiritual guidance.

As a means of looking inside myself to better understand me.

When I want to accept the gift of my emotions, I will look within.

When I want to know what the people in my life are reflecting about me living in this world.

To investigate the underlying cause of emotion by using my mind-body connection.

To seek guidance and direction through insight by communicating with/through my heart.

When I want to connect with the therapist inside of me and have a conversation.

Connection with self

When I am getting messages from my heart presenting as pain in my mind.

When I am getting messages from my cells presenting as pain in my body.

To improve my well-being by strengthening my mind-body connection.

When I realize my best friend in the world is me.

When I need a little reminder that I am the only one responsible for my happiness.

When I am ignoring my own needs and wants because I am too busy giving, responding, reacting, and attending to other people's needs.

When I want to communicate with the real me and find out what it is I need to be happy.

When I have physical, mental, or emotional symptoms of being out of balance.

When I want to be comfortable in my heart feeling, rather than spending so much time in my head analyzing, deciding, strategizing, judging, and second-guessing.

When I want to trust my unseen energy rather than spending so much time analyzing, deciding, strategizing, judging, and second-guessing.

When I realize that my connection with animals is more tangible than it is with my authentic self.

Connection with others

Connection with others and life on the planet allows me to recognize we are all one source with unique presentations.

When I want to express my essence, my Source energy, I can respect others' freedom and the right to express their essence in the way they choose.

To nurture my relationships by seeing others as divine in essence and physical in their presentation.

To help me recognize my core beliefs, reflected in the world around me.

When I want to know what I am projecting into the world.

When I want to know how I am judging, criticizing, and condemning myself, I can see how I do this to another.

When I want to find out what it is I would like to change about me in this world.

When I want to expand my integrity and compassion for all of life.

When I want to remember my connection with Mother Earth and appreciate this connection.

To enjoy the connections, I have with those who reflect love and acceptance back to me.

When I want to support another who is finding their life difficult to manage.

When I want support from another because I am finding my challenges difficult to manage.

When I want to recognize my energetic connections with others.

When I feel another's pain and discomfort, and I want to offer an energetic message of unconditional love.

When I recognize the pain and angst expressed by large numbers of the collective, and I want to respond with courage, wisdom, and depth rather than resistance.

When I want to hold myself in a place of understanding and certainty and come from a place of compassion while observing another's fear, insecurity, and vulnerability.

Connection with Spirit and the unseen

When things become difficult and I am feeling like the victim, I remember with the Spirit of all things and all things that are Spirit.

When I become so caught up in being a physical body, I cannot feel like I am enough.

When I want to be physical.

When I marvel at the awesomeness of the universe and the M.A.G.I.C. of life connected to this planet, I want to express my appreciation.

When I recognize that in many ways, I am but a speck in the universe amongst many universes, while recognizing my unlimited divinity.

When I want to strengthen my appreciation for and connection with my spiritual self.

When I desire to recognize, connect with, and interact with those who have gone before me.

When I am seeking guidance, advice, and support from the part of me not caught up in the analysis of the drama I perceive.

When I want to connect with the many forms of life that contribute to my experience on this planet.

When I want to connect with the energy known as Earth and allow her to comfort and heal my physical expression.

When I want to offer healing and love to Mother Earth as caring, compassion, and sensitivity.

When I recognize the importance of letting go of control and handing the reins over to the Spirit of all-knowing.

When I want guidance to cook a meal, I go to a connection with the spirits I once called Nana, Mum, and Aunty.

When I want guidance of a practical, mechanical, or logical nature, I call on the spirits I once called Dad, Uncle, and Cousin.

When I am seeking guidance with a client, I go to a connection with the spirits I call "my team" to collaborate with my client's "team."

When I am tired of messing up, I go to "my team" as I hand over everything to their management.

CHAPTER 17

Extra M.A.G.I.C. tricks

Extra M.A.G.I.C. tricks

> *M.A.G.I.C. IS THE MUSIC, IT IS NOT THE SONG.*
> *IT WILL GET YOU IN THE GROOVE FOR THE SONG.*
> *- PAUL DUNNE*

Most people are familiar with the experience of having plans sabotaged by an unknown source. We often blame some internal aspect of the self without really knowing what that means. Practicing M.A.G.I.C. is no different from any other activity we might engage in. Considering this, it might be helpful to talk about some of the potential challenges known to arise as we begin this practice. It is helpful to start by reminding ourselves that this practice does not differ from any other practice or training activity. This is retraining our brains to think differently. It acknowledges the realities of living in a physical world while highlighting our personal power to create the life we want.

The following are not to be seen as expected challenges, but as potential challenges that some people—may be not you, but some people—will encounter. As human beings, our ego will insist that it needs to be in control of all our affairs, and when we make decisions that align with the authentic self, there is likely to be trouble. There is an ongoing battle waged by the ego to maintain control, not just of our physical safety, but of all our physical, emotional, and spiritual matters. The following are some possible sabotage-thinking strategies used by our ego in the event of starting a new practice.

Vulnerability

Most days, most people show up for work, study, or play. We will show up to support a friend or love a pet. But when it comes to showing up for our own expansion, our own growth, being our bestest friend in the entire world, we often fail to show up. As has been mentioned previously, our ego minds are not necessarily into doing the best thing for our highest good and spiritual growth. It is because the ego mind is not into experiencing pain, and it is certainly not into spiritual growth. It will lead us in ways that avoid pain, even if it means not giving ourselves the most loving and empowering experience. The ego mind is more into disempowerment and background-trauma-related pain. This leaves us with a sense of vulnerability that can cause most of us to retreat from what we need to do most for our own well-being. Vulnerability often presents as the sense of being in danger of physical, mental, emotional, or spiritual attack. The ego believes that we are alone and separate in this world, and it says, "I am open to attack by just about anything and anybody—and I'm not wearing any protection!"

Veteran social researcher, storyteller, and vulnerability advocate Brené Brown[157] says, "Vulnerability is having the courage to show up when you can't control the outcome. And, sometimes the bravest and most important thing you can do is just show up." M.A.G.I.C. has a loving and gentle way of allowing us to show up. It does this by opening us up to inner guidance so that we can courageously acknowledge our vulnerability and move through it with dignity and integrity. We are reassured through the practice of connection of the presence of a spiritual self, a connection with the One Energy of all of life, and the connection we recognize between us and our Creator. Through the practice of mindfulness, we are able to let go of past and future fear-based thinking while we enjoy the present.

Sabotage is a setup

We provide the ego mind with ammunition for sabotaging our plans as we hold onto attachments and expectations. This applies to you practicing M.A.G.I.C. What often happens is that we will set up expectations for our practice, then lock our sights on reaching those expectations. This is not a "bad" thing, and in fact, it can even prove beneficial. The problem develops when we become so attached to one or more of these outcomes that we focus all our energy on realizing these outcomes, no matter what. As we do this, we are increasing the level of resistance to any chance of failing in our mission. It is this resistance to failing that provides energy and momentum in the opposite direction from our desired outcome.

By focusing on what we don't want rather than what we do want, we end up activating what we don't want. Remember what Carl Jung alluded to and what is so eloquently expressed by Neale Donald Walsch, "What you resist, persists. What you look at disappears. It ceases to have its illusory form. You see it for what it is."[158] The trick, then, is to let go of all attachment to expectations we might have regarding our practice. We know the "why"; now we need to trust it as the driving force to reach our goal point. When we allow the practice to take us where we need to go, the flow will be as it should. Experiment, explore, and play with the practice with a mindset of wonderment, and see what comes out of it. There is no "must," "should," "have to," or "or else" in this practice. Only play and see, play and see.

The evolution and expansion

An adapted Zen proverb says, "Before enlightenment, chop wood, carry water. After enlightenment, chop wood, carry water." The wisdom drawn from this proverb might read, "Before I practiced M.A.G.I.C., there was lots of dedicated effort, and then when I practiced M.A.G.I.C., there was more dedication and effort." After practicing M.A.G.I.C. for a while, it will become clear. We notice the dedication is sweeter; we want to practice, and the effort comes out of inspiration rather than motivation.

One individual who practices M.A.G.I.C. told how he moved past a sense of hopelessness and helplessness. "As I practiced, I was aware of the change. Initially, the feelings of hopelessness and helplessness went away. Altogether! But one day, to my astonishment and disappointment, I noticed a sense of helplessness and hopelessness, but now it was different. It was different because now the pain was different. Sounds weird, but it was like I had visited an old friend. Somehow, I learned to appreciate these experiences. Now I understand that chopping wood and carrying water is the destination and the journey in one. Life is perfect as it is." And from a Zen student: "Before I had studied Zen for thirty years, I saw mountains as mountains and waters as waters. When I arrived at a more intimate knowledge, I came to the point where I saw mountains are not mountains, and waters are not waters. But now that I have got its very substance, I am at rest. For it's just that I see mountains once again as mountains, and waters once again as waters."[159]

Need for conscious living

Becoming aware that we have returned to an old pattern of thinking or behaving that doesn't serve us can come as a surprise. *Conscious living* is a term to describe our awareness of the events happening around us, along with our thinking at any moment. Our feeling in these moments, and the manner in which we are responding or reacting, are our clues to what we are believing about ourselves living in this world. Conscious living allows us to notice our emotional state and the triggers responsible for activating these emotions. Being in an emotional state is our state of being. When we are aware of our current state of being, there is real-time conscious awareness of our capacity and power to choose the way we react to triggers. Choosing to live more consciously in any moment is really about choosing to use our free will. It is a benefit of practicing M.A.G.I.C. that we retrain ourselves to choose more consciously while raising the frequency of our state of being.

A favorite quote of mine comes from Viktor E. Frankl: "Between stimulus and response, there is a space. In that space is our power to choose our response. In our response lies our growth and our freedom."[160] It is in this space that we find our greatest gift: the gift of choice, the gift of free will. As freedom-seeking beings, this then becomes the moment of opportunity for becoming aware, conscious creators. It is in this place that we have the opportunity to choose whether we want to play the victim or play the god. It is the combination of these individual spaces which creates our life experience. Practice conscious living by being present using M.A.G.I.C.

Engage the heart before the head

"The soul conceives, the mind creates the body's experiences. The circle is complete. The soul then knows itself in its own experience." Also, "The function of the soul is to indicate its desire, not impose it. The function of the mind is to choose from its alternatives. The function of the body is to act out that choice."[161]

Practicing M.A.G.I.C. allows the natural process of flow to occur while not supporting what is often considered the normal process. For most of us, the normal process involves using our heads to think our way through, over, and around problems. We learn to ignore our inner knowing, our intuition, and our wiser self, which is the natural way. The natural process is when there is flow in life when the painting is evolving into a masterpiece when the game is played by instinct through the head and hands. It is important to engage the heart first, then allow our heads to support the process by working out strategies and solving problems. This way, we are following our hearts and allowing our onboard computer, our heads, to support the process, rather than the other way around. This is a good blueprint for life. M.A.G.I.C. is exactly this: an experience our body has after our mind has created a practice that our soul conceived. Our mind needed inspiration, guidance, a concept before it could begin the process of creating something that our body could experience.

Nonattachment

Holding expectations of ourselves, or of something we want to be, do, or have, can easily grow into an attachment. Some would argue this is a good thing because it keeps us focused on the outcome. If it reminds us of the feeling, then we know when we reach this goal, and this is a good thing. The problem arises when we are energized toward the outcome with resistance to failure. When this happens—when we develop this resistance to failure—our energy is in resisting, not in reaching the outcome. And what we resist will persist and grow stronger. Our energy is now going in the opposite direction from what we want. It is taking us towards what we don't want rather than what we do want.

Being attached to these expectations rather than flowing with the music of life limits our options, along with our chances for true happiness. This is important as we practice M.A.G.I.C., because as with any practice when we resist (failure), we limit ourselves from receiving the complete essence of the practice. Do the practice for its benefit, and let go of the ego's expectations. So, we say, play, play, play. When we play, we let go of the need to achieve. Siddhartha Gautama, the Lord Buddha, is credited with the philosophical truth that attachment (acquisition) is the root of all suffering. M.A.G.I.C. is meant to be fun. Life is meant to be fun. Let go of attachments and feel the freedom of the ride.

Way of living

M.A.G.I.C. is to be designed by you for your life. It is to be lived and practiced by you in your everyday routine. While practicing once a day for an extended period is a powerful option, it is not the main focus of this practice. In some ways, it limits the effect of the practice to use it once each day, like a meditation or yoga practice. It is designed to be a part of your all-day, everyday affairs. This practice is a way of living.

It may surprise some to find that in so many ways, each of us already exercises the individual practices in some form or another. Everyone practices mindfulness, whether it be listening to music or as a form of meditation. We each practice appreciation at different times, even if this appreciation is practiced only in relation to a pet, or music, or nature. It would be safe to say that everyone feels the effects of grounding when in a nature setting, whether this presents a sense of connection or oneness with nature or simply a nice feeling that doesn't need to be explained. With the addition of a little focus and awareness, you will find you are practicing some if not all of these practices in your life. By all means, practice M.A.G.I.C. as a concentrated meditation at a focused time, but more than this, allow the practice to be integrated into the hours of your day. Even better still, allow your day to be integrated into your practice.

Let go of ego

Life is a type of dance. The ego is unwavering with its need to make sure everything is tangible, explainable, practical, logical, and rational, based on our life experiences and a collection of fictional stories gathered over time. Because the ego mind grows out of our life experiences and the stories we have formed from those experiences, it has a database of made-up stories—fictional stories that have come from science, religion, politics, school, government authorities, and loving or not-so-loving parents. The ego is a fictional work, a work in progress from before birth to death. We are not our egos, but we can represent the result of our ego's limited belief system. The M.A.G.I.C. practice engages the authentic self while respecting the ego's role in our physical experience. The dance comes out of managing our ego mind and following the guidance of our authentic self. This way, we live as a creation in the mind of universal Love.

Allow yourself to experience

When engaged as a practice, M.A.G.I.C. is an experience and needs to be experienced; it is not something to be "done." Rather than attempting to understand, analyze, or judge this practice, the seeker needs to allow him or herself to engage with the practice and experience the results. Words cannot teach! We can tell someone what it was like to walk across hot coals, zone out at a music festival, or sit on a tractor for twelve hours a day, but until they experience it for themselves, they can't fully appreciate the essence of the event. After all, it is the journey, the exhilaration of the ride we are chasing. M.A.G.I.C. is an experience unique to our individual journeys, and letting go of our ego's illusion allows us to recognize the journey.

This is not to say that it is not okay or beneficial to question and experiment with any practice we engage with, like yoga, Tai Chi, meditation, or any regularly engaged in activity that integrates our physical, mental, emotional, and spiritual aspects. However, it is unhelpful to debate and intellectualize the practice while looking for its benefits. If we hope to investigate, understand, or historicize this practice, there is certainly a wide scope of information out there to fill the most skeptical and intellectual of minds.

Because each of the individual practices comes from a spiritual base, promoting spiritual awareness, M.A.G.I.C. is open to contemplation, meditation, introspection, deep and meaningful discussion, and most of all, experiencing. For those who enjoy (do not depend on) science, there is plenty of research and evidence available to nourish the mind. Taste it and play with it, at least until you have some sense of its potential in your life, and then feel free to analyze, intellectualize, and debate it, if that is your thing.

Skeptical is good

This isn't about believing everything written here. Rather, it is about taking what you, the seeker, feel comfortable with and developing your own practice. Remaining skeptical about everything here isn't about being narrow-minded or biased to the point where you cut off your nose to spite your face or the other way around. Skepticism is good, but there comes a point where skepticism can become an arrogant, ego-based fear that closes us off from the essence of life and our full potential as spiritual beings in physical form.

GUIDANCE BEHIND THE BOOK

Guidance behind the book

The following words of guidance were provided by my nonphysical team leading up to and while writing the book. Overall, I received seven separate insightful meditations, which inspired me to continue my journey to empower all young people. In the third message, the book *I Am Made for M.A.G.I.C.* was noted specifically.

I provide the following extracts from the seven meditations as an encouragement to you, the reader, for connecting with your spiritual team. In addition, I wanted to open the doors for all individuals who have an inner voice calling out to them to empower young people in this world.

Message
Learn what others do for reflection and invention.
The children are working with you now. Some you will not meet on this plane.
These 'children' teach from a distance, as your grandchildren have demonstrated.
The children will teach and direct you. These children will facilitate your learning.
Engage – Connect!
Some will want physical reassurance through child focused instruments... books, films, play, computer games, all will want to know and hear about their own bodies.
Listen with the heart so that you learn the language.
Each child will need to find a way to communicate their "feelings" - urgency to care givers.
See past the physical plane, for it will distract you from the entrance to the cave; You are looking for the opening – the way to the garden.
Each spirit team will guide you.
Your focus is to be pure intent, for this will be your light.
You are never alone. We are always with you. Anywhere – Anytime. Everywhere – All the time.
(Keep this channel open please)

Message
Me: What do you want me to do?

Team: The time has come to facilitate an opportunity for the children to speak. It is time to open up to the teachings that flow through the young ones. This isn't about global warming, peace, politics, health, or social exclusion. This is about the new energy that the Earth resonates with. It is time to let go of the old ways and introduce the children of the fifth dimension.

Me: Why is it important for me to do this?

Team: You have an established connection with the children. It was your intention, from the beginning to lift all children to their grandest versions of their greatest selves. It has been your learning, your training, to come to this place where your involvement will empower all young people.

Me: Will I have a team of like-minded beings in the physical form to work with me?

Team: The team has been assembled. They are waiting for you to open the doors.

Me: What is it I need to do to "open the doors"?

Team: Make a firm commitment to engage and empower young people. Offer resources and a place of acceptance and (empowerment) reassurance with a community of "oneness." Follow your heart. Trust in us to direct, support, and facilitate your training. Know that you will be looked after and are looked after in this. Let go of the fears and doubts that plague you.

Me: I don't know where to start. Where do I start?

Team: You understand how things work. This has been shown to you, demonstrated many times. As recently as with the interaction with the medical facility. Move forward with a commitment to follow the light, and we will ensure you see the light.

Me: Is there anything specific I need to do now?

Team: Keep this channel open. We want to communicate with you. Make it your place to look for the messages. This will be a strengthening process.

Me: I am aware of your presence and presents.

Team: You are on the right path. In this space and time, where you calm your mind and your awareness is intensified, this conduit is cleared and tuned—tapped in, turned on, tuned in. Trust the process as you allow the frustration and impatience to dissolve. Explore your travel; your freedom options from a place of knowing.

Message

We have come in love and peace for humanity. It is our intention to show you a way of uniting those young people, the children of Gaia. It is important for the children of the Earth to be reminded of their purpose and mission on Earth. While the individual and collective mission is to experience the joy of expanding as physical expressions of the One Source, each has a particular part to play in the ascension of humanity and the Earth. Through your involvement with these children, the world will come to realize the ascension process and the new Earth.

There are a number of stages in this process you will be involved with. And yes, there is a team you will work with awaiting the time. We have told you they are waiting for you to open the doors. This is true. We haven't told you what this means, to open the doors. There is a need for a light to be expressed across this planet of yours to unite all teachers and supporters. It is this light that will open the doors of enlightenment to the team.

For this to happen, you must produce your book of magic. It will be through this practice of enlightenment that each member will be awakened to his or her role. The doors represent passing through a wall of heaviness from the 3D expression into the 5D dimension. Your book, your practice, will be the key that opens this for your team. We will guide the process. Continue to trust your inner being to guide you through this process. We will be there arranging the necessary resources for its manifestation. Trust us, and trust your inner being. You are here to allow this to happen. It is written.

Message

The way to open the doors

Unlike the doors you are generally accustomed to, these doors do not lock or unlock. They, however, are activated to open and close. You have the power to activate these doors with your energy field. Thinking and wishing the doors to open is fruitless. Effort has only one effect, and that is to maintain the integrity of the closed doors.

Become clear about your intention. Be so clear about your intention when those doors open. Know you will not have any option other than to go with the flow coming through the doors. While the outcomes are not able to be altered due to the momentum, the journey is totally flexible. This flow into the house will have a momentum out of its own nature. It will evolve and expand to compliment those who enter.

How is it that you maintain pure intention? How will you know? You will know when you recognize your light. When the head, the hands, and the heart are acting as one, there will be an expression of light. Your only job is to express your light. Allow the doors to be as they will. This you will need to practice regularly. Set aside time and place to focus on activating your light. Trust all is as it should be.

Message

Question: What is it, the one thing young people need to know more than anything else?

Answer: Because they are young in earthly years confuses both the way in which they are perceived and the manner in which they are perceived themselves.

Living in a time-space reality always limits the ability to see the true enormity of the truth. Because children grow into this perspective – this limiting mindset, a mindset where they trust their guardians - their limiting mindset is established.

They desire and need for love, acceptance, safety, and acknowledgement, overwhelming any knowing – any memory of their origins. The physicality of a 3D reality combined with the sensations associated with emotions stimulated within relationships dominates the freedom of choice. Most people spend the rest of their life seeking that freedom in choice.

The first thing important for young people to hear is they came from Source energy into a reality that denies their authentic being.

They came as powerful light beings into a reality which demands they "fit in".

Each young person needs to hear they are more than what they see in the mirror. More than his or her physical being, their feeling self, or even their thinking self, they are an energetic experience.

Hearing this will not be enough for most. Each will need to experience this truth to assimilate it into his or her life experience. Hearing this, reflecting upon it, discussing it and testing its authenticity in everyday life is necessary to "know" is as their truth.

Provide questions and activities as everyday experiences that open his or her mind to the possibilities, the potential within. Allowing each to activate her or his innate curiosity will offer the option of personal empowerment. It is important to remind and re-establish each young person's God-given power.

Question: What is the thing, the one thing most if not all young people want to hear, or think they want to hear?

Answer: within each young person's mind is "are they alone, separate from and altogether different to all other young people?"

Everyone wants to "fit in" be accepted while needing to be an individual – unique and special. This is a seemingly nonnegotiable internal conflict. There is pain.

Question: What is the thing, more than any other thing, that young people do not want to hear?

Answer: They, and they alone, are totally responsible. They have total responsibility for accepting their individual divinity and using it for the greater good of all of life on this planet.

The courage to accept responsibility for this limitless power has been diluted by the limiting beliefs accumulated by previous generations. The courage to accept his or her role as divine influencer on earth demands a willingness to challenge the very individuals he or she looks to for acceptance, acknowledgement, love and the "things" that are said to give happiness.

It is believed, choosing to accept personal responsibility is choosing to live without all the components that go into making personal happiness. The dominant paradigm has individuals looking outside of themselves for happiness. Looking for love, in all the wrong places.

When he or she rallies the courage to trust and engage their own inner wisdom, their inner knowing, they meet opposition. There is opposition presented from the external world and there is opposition presented from within.

The external world is coming from a place of fear. Fear-based thinking demands we secure control over our situations and circumstances, and maintain that control. Unless the belief goes, I can control how and when my environment (people, places, events & circumstances) within change, I should be afraid of what will happen to me.

There is a continuous and vigorous attack on any individual's mind through mass media machines fueled by a single-focused attempt to gain control. It matters not whether you consider this to be a conscious play or a coincidence. What matters, and we mean that literally, is what you the population think about and the way you think about it. What you think about, where you focus your energy, is what becomes matter. (It matters because - it becomes matter)

This is never about pointing a finger at an external cause. You are the cause and the effect. Time and time again it has been highlighted. You experience what you create, nothing more and nothing less. Address the external forces by acknowledging and using your internal sources. What Yoda says, "The Force is with you... use it."

NOTES ABOUT THE AUTHOR

Notes about the author

Paul Dunne practiced as a registered psychologist from 1992 to 2019. Over the years, Paul placed a particular emphasis on and around the youth sector, providing face-to-face counseling for children, young people, caregivers, and workers with young people. Throughout his years as a practitioner, Paul adopted a holistic, spiritual approach, integrated with a quantum-psychology response for building resilience and personal empowerment.

Paul's work shifted focus, from issues faced by young people, such as suicide and self-harming behavior, through to the reality of life-and-death issues of palliative care and aged care. He also supported individuals who were victims or perpetrators of domestic and family violence. His career has continually allowed him to focus on groups of individuals facing extreme challenges, such as homelessness, domestic and family violence, suicide, long-term unemployment, bullying, and death and dying.

His work has maintained a consistent theme: to challenge the boundaries that serve only to protect the mundane and to promote the empowerment of individuals and communities. This resulted in a search for efficient and effective ways to empower individuals. This journey has been his own expansion, empowerment, and spiritual awakening while serving as a guide to others.

These days, Paul has turned his focus towards writing and teaching with an emphasis on empowering young people to take responsibility for their own divinity in a world that denies their spiritual origins.

REFERENCES

References

1. Dyer, W.W. (4 October 2001). You'll See It When You Believe It: The Way to Your Personal Transformation. HarperCollins US; 1st edition.
2. Walsh, N.D. (1995). Conversations with God: An Uncommon Dialogue. Book 1. Hodder. pp.3.
3. Carpenter, T & L. (1992). Dialogue on Awakening: Communion with a loving brother. The Carpenters' Press, Princeville, Hawaii. 96722. pp. 71.
4. Eckhart Tolle Quotes. (n.d.). (August 12, 2021). BrainyQuote.com. Retrieved from BrainyQuote.com website: https://www.brainyquote.com/quotes/eckhart_tolle_786638
5. Maltz, Maxwell. (1960). Psycho-Cybernetics. Simon & Schuster. ISBN 978-0671700751.
6. Hill, Napoleon. (1937, March). Original copy. Think and Grow Rich. Vermilion - mass market. ISBN-10: 0091900212; ISBN-13: 978-0091900212.
7. Murphy, Joseph. (1963). The Power of Your Subconscious Mind.
8. Campbell, Joseph. (2021, November 30). The Power of Myth with Bill Moyers. KNOPF US; Anchor Books edition. Retrieved from https://www.jcf.org/about-joseph-campbell/follow-your-bliss/ (pp. 148)
9. A Course in Miracles. (2007). Workbook. Part I, Lesson 31. (https://acim.org/acim/en/s/433)

10. A Course in Miracles. (2007). Text / Chapter 3: The Innocent Perception / IV. Error and the Ego. The Foundation for Inner Peace. 448 Ignacio Blvd., #306, Novato, CA 94949, www.acim.org and info@acim.org, used with permission. (https://acim.org/acim/en/s/74).
11. Hicks, E. & J. (2004). Ask and It Is Given: Learning to Manifest Your Desires. Hay House Inc.
12. Haanel, Charles, F. (2000). The Master Key System. MDG International, Inc., pp. 4.
13. Allen, James. (1903). As a Man Thinketh. Innovative Eggz LLC. Complete original text paperback reprinted January 31, 2006.
14. Coué, Emile. (1922). Self Mastery Through Conscious Autosuggestion. Published January 30, 2019, by Routledge.
15. Initiates, T. (1912). The Kybalion. Retrieved from https://www.sacred-texts.com/eso/kyb/index.htm.
16. Initiates, T. (1912).
17. Retrieved from https://www.goodreads.com/author/quotes/278.Nikola_Tesla
18. Haanel, Charles, F. (2000). The Master Key System. MDG International, Inc., pp. 4.
19. Initiates, T. (1912). The Kybalion. Retrieved from https://www.sacred-texts.com/eso/kyb/kyb14.htm
20. Twyman, James F. (2010). The Art of Spiritual Peacemaking: Secret Teachings from Jeshua Ben Joseph. Original text - 33 lessons in 99 days.
21. A Course in Miracles. (2007). Text / Chapter 4: The Illusions of the Ego. II. The Ego and False Autonomy. (https://acim.org/acim/en/s/81). The Foundation for Inner Peace. 448 Ignacio Blvd., #306, Novato, CA 94949, www.acim.org and info@acim.org, used with permission.
22. Lipton, Bruce. (2005). The Biology of Belief: unleashing the power of consciousness, matter & miracles. Published by Mountain of Love/Elite Books. Santa Rosa, CA 95404. pp. 38.

23. Stussman BJ, Black LI, Barnes PM, Clarke TC, Nahin RL. Wellness-related Use of Common Complementary Health Approaches Among Adults: United States, 2012. Natl Health Stat Report. 2015 Nov 4;(85):1-12. PMID: 26556396.
24. Morris, Z. S., Wooding, S., & Grant, J. (2011, December 16). The answer is 17 years, what is the question: understanding time lags in translational research. Retrieved from https://journals.sagepub.com/doi/full/10.1258/jrsm.2011.110180
25. Campbell, Joseph. (2021, 30 November). The Power of Myth with Bill Moyers. KNOPF US; Anchor Books edition. Retrieved from https://www.jcf.org/works/quote/being-helped-by-hidden-hands/
26. Doidge, N. (2007, March 15). The Brain that Changes Itself: Stories of Personal Triumph from the Frontiers of Brain Science. Penguin Books.
27. Craig, G. (2022) The Gary Craig Official EFT Training Centers. Retrieved from https://www.emofree.com/unseen-therapist/prelim/read-this-first.html. © 2017 - 2022 Gary Craig. All Rights Reserved.
28. McCraty, R., Atkinson, M., & Tomasino, D. (2001). Science of the Heart. Exploring the Role of the Heart in Human Performance. HearthMath Research Centre, Institute of HearthMath. An Overview of Research Conducted by the HeartMath Institute. Publication number 01-001. Boulder Creek, CA.
29. McCraty, R., et. al. (2001).
30. Sandelin, R. (2015, November 13). Candace Pert's Molecules of Emotion (documentary film project). YouTube video. Retrieved from https://www.youtube.com/watch?v=WyCyzHyueLM
31. McCraty, R., et. al. (2004). Electrophysiological Evidence of Intuition: Part 1. The Surprising Role of the Heart. Journal of Alternative and Complementary Medicine 2004; 10(1): 133-143.
32. McTaggart, L. (2008, January 2). The Field: The Quest for the Secret Force of the Universe. Harper Perennial; updated edition (January 2, 2008).

33. Miller, L. with Barker, T. (2015). The Spiritual Child: The New Science on Parenting for Health and Lifelong Thriving. Bluebird books for life.

34. Miller, L. with Barker, T. (2015). The Spiritual Child: The New Science on Parenting for Health and Lifelong Thriving. Bluebird books for life.

35. Chödrön, Pema (2016, June 7). When Things Fall Apart: Heart Advice for Difficult Times. Chodron, Pema; 20th Anniversary Edition.

36. Kabat-Zinn, J. (2005, January 5). Wherever You Go, There You Are: Mindfulness Meditation in Everyday Life. Retrieved from https://www.goodreads.com/author/quotes/8750.Jon_Kabat_Zinn

37. Spalding, T. L. (2020, November 1). A Year of Forgiveness: A Course in Miracles Lessons with Commentary from Jesus. Lesson 214. Light Technology Publications.

38. Spira, R. The Essence of Non Duality: Guided Meditations and Conversations on the Source of Happiness and the Nature of Reality. Retrieved from https://rupertspira.com/teachings?player=video

39. Spira, R. (2010, February 9). How do I just let go and be? Q&A: A question about letting go. Retrieved from https://rupertspira.com/nonduality/blog/article/how_do_i_just_let_go_and_be

40. Renard, Gary. R. (2004, November 1). The Disappearance of the Universe: Straight Talk about Illusions, Past Lives, Religion, Sex, Politics, and the Miracles of Forgiveness. Hay House Inc.

41. Dispenza, J. (2013, February 15). Breaking the Habit of Being Yourself: How to Lose Your Mind and Create a New One. Hay House Inc.

42. Walsh, N.D. (1995). Conversations with God: An Uncommon Dialogue. Book 1. Hodder. pp.167.

43. Boccia M, Piccardi L, Guariglia P. The Meditative Mind: A Comprehensive Meta-Analysis of MRI Studies. Biomed Res Int.

2015; 2015:419808. doi: 10.1155/2015/419808. Epub 2015 Jun 4. PMID: 26146618; PMCID: PMC4471247.

44. Various references from Google Scholar search for functional MRI (fMRI) studies. https://scholar.google.com.au/scholar?as_vis=0&q=fmri+and+meditation&hl=en&as_sdt=0,5

45. Svend Davanger, Øyvind Ellingsen, Are Holen, Kenneth Hugdahl. (2010, August 1). Meditation-Specific Prefrontal Cortical Activation During Acem Meditation: An FMRI Study. Sage Journals. Retrieved from https://journals.sagepub.com/doi/abs/10.2466/02.04.22.PMS.111.4.291-306

46. Goyal M, Singh S, Sibinga EMS, et al. Meditation Programs for Psychological Stress and Well-Being: A Systematic Review and Meta-Analysis. JAMA Intern Med. 2014;174(3):357–368. doi:10.1001/jamainternmed.2013.13018

47. Davidson, Richard J., PhD; Kabat-Zinn, Jon, PhD, et al. Alterations in Brain and Immune Function Produced by Mindfulness Meditation, Psychosomatic Medicine: July 2003 - Volume 65 - Issue 4 - p 564-570 doi:10.1097/01. PSY. 0000077505.67574.E3

48. Jha, A.P., Zanesco, A.P., Denkova, E., et al. (2020). Bolstering Cognitive Resilience via Train-the-Trainer Delivery of Mindfulness Training in Applied High-Demand Settings. Mindfulness 11, 683–697. https://doi.org/10.1007/s12671-019-01284-7

49. Blaine Ditto, PhD, Marie Eclache, BA, and Natalie Goldman, BA. (2006). Short-Term Autonomic and Cardiovascular Effects of Mindfulness Body Scan Meditation. Society of Behavioural Medicine. Department of Psychology. McGill University.

50. Vieten, Cassandra, et al. (2018, November 17). Future directions in meditation research: Recommendations for expanding the field of contemplative science. PLOS ONE. https://doi.org/10.1371/journal.pone.0205740. Retrieved from https://journals.plos.org/plosone/article?id=10.1371/journal.pone.0205740

51. Garland EL, Manusov EG, Froeliger B, Kelly A, Williams JM, Howard MO. (2014 Jun;82(3)). Mindfulness-oriented recovery enhancement for chronic pain and prescription opioid misuse:

results from an early-stage randomized controlled trial. J Consult Clin Psychol. 448-459. doi: 10.1037/a0035798. Epub 2014 Feb 3. PMID: 24491075; PMCID: PMC4076008. Retrieved from https://pubmed.ncbi.nlm.nih.gov/24491075/

52. Vieten, Cassandra, et al. (2018, November 17).
53. Vieten, Cassandra, et al. (2018, November 17).
54. Thich Nhat Hanh. (2012, 3 December). The Pocket Thich Nhat Hanh Paperback. SHAMBHALA - TRADE; 1st edition. pp. 30.
55. Getting Started with Mindfulness. Mindful: healthy mind, healthy life. Mindful Communications. Retrieved from https://www.mindful.org/meditation/mindfulness-getting-started/
56. Harris, R. (2007, March 1). The Happiness Trap: Stop Struggling, Start Living. Publisher Little Pink Dogs. Retrieved from https://thehappinesstrap.com/preview/
57. Kabat-Zinn, J. (2018, September 27). Defining Mindfulness: What is mindfulness? The founder of Mindfulness-Based Stress Reduction explains. Mindful: healthy mind, healthy life. Retrieved from https://www.mindful.org/jon-kabat-zinn-defining-mindfulness/
58. Tolle, E., (2004, August 1). The Power of Now: A Guide to Spiritual Enlightenment. New World Library.
59. Dragon Rising: It's All About Modern Energy. Retrieved from https://dragonrising.com/
60. Grout, Pam. (2016). Thank and Grow Rich: A 30-Day Experiment in Shameless Gratitude and Unabashed Joy. Hay House Inc.
61. Grout, Pam. (2016). Thank and Grow Rich: A 30-Day Experiment in Shameless Gratitude and Unabashed Joy. Hay House Inc.
62. Emmons, R. (2010, November 16). Why Gratitude Is Good. Greater Good Magazine: Science-Based Insights for a Meaningful Life. Retrieved from https://greatergood.berkeley.edu/article/item/why_gratitude_is_good

63. Anka, D., channel for Bashar. Website https://www.bashar.org/
64. Fearless Soul. Follow Your Heart... Your Brain Is Stupid. YouTube channel https://www.youtube.com/channel/UC0nOQ1R3Z-vRO7K6g-W7Jkg
65. Gordon, AM. (2013, April 29). Five Ways Giving Thanks Can Backfire. Greater Good Magazine: Science-Based Insights for a Meaningful Life. Retrieved from https://greatergood.berkeley.edu/article/item/five_ways_giving_thanks_can_backfire
66. Yoda quotes. (2005). From Star Wars III - Revenge of the Sith. Retrieved from https://www.yodaquotes.net/train-yourself-to-let-go-of-everything-you-fear-to-lose/
67. Carpenter, Tom. (1992). Dialogue on Awakening: Communion with a Loving Brother. The Carpenters' Press. Princeville, Hawaii. pp. 47.
68. Williams, M. (1997, April 2). Return to Love: Reflections on the Principles of "A Course in Miracles." Harper One.
69. Emmons, R. (2015, November 25). Gratitude is good medicine: Practicing gratitude boosts emotional and physical well-being. UC Davis Health, Medical Center.
70. Fisk, G.M. (2009, December 16). "I want it all and I want it now!" An examination of the etiology, expression, and escalation of excessive employee entitlement. Human Resource Management Review. Volume 20, Issue 2, June 2010, pp. 102-114. Retrieved from Science Direct https://www.sciencedirect.com/science/article/abs/pii/S1053482209001077
71. Emmons, R. (2017, October 11). Three Surprising Ways that Gratitude Works at Work. Greater Good Magazine: Science-Based Insights for a Meaningful Life. Retrieved from https://greatergood.berkeley.edu/article/item/three_surprising_ways_that_gratitude_works_at_work
72. Emmons RA, McCullough ME. Counting blessings versus burdens: an experimental investigation of gratitude and subjective well-being in daily life. J Pers Soc Psychol. 2003 Feb;84(2):377-89.

doi: 10.1037//0022-3514.84.2.377. PMID: 12585811. Retrieved from https://pubmed.ncbi.nlm.nih.gov/12585811/
73. Allen, S. (2018, May). The Science of Gratitude. A white paper prepared for the John Templeton Foundation by the Greater Good Science Center at UC Berkeley. Retrieved from https://ggsc.berkeley.edu/images/uploads/GGSC-JTF_White_Paper-Gratitude-FINAL.pdf
74. Why Gratitude is Good for Your Health. Exploring Your Mind. Retrieved from https://exploringyourmind.com/gratitude-is-good-health/
75. Retrieved from https://www.ncbi.nlm.nih.gov/pubmed/28128978
76. Wood AM, Joseph S, Lloyd J, Atkins S. Gratitude influences sleep through the mechanism of pre-sleep cognitions. J Psychosom Res. 2009 Jan;66(1):43-8. doi: 10.1016/j.jpsychores.2008.09.002. Epub 2008 Nov 22. PMID: 19073292.
77. Ackerman, CE. (2021, June 22). 28 Benefits of Gratitude & Most Significant Research Findings. Positive Psychology. Retrieved from https://positivepsychology.com/benefits-gratitude-research-questions/
78. McCraty, R. (2002, January). The Appreciative Heart: The Psychophysiology of Appreciation. 1998. https://www.researchgate.net/publication/232478613.
79. Twyman, James F. (2010). The Art of Spiritual Peacemaking: Secret Teachings from Jeshua Ben Joseph. Original text - 20 lessons in 99 days.
80. Choquette, Sonia. (2008). The Answer Is Simple: oracle cards guidebook. pp. 115. Hay House Inc. Sydney.
81. Grout, Pam. (2016). Thank and Grow Rich: A 30-Day Experiment in Shameless Gratitude and Unabashed Joy. Hay House Inc.
82. Dyer, WW. Retrieved from https://www.goodreads.com/author/quotes/2960.Wayne_W_Dyer

83. Robbins, T. Making Great Changes Together. Posted by Team Tony. Retrieved from https://www.tonyrobbins.com/stories/unleash-the-power/making-great-changes-together/
84. HeartMath Institute. Quick Coherence Technique. Retrieved from https://www.heartmath.com/quick-coherence-technique/
85. Tzu Lao. Quotes from Goodreads. Retrieved from https://www.goodreads.com/quotes/119283-life-is-a-series-of-natural-and-spontaneous-changes-don-t
86. Twyman, J. (2006, April 1). The Art of Spiritual Peacemaking: Secret Teachings from Jeshua ben Joseph. Findhorn Press.
87. Rudd, R. (2013, May). Gene Keys: Unlocking the Higher Purpose: Embracing Your Higher Purpose. Watkins.
88. Hicks, E & J. (2008, September 1). Money and the Law of Attraction: Learning to Attract Wealth, Health and Happiness. Hay House Inc.
89. Robbins, Tony. Retrieved from https://www.tonyrobbins.com/career-business/where-focus-goes-energy-flows/.
90. A Course in Miracles. (2007). Text. Chapter 12: The Holy Spirit's Curriculum. VII. Looking Within (https://acim.org/acim/en/s/161). The Foundation for Inner Peace. 448 Ignacio Blvd., #306, Novato, CA 94949, www.acim.org and info@acim.org, used with permission.
91. Chevalier G, Sinatra ST, Oschman JL, Sokal K, Sokal P. (2012, January 12). Earthing: health implications of reconnecting the human body to the Earth's surface electrons. Journal of Environmental and Public Health, 2012, 291541. https://doi.org/10.1155/2012/291541.
92. Rudd, R. (2013, May). Gene Keys: Unlocking the Higher Purpose: Embracing Your Higher Purpose. Watkins.
93. Sokal K., & Sokal P. (2011). Earthing the human body influences physiologic processes. Journal of Alternative and Complementary Medicine (New York, N.Y.), 17(4), 301–308. https://doi.org/10.1089/acm.2010.0687

94. Chevalier G, Patel S, Weiss L, Chopra D, Mills P. (2018). The Effects of Grounding (Earthing) on Bodyworkers' Pain and Overall Quality of Life: A Randomized Controlled Trial. EXPLORE. 15. 10.1016/j.explore.2018.10.001.
95. Sinatra ST, Oschman JL, Chevalier G, Sinatra D. Electric Nutrition: The Surprising Health and Healing Benefits of Biological Grounding (Earthing). Altern Ther Health Med. 2017 Sep;23(5):8-16. PMID: 28987038.
96. Ober, C. ESD Journal. Retrieved from http://www.esdjournal.com/articles/cober/bio.htm
97. Chevalier G, Sinatra ST, Oschman JL, Sokal K, Sokal P. (2012). Earthing: health implications of reconnecting the human body to the Earth's surface electrons. Journal of environmental and public health, 2012, 291541. https://doi.org/10.1155/2012/291541.
98. Down to Earth Film. (2019, November 14). Down To Earth Collective. https://downtoearthfilm.com/payl?flag-block=1#flag-block
99. Grounded - An independent documentary about grounding. Found at https://www.groundology.co.uk/videos?show=grounded-documentary#video
100. Ghaly M, Teplitz D. The biologic effects of grounding the human body during sleep as measured by cortisol levels and subjective reporting of sleep, pain, and stress. J Altern Complement Med. 2004 Oct;10(5):767-76. doi: 10.1089/acm.2004.10.767. PMID: 15650465.
101. Tafet GE, Toister-Achituv M, Shinitzky M. Enhancement of serotonin uptake by cortisol: a possible link between stress and depression. Cogn Affect Behav Neurosci. 2001 Mar;1(1):96-104. doi: 10.3758/cabn.1.1.96. PMID: 12467107.
102. Latz, T. & Ross, M. (2012, August 20). Shifting Lives Through Earthing – A Psychiatrist's Perspective. Retrieved from https://www.shiftyourlife.com/shifting-lives-through-earthing-a-psychiatrists-perspective/

103. Chevalier G, Sinatra ST, Oschman JL, Delany RM. (2013). Earthing (grounding) the human body reduces blood viscosity—a major factor in cardiovascular disease. Journal of alternative and complementary medicine (New York, N.Y.), 19(2), 102–110. https://doi.org/10.1089/acm.2011.0820.
104. Chevalier G, Sinatra ST, Oschman JL, Sokal K, Sokal P. (2012). Earthing: health implications of reconnecting the human body to the Earth's surface electrons. Journal of environmental and public health, 2012, 291541. https://doi.org/10.1155/2012/291541.
105. (2018, July 11). Grounding: Definition – What does Grounding mean? Retrieved from https://www.yogapedia.com/definition/10615/grounding
106. Dyer, W.W. (2004, August 1). The Power of Intention: Learning to Co-Create Your World Your Way. Hay House Inc.
107. Millman, D. (2000, October 10). Way of the Peaceful Warrior: A Book that Changes Lives. H J Kramer.
108. Lipton, Bruce. (2005). The Biology of Belief: unleashing the power of consciousness, matter & miracles. Published by Mountain of Love/Elite Books. Santa Rosa, CA 95404.
109. Rudd, R. (2013). Gene Keys: Unlocking the Higher Purpose: Embracing Your Higher Purpose. Watkins.
110. Klein, G. (2015, June 4). The Insight Stance: Boosting Your Insights, Part 2. Psychology Today. Retrieved from https://www.psychologytoday.com/au/blog/seeing-what-others-dont/201506/the-insight-stance
111. McCraty, R., Atkinson, A. & Tomasino, D. (2001). HeartMath Institute. Coherence and the Surprising Role of the Heart. Science of the Heart. Exploring the Role of the Heart in Human Performance. An Overview of Research Conducted by the HeartMath Institute. https://www.heartmath.org/research/science-of-the-heart/
112. Bradley RT, McCraty R, Atkinson M, Gillin M. (2008). Non-local Intuition in Entrepreneurs and Non Entrepreneurs: An Experimental Comparison Using Electrophysiological Measures.

Retrieved from https://www.heartmath.org/research/research-library/intuition/nonlocal-intuition-in-entrepreneurs-and-non-entrepreneurs/

113. Rezaei, S., Mirzaei, M., & Zali, M. R. (2014). Nonlocal Intuition: Replication and Paired-Subjects Enhancement Effects. Global advances in health and medicine, 3(2), 5–15. https://doi.org/10.7453/gahmj.2014.012.

114. McTaggart, L. @ lynnemctaggart.com. Retrieved from https://lynnemctaggart.com/intention-experiments/evidence/

115. Orloff, J. (2017, April 4). The Empath's Survival Guide: Life Strategies for Sensitive People. Sounds True Publishing.

116. Hartmann, S. (2003, February). Oceans of Energy. The Patterns & Techniques of EmoTrance. E-Book Edition V 1.0. Code No. 90041E. Published by Dragon Rising. Retrieved from https://epdf.pub/oceans-of-energy-emotrance.html

117. Taken from Oceans of Energy: The Patterns and Techniques of EmoTrance by Silver Hartmann. Original document is out of print. Information can be found at https://dragonrising.com/

118. McCraty R, Atkinson M, Bradley RT. Electrophysiological evidence of intuition: part 1. The surprising role of the heart. J Altern Complement Med. 2004 Feb;10(1):133-43. doi: 10.1089/107555304322849057. PMID: 15025887.

119. Gin RH, Green BN. George Goodheart, Jr., D.C., and a history of applied kinesiology. J Manipulative Physiol Ther. 1997 Jun;20(5):331-7. PMID: 9200049.

120. Nelson, B. (2019, June 10). The Emotion Code: How to Release Your Trapped Emotions for Abundant Health, Love, and Happiness. St Martin's Press.

121. Rossi, E., & Cheek, D. R. (1988). Mind-Body Therapy: Methods of Ideodynamic Healing in Hypnosis. W.W. Norton & Company. New York. London.

122. Shenefelt, P. D. Ideomotor signaling: from divining spiritual messages to discerning subconscious answers during hypnosis and hypnoanalysis, a historical perspective. Am J Clin Hypn.

2011 Jan;53(3):157-67. doi: 10.1080/00029157.2011.10401754. PMID: 21404952.
123. Littrell, J. The mind-body connection: not just a theory anymore. Soc Work Health Care. 2008;46(4):17-37. doi: 10.1300/j010v46n04_02. PMID: 18589562.
124. Tolle, E. (2004, August 1). The Power of Now: A Guide to Spiritual Enlightenment. New World Library.
125. Spira, R. Rubert Spira teachings. Retrieved from https://rupertspira.com/teachings?player=video
126. Vanilla Papers. Website of Dee. 17 Journaling Tips for Beginners (and How to Start). Retrieved from https://vanillapapers.net/2019/11/13/journaling-tips/
127. HeartMath Institute YouTube channel. The Heart's Intuitive Intelligence: A path to personal, social and global coherence. Retrieved from https://www.youtube.com/watch?v=QdneZ4fIIHE
128. Retrieved from HeartMath Institute website: https://www.heartmath.org/gci/gcms/live-data/
129. McCraty R, Deyhle A, Childre D. The global coherence initiative: creating a coherent planetary standing wave. Glob Adv Health Med. 2012 Mar;1(1):64-77. doi: 10.7453/gahmj.2012.1.1.013. PMID: 24278803; PMCID: PMC3833489.
130. The Global Consciousness Project. Meaningful Correlations in Random Data. The Global Consciousness Project, created originally in the Princeton Engineering Anomalies Research Lab at Princeton University, is directed by Roger Nelson.
131. Al-Achrafi, S. Retrieved from Marmalade Fish website @ https://www.marmaladefish.com/insights/
132. A Course in Miracles. (2007). Workbook. Part I. Lesson 95. The Foundation for Inner Peace. 448 Ignacio Blvd., #306, Novato, CA 94949, www.acim.org and info@acim.org, used with permission (https://acim.org/acim/en/s/499)
133. Taylor, S. (2017, March 1). The Leap: The Psychology of Spiritual Awakening. New World Library.

134. Lipton, B. H. (2012, June 7). The Wisdom of Your Cells. Retrieved from https://www.brucelipton.com/the-wisdom-your-cells/
135. Sanders, C. L. (2014, May 19). Speculations about Bystander and Biophotons. Dose Response. 2014 May 19;12(4):515-7. doi: 10.2203/dose-response.14-002.Sanders. PMID: 25552952; PMCID: PMC4267444.
136. Popp FA, Li KH, Mei WP, Galle M, Neurohr R. (1988, July 15). Physical aspects of biophotons. Experientia. 1988 Jul 15;44(7):576-85. doi: 10.1007/BF01953305. PMID: 3294033.
137. Lipton, Bruce. (2005). The Biology of Belief: Unleashing the power of consciousness, matter and miracles. Published by Mountain of Love/Elite Books. Santa Rosa, CA 95404. pp. 112.
138. Murray G, La Pira F, McCraty R, Bradley R, Atkinson M, Simpson D, Scicluna P. (2007). Before Cognition: The Active Contribution of the Heart/ANS to Intuitive Decision Making as Measured on Repeat Entrepreneurs in the Cambridge Technopol. Retrieved from https://www.heartmath.org/research/research-library/intuition/before-cognition-the-active-contribution-of-the-heart/
139. McCraty R, Atkinson M, Bradley RT. Electrophysiological evidence of intuition: part 1. The surprising role of the heart. J Altern Complement Med. 2004 Feb;10(1):133-43. doi: 10.1089/107555304322849057. PMID: 15025887.
140. Diamond, J. (2019, April 17). The Placebo Effect. All true healing should occur through what we may call the intentional or purposeful placebo effect. Retrieved from https://medium.com/@JohnDiamondMD/the-placebo-effect-c619a5016e39
141. A Course in Miracles. (2007). Text, Chapter 21: Reason and Perception. Introduction. The Foundation for Inner Peace. 448 Ignacio Blvd., #306, Novato, CA 94949, www.acim.org and info@acim.org, used with permission. (https://acim.org/acim/en/s/251)
142. McCraty, R. (2003, July). The Energetic Heart: Bioelectromagnetic Interactions Within and Between People. The Neuropsychotherapist 6(1):22-43. Retrieved from https://www.research-

gate.net/publication/274451622_The_Energetic_Heart_Biolectromagnetic_Interactions_Within_and_Between_People
143. McCraty, R., Atkinson, M. & Tomasino, D. (2001). Science of the Heart. Exploring the Role of the Heart in Human Performance. An Overview of Research Conducted by the HeartMath Institute. Chapter 6: Energetic Communication. Publication No. l 01-001. Boulder Creek, CA.
144. A Course in Miracles. (1975, January 1). ACIM. Workbook, Part I, Lesson 19 (https://acim.org/acim/en/s/421)19.2:3. The Foundation for Inner Peace. 448 Ignacio Blvd., #306, Novato, CA 94949, www.acim.org and info@acim.org, used with permission.
145. Walsch, N.D. (1996, October 29). Conversations with God: An Uncommon Dialogue, Book 1.
146. A Course in Miracles. (1975, January 1). ACIM. Text: Chapter 13: The Guiltless World. V. The Two Emotions (https://acim.org/acim/en/s/169). The Foundation for Inner Peace. 448 Ignacio Blvd., #306, Novato, CA 94949, www.acim.org and info@acim.org, used with permission.
147. Retrieved from Facebook page, Abraham Hicks Daily Teachings @AbrahamDailyX·Community. https://www.facebook.com/AbrahamDailyX/
148. Tolle, E. (2004, August 1). The Power of Now: A Guide to Spiritual Enlightenment. New World Library.
149. Miller, L. & Barker, T. (2015). The Spiritual Child: The New Science on Parenting for Health and Lifelong Thriving. Bluebird books for life. pp. 25.
150. Miller, L. & Barker, T. (2015). The Spiritual Child: The New Science on Parenting for Health and Lifelong Thriving. Bluebird books for life. pp. 26.
151. Maathai, W. 103 Motivational Wangari Maathai Quotes that Show Things in Right Perspective. Retrieved from https://quotes.thefamouspeople.com/wangari-maathai-4188.php

152. Twyman, J. (2006, April 1). The Art of Spiritual Peacemaking: Secret Teachings from Jeshua ben Joseph. Findhorn Press; First Edition.
153. A Course in Miracles. (2007). Workbook. Part I. Review VI. Lesson 201. The Foundation for Inner Peace. 448 Ignacio Blvd., #306, Novato, CA 94949, www.acim.org and info@acim.org, used with permission. Workbook. (https://acim.org/acim/en/s/610)
154. Wade, T. (2019, December 19). Website Antara Healing: A powerful alliance of mind, body and spirit. Retrieved from https://antarahealingarts.com/category/unabridged-articles/unabridged-your-cells-are-listening-how-talking-to-your-body-can-help-you-heal
155. Nelson, B. (2020, July 14). Dr. Bradley Nelson's blog post. Do you have a heart wall? Retrieved from https://drbradleynelson.com/do-you-have-a-heart-wall/
156. Rudd, R. Articles from the Gene Keys website. Glossary of Empowerment. Retrieved from https://genekeys.com/articles/glossary-of-empowerment/
157. Brown, B. (2010, June). The Power of Vulnerability. Talk at TEDxHouston. Retrieved from https://www.ted.com/talks/brene_brown_the_power_of_vulnerability?utm_campaign=tedspread&utm_medium=referral&utm_source=tedcomshare
158. Walsch, N. D. (1996, January 1). Conversations with God: An Uncommon Dialogue, Book 1. Tarcherperigee; 1st edition. pp. 70.
159. Qingyuan Weixin (Zen master). Found in Lopez, DS. (2010, September 15). Buddhism and Science: A Guide for the Perplexed. University of Chicago Press.
160. Viktor E. Frankl Quotes sourced from Brainy quote. Retrieved from https://www.brainyquote.com/authors/viktor-e-frankl-quotes

161. Walsch, N. D. (1996, January 1). Conversations with God: An Uncommon Dialogue, Book 1. Hodder Headline Australia Pty Ltd. pp.133.

www.ingramcontent.com/pod-product-compliance
Lightning Source LLC
Chambersburg PA
CBHW030253010526
44107CB00053B/1690